Zelda Sayre Fitzgerald

Zelda Sayre Fitzgerald

LINDA WAGNER-MARTIN

LUME BOOKS

LUME BOOKS

This edition published in 2021 by Lume Books
30 Great Guildford Street,
Borough, SE1 0HS

ISBN 978-1-83901-382-9

Typeset using Atomik ePublisher from Easypress Technologies

www.lumebooks.co.uk

For Doug, Tom, and Andrea once again

We all knew about each other in Jeffersonville: how each other swam and danced and what time our parents wanted us to be home at night, and what each one of us liked to eat and drink and talk about ...

Zelda Sayre Fitzgerald, "Southern Girl"

From the orchard across the way the smell of ripe pears floats over the child's bed. A band rehearses waltzes in the distance. White things gleam in the dark — white flowers and paving-stones. The moon on the window panes careens to the garden ... The world is younger than it is ...

Zelda Sayre Fitzgerald, *Save Me the Waltz*

Table of Contents

Preface

Most biographers conceive of their subjects' lives as being formed by their origins; biographies often begin at the birth of the subject/protagonist/character. In the case of Zelda Sayre, however, in most of the dozen biographies about her and her husband, F. Scott Fitzgerald, Zelda's first appearance is at the age of seventeen, when her future spouse sees her at a dance in her hometown of Montgomery, Alabama.

Of the early studies, only Nancy Milford's 1970 biography, *Zelda*, begins with the Sayre family history, and includes a brief description of the town of Montgomery in 1900, when Zelda was born.[1]

Milford, like all the early critics who studied the Fitzgeralds and their writing, was not Southern. Scott Fitzgerald, born in St. Paul, Minnesota, living his early life both there and in Buffalo, New York, was also not Southern. His path of social climbing

---

[1] Excepting Sara Mayfield's 1971 *Exiles from Paradise, Zelda and Scott Fitzgerald, a personal biography* filled with information about the South, and the recent Sally Cline, *Zelda Fitzgerald, Her Voice in Paradise* (2003).

moved him to the East, to the revered Atlantic seaboard, and eventually to Princeton University. Unlike his contemporary Ernest Hemingway, Fitzgerald never expressed interest in going west—to either the mountains or the Pacific coast—or in going to any place exotic: instead of Key West and Cuba, Fitzgerald chose Baltimore.

To identify Fitzgerald as a writer innately fascinated with the South is to misrepresent his interests. To identify Zelda Sayre as anyone except a Southerner is to misrepresent her. Until she left Montgomery to travel to New York for her wedding, accompanied then by her older married sister, Zelda had never spent a night away from her parents' home (except for dances at Southern colleges and cities, where she reigned as a relatively famous "belle").

This book aims to place Zelda within the environs of the turn-of-the-century South, the Deep South of which Montgomery, Alabama still (in the twenty-first century, more than a century later) remains representative. As the Capitol of the Confederacy, Montgomery still proudly displays a statue of Jefferson Davis, and the house he and his wife Varina occupied—moved to be a part of the cluster of state office buildings and the Alabama Capitol itself—was a house built and designed by Zelda Sayre's great-uncle. Homes in the Garden District, to either side of Perry Street, are much as they were when Zelda was growing up (1900-18), roller-skating her risky path past the Governor's house on Perry Street, then reversing and heading to Court Street where cobblestones made her foray even more dangerous. The lush physical beauty of the tree-shadowed streets, like the relentless spring and summer heat, made Zelda an outdoor child, as well as a crack swimmer and diver. Every white Montgomery child had access to pools at the country club, the city park, or the YMCA: when Zelda strutted to the diving board in her form-fitting Annette Kellerman swimsuit, she was being (conventionally) shocking. She was showing off—her small but good figure, her athletic ability, her saucy disregard for the oughts and shoulds of the culture of the Southern lady. Yet, in fact, Zelda Sayre was the quintessential Southern lady.

What lay ahead for Zelda in the manic and hard-drinking 1920s, caught between the impersonal urban life of New York and Paris and the less frenetic living in Minneapolis, the south of France, and Baltimore, was so unexpected that it helped to undermine the confidence, the joy, that had characterized her childhood and adolescence.

This is that story.

Short Titles and Abbreviations

The following short titles and abbreviations are used throughout this book:

CT—"Caesar's Things", unpublished novel by Zelda Sayre Fitzgerald, available at Princeton University Library

CU—F. Scott Fitzgerald's *The Crack-Up*, edited by Edmund Wilson (New Directions, 1945)

CW—*The Collected Writings of Zelda Fitzgerald*, edited by Matthew J. Bruccoli (University of Alabama Press, 1997, reissue of 1991); includes *Save Me the Waltz* (noted separately as **SMTW**), *Scandalabra*, and all short fiction and essays

DS, DZ—*Dear Scott, Dearest Zelda: The Love Letters of F Scott and Zelda Fitzgerald*, edited by Jackson R. Bryer and Cathy W. Barks (St. Martin's Press, 2002)

Exiles—Sara Mayfield's *Exiles from Paradise, Zelda and Scott Fitzgerald* (Delacorte, 1971)

Fool—Scott Donaldson's *Fool for Love: F. Scott Fitzgerald* (Congdon & Weed, 1983)

Life—*F Scott Fitzgerald, A Life in Letters*, edited by Matthew J. Bruccoli (Scribner's Sons, 1994)

Milford—Nancy Milford's *Zelda, A Biography* (HarperCollins, 1970)

PUL—Princeton University Library's archive of manuscripts, letters, photos, and miscellanea for both Zelda and Scott Fitzgerald

S—*Scottie, The Daughter of ...* by Eleanor Lanahan (HarperCollins, 1995)

SMTWZeldaFitzgerald's*Save Me the Waltz*,pagedasin CollectedWritings

SSEG—Matthew J. Bruccoli's biography *Some Sort of Epic Grandeur, The Life of F. Scott Fitzgerald*, second revised edition (University of South Carolina Press, 2002)

Zelda—*Zelda: An Illustrated Life*, edited by Eleanor Lanahan (Harry N. Abrams, 1996)

The notes also use abbreviations of book titles in the Bibliography.

ONE - The Belle

There are few more memorable wives in twentieth century American culture than Zelda Sayre Fitzgerald, who was married to the successful young author F. Scott Fitzgerald in 1920. His first novel, *This Side of Paradise*, had appeared a few weeks before their marriage. Because of his popularization of the Jazz Age, complete with its New York partying, elite college society, and alcohol, dancing, and flappers, readers tended to locate his beautiful Southern bride with the exotic name—Zelda—within those fictional contexts. The reality of the Zelda Sayre story was that she had never been to New York City until she traveled there, accompanied by her older married sister, to wed Fitzgerald. Neither had she gone to college, nor had she been abroad. In fact, she had seldom spent a night away from her father's house: Zelda Sayre was a Montgomery, Alabama, girl, whose father was a judge there in the state capitol. But more than that, Zelda Sayre was a highly visible Alabama belle.

To change the definition of Zelda from "flapper" to "belle" is to move from the sensationalized and risqué image of woman as fast, easy, a "speed," to that of the highly desirable but more traditional and consistently protected beauty. Flirtatious and flamboyant, the Southern belle was often a local celebrity. She was, however, the woman one courted, and she was never assumed to be available.

In the candid words of Virginia Foster Durr, who grew up in Birmingham, Alabama, belles "were almost like visiting movie stars ... the epitome of success." Of Zelda Sayre, Durr wrote "she was just gorgeous. She had a golden glow around her ... The boys would line up the whole length of the ballroom to dance with her for one minute. She was just pre-eminent. And we recognized it."[2]

The belle is peculiar to the South. Because Fitzgerald grew up in St. Paul, Minnesota and Buffalo, New York; and went to schools in the East, he knew little about belledom. Born into a high enough class to be financially secure, so that having suitable clothes, money for train travel, and leisure free from work was one of the requisites of this kind of time-consuming status. Several dozen callers on Sunday afternoons, as many letters daily, boxes of long-stemmed red roses, small square boxes of corsages, and the offers of fraternity pins, club insignias, and engagement rings—not to mention the actual dates, parties, and dances—kept the true belle busy from morning to night, and into the next morning. The orderliness of the custom may have been difficult for outsiders to fathom, but within each social circle, rituals were firm: "town girls" could not be belles (again, social class, with a proper and recognizable family name, was crucial); neither could "fast" girls. The existence of the belle was a tribute to

---

[2] Virginia Foster Durr, Outside the Magic *Circle* (1985), pp. 30, 64.

the power, and the self-conceit, of the higher classes within the South: it reaffirmed patriarchy.[3]

Having some money was not the most significant part of being from the right social class. In the South, people knew which families were which—and in Montgomery, the Sayres were important people.[4] Being so popular as a teenager and a debutante was a way of ensuring that the woman in question was the right sort of girl, a candidate to be one's marriage partner—for, ultimately, belles were to take on the roles of wives and, particularly, of mothers. Southern bloodlines, like Southern manners, were not to be corrupted. Stemming from the aftermath of the Civil War, when the barriers between the white race and the black became even more firmly entrenched—and horribly enforced through lynching—the politics of marriage grew increasingly significant. Because fortunes had been lost during both the Civil War and Reconstruction, social position was maintained largely on the basis of family name, and through one family's partnership in marriage with another stable and well-placed family.

Belledom, then, was not only an individual triumph: "These great Southern belles became an institution. A man was proud to be seen with them. It gave him status. Their cities were proud of them."[5] The formation of the Zeta Sigma "fraternity" at Auburn University, for example, designed to honor those

[3] Durr, *Magic Circle*, pp. 29-30; Sara Haardt, "Southern Souvenir" in Southern Souvenirs (1999), p. 298; Kendall Taylor, *Sometimes Madness* (2001), pp. 2-3; Tallulah Bankhead, *Tallulah* (1952), p. 27; CT.

[4] Milford, pp. 10-11; Exiles, pp. 5-6.

[5] Durr, Magic Circle, p. 30; S, pp. 18-19; Exiles, pp. 2-3, 223-5.

college men who had been or were in love with Zelda Sayre (note the initials ZS), was more of a tribute than it was a joke: membership meant that certain undergraduate men had moved in the elite social circle of Miss Zelda Sayre of Montgomery.

Zelda was the youngest of four daughters; none of her three sisters had been belles. The oldest, Marjorie, born 1885, was fragile and serious, bothered with nerves throughout her life. The middle sisters, Rosalind and Clotilde, born in 1889 and 1891, were attractive but not inordinately popular. They showed some independence, however, when—unlike most of their friends—they chose to work in Montgomery until their respective marriages. Zelda's older sisters were fourteen, eleven, and nine years older than she; she was closest in age to her only living brother, Anthony, who was six years older than she.[6]

The other belle in the Sayre household had been Minnie Buckner Machen (of the Scottish MacHens), wife of Judge Sayre, their mother. More artistic than she was orderly, Minnie sang and played the piano; she had written poems and was once contacted by a publisher about writing a novel. After graduating in 1878 from the Montgomery Female College, she had gone from Eddyville, Kentucky, from her father's estate of 3000 acres (called "Mineral Mount") to Philadelphia to be "finished", and had there been offered a part in a stage production—at which point her father brought her home: No Machen daughter would be an actress. Her beauty and talents seemingly submerged under the strict control of her lawyer husband, a Sayre who brooked no frivolity in his household, Minnie managed to carry out her roles in Montgomery society—though she was

[6] Exiles, p. 21; SMTVV, PUL.

known to be sometimes unsocial, and most of the city recognized that Judge Sayre's family was not wealthy. In fact, this branch of the Sayres never owned any of the houses they lived in, though they managed to rent homes in the Silk Hat section of Montgomery. They were not, however, living in the Garden District or in Cloverdale.[7]

Zelda was the Sayres' last child, probably unplanned. Born when Minnie was nearly 40, the baby was one of the prettiest children in town. Seeing Zelda's beauty and coloring (which was fair like hers, in contrast to the dark complexions of the other children), Minnie began an unconscious program of favoring Zelda. She made her beautiful clothes ("Baby" did not often wear the hand-me-downs of her older sisters), she saw that she had all the dance lessons she wanted, she encouraged her daughter's flirtatious ways, she gave her permission to be out late at social events while she was still in high school, she protected Zelda from her father's anger, and she herself enjoyed the boys and men who came to call. If there had ever been any consideration of Zelda's going to college, it was erased by her quick, early popularity that left the family exhausted monitoring the surge of activity—getting the mail, answering the telephone, opening the door for telegram delivery and florists, making the new gown for the next dance, serving lemonade and cookies on the porch to the bevy of suitors, worrying about who was driving the cars on the highways, or whether or not the train reached its destination on

---

[7] Exiles, pp. 4-7; Helen F. Blackshear, "Mamma Sayre," Georgia R., pp. 466-7; and see Scottie Fitzgerald Smith, "The Maryland Ancestors of Zelda Sayre Fitzgerald," Maryland Historical Magazine (1983), pp. 217-28.

time. For finally, even in 1918 and 1919, Southern daughters were pointed toward making good marriages.[8] In Virginia Durr's cryptic assessment, "Life without a husband meant a life of poverty ... The consequences of not being loved were plain: you didn't get married. You got to be an old maid."[9] In Judge Sayre's modest household, sending any daughter to college would have meant careful reallocation of finances. The road in front of Zelda Sayre was clear, and it went to only one destination.

Life in the Sayre Household

Anthony Dickinson Sayre was the son of proud families. His mother was Musidora Morgan Sayre, the sister of Senator John Tyler Morgan, brigadier general in the Confederate army who later served in the United States Senate as an Alabama senator. She was also related to John Hunt Morgan, the famous Confederate raider. In 1835 Musidora married Daniel Sayre, a journalist who had founded and edited a small paper in Tuskegee and later edited the *Montgomery Post*. The more prominent of the Sayre children was William, a lawyer who designed and built a mansion for himself that later became the first White House of the Confederacy. William rented the house to the Committee of the Confederacy for the use of Jefferson Davis, for $5000 a year; and the house is preserved today near the Capitol complex in the heart of Montgomery. The city honored the family name by calling one of the Silk Hat streets "Sayre

---

[8] Blackshear, "Mamma Sayre," p. 465; Jacqueline Tavernier-Courbin, "Art as Woman's Response," Southern Literary Journal (1979), p. 25.

[9] Durr, Magic Circle, p. 66.

Street"; the elementary school in that area, originally known as Chilton Grammar School, became "the Sayre Street School."

Anthony Sayre was well educated. Living modestly on Court Street, in a household which emphasized reading and education, he attended a small private school, and then went to Roanoke College in Salem, Virginia. Taking honors in both Greek and mathematics, he was Valedictorian of the Class of 1878. He taught mathematics at Vanderbilt University for a year, and then returned to Montgomery to read law. He was admitted to the bar in 1880. In 1883 he was appointed clerk of the city court, so with that steady income in 1884 he married Minnie Machen at Mineral Mount.[10]

Thirteen months after their wedding, Marjorie was born; then came Daniel, named for his grandfather, a child who died at eighteen months of spinal meningitis. In the quasi-breakdown Minnie experienced, she went to her room and stayed there. Finally, their doctor, an older general practitioner, forced his way in and entreated her to live for Marjorie's sake.

For Minnie Machen Sayre, who had been considered glamorous by her admirers, life as the wife of a busy clerk of courts—responsible for keeping house, training servants, cooking, and rearing infants—was never pleasant. She went from being a popular and talented young woman to a matron, and she never felt at home in Montgomery: she always referred to herself as a Kentuckian. Part of her isolation accrued from her husband's personality. Orderly to a fault, Anthony lived on a pristine schedule, regardless of which child was ill or what household catastrophe had occurred. Later in life, he was known to start

---

[10] Milford, pp. 5-7; Exiles, pp. 5-9; S, pp. 19-20.

for bed each night at 8.30 p.m. Throughout his married life he rode from the Sayre Street-Pleasant Street neighborhood on the same streetcar each morning, and returned every evening at the same time. There would be a quiet dinner, which Minnie would have ready; and then the father of the Sayre family might play a game of chess with his neighbor, Judge Mayfield. Then he retired. He was clearly head of the family, but it was Minnie who cared for the children and made what arrangements she could to give them the freedom she thought they needed to grow up healthily.

After Daniel's death, Minnie and Anthony had four more children—the two daughters, Rosalind and Clotilde, and then in 1894, Anthony (not so strong as his brother had been, but able to survive through several years of college at Auburn in civil engineering and fraternity life). By the time of Zelda's birth early on July 24, 1900, Minnie was tired of her necessary daily life, of providing meals, seeing that the laundry was done, that the shirts and middies, table linens and bedding were ironed, that the children had suitable outfits for holidays and church, and that Anthony—by now a respected judge in the Alabama court system—wore appropriate clothing and had timely haircuts, as well as meals that he liked. Whereas observers saw Judge Sayre's life as controlled to the point of obsessiveness, the reality of life at the various houses they rented on, first, Sayre Street and then Pleasant, was chaotic. Roller skates in the hallway, creaky swings and metal chairs on the wide porches, bicycles with spent tires and no way to transport them to a repair shop, too many children to watch to know where they all were at any given time, misplaced hair ribbons and borrowed cosmetics … Minnie handled daily life, and its disarray, on her own.

During the years when the children were young the Sayre

household also included Anthony's mother, Musidora (famous in the neighborhood for her "whipping tongue"[11]); his bachelor brother, Reid, and Minnie's sister Marjorie, their father having been killed in Kentucky in a riding accident. Minnie's staff consisted of a cook, however sporadic her presence may have been; a laundress; a yardman (even modest houses had large yards); and a nanny, often an African American, as were the other household employees. The nanny cared for the children; she was not a tutor. Whereas Minnie and her sister would have been expected to prepare some foods and do housework, as would the older children have been so expected, Musidora Sayre as mother-in-law would have been exempt from most work. Just as Anthony was worried about the expenses of the large household, Minnie was worried about juggling its management—to his and his mother's satisfaction.

Many of the positions Anthony Sayre assumed in his law career may have resulted from his need for more money. He was a member of the Alabama House of Representatives for four years; he was then elected to the state Senate, and was chosen as its president during his last year in office. By 1897 he was elected judge of the city court in Montgomery, when his title of "judge" then usurped his name—everyone, even Minnie, called him Judge Sayre. In 1909 he was appointed associate justice of the Alabama Supreme Court, with an annual salary of $6500.

During these twenty-five years of Anthony's involvement in his law career, Minnie was devoting twenty-five years to playing the role of competent wife and mother. She played the part

---

[11] Quoted in Milford, p. 7

well, except that she was often ill during pregnancy, and she breast-fed her children, perhaps responding to the belief that lactating women could not become pregnant. Given the state of birth control at the turn of the century, with the Comstock prohibitions against sharing information about that process, Minnie may have nursed Zelda for the long period (though indeterminate, it may have been two or three years, given its legendary status in the Fitzgerald stories) as a means of ensuring that Zelda was the last child born to the Anthony Sayres.

Zelda's Childhood

To find herself little more than a housewife would have been sobering for Minnie Machen, who had known growing up on her father's estate that her life was planned to be privileged. She had been sent to Montgomery for her secondary school education, and it was in Montgomery at a New Year's Ball that she had met Anthony Sayre.[12] But she had then gone to Philadelphia for more instruction in voice, music, and diction. When she married and came to live in a series of rented, old houses in Montgomery, in locations chosen so that everyone in the family could take the streetcar, she realized that the snobbery of the Sayres was founded on little except pride.

The Sayre family stories about the move from New Jersey through Ohio and into Alabama at the time of that territory's becoming a state—a narrative of the pioneering spirit—held little interest for her. Her own family stories were more dramatic. It was her father who migrated to Kentucky from South Carolina and had several careers—in iron refining, in building turnpikes,

---

[12] Exiles, pp. 4-5.

in the law. He was a state senator when the Civil War broke out, and he sided with the secessionists, even though Kentucky chose to be Union. Elected to the Confederate Congress, Machen fled to Canada when the Confederacy was defeated, because he was afraid of reprisals. His third wife, Minnie's fragile mother, took Minnie and Marjorie with her to Canada and lived in fear there—the family had little to eat and Minnie thought that her mother's health was broken during those months. When her father was granted amnesty and they returned to Kentucky, her mother eventually committed suicide.

Her father, on his return, was elected to the United States Senate and, after serving for only four months, was a nominee for the candidacy for Vice President of the country. He lost that nomination, returned to his estate, and served as a member of the powerful Kentucky railroad commission from 1880 on. There he raised tobacco and looked after his youngest children, Minnie and Marjorie.

Because in part Zelda looked like the blonde Machen children, and in part because Minnie knew Zelda would be her last child, she tried to replicate her own girlhood in Zelda's life. By this time, 1900, the marriage of Anthony Sayre and Minnie Machen had established its own patterns: the Judge didn't care to interfere in Minnie's decisions about the children, even had he understood what those decisions were. His focus was entirely on how Minnie spent money, how costly the meals were, how difficult earning more money was for him as he aged. And he was ill-prepared to think about rearing children because his own childhood, as the son of the sharp-tongued mother and the talented but passive writer-husband, had been shaped almost entirely by ambition—his own and his parents' for him. To excel,

11

to graduate from college at age nineteen with the remarkable academic record, to teach at Vanderbilt University—Anthony Sayre had succeeded. The quality of happiness hardly came into his calculations.

Part of the reason the Judge did not interfere with Minnie in child raising was that most of their children were daughters. With the age-old preference for sons, and traumatized as much as Minnie over Daniel's death, Judge Sayre found that it mattered little what Minnie did with the girls—so long as they were quiet at mealtimes and respectful at church (to which he did not go) and to his mother and brother. The modest Southern verities of good manners and good morals were the scaffolding of child rearing in the late nineteenth century, and it was only Zelda who was born, barely, in the twentieth. She too would be raised as though she were a nineteenth century child.

That the children were not comfortable with their father and their living situation may be inferred from the fact that their memories are shadowed with the solemnity of the Judge's life, his rules that strict order be imposed (and the fact that they all feared waking him from his post-lunch nap), and their recognition that their mother made the decisions that mattered. Rather than being parents who were united in efforts concerning the children, Anthony and Minnie were distinct and separate. When Zelda came later to refer to her father as "Old Dick," it was a mark of the way his stern demeanor fostered subversion in, at least, his youngest child. What Zelda learned from the model of her parents' relationship was that wives were to be submissive—on the surface. Shading the truth, omitting explanations, lying when necessary—Minnie's behavior could be justified if the modus operandi was "getting around" the Judge (and his strictures about spending money). Zelda also observed her father's denigration of the arts—he was brilliant, her mother was talented in other ways. But Zelda knew early that "those ways" did not count for much: Anthony Sayre, defining his success as the product of hard study and real intellect, could not understand why it was important that Zelda began ballet when she was only nine years old. Minnie had wanted Zelda to start first grade when she was six, but when the child returned home and said she would not go back (she claimed she already knew the things they had talked about), Minnie agreed. So Zelda started school at seven.[13]

Zelda learned, too, that the prominence that counted was what society could observe. Her father's faithful regularity, waiting for the streetcar, walking to and from the car stop, lying down for his afternoon nap, playing chess with a man as socially prominent as he was—these were the events that had cultural significance. They were important because Judge Sayre was paid a salary for his work. Women's work, partly because it went unpaid, was seldom titled "work." Women had so little power that people didn't even use the word "power" to discuss their options: "power" existed only within the important institutions the law, the work place, the church. Women who worked at home, rearing children and running households, had none.

Alice Miller has done thorough work on what she calls "the drama of the gifted child,"[14] pointing out that this child (like most children) will fear abandonment. The child learns quickly, well before it can speak, that the shortest route to

---

[13] Sara Haardt, "June Flight," Southern Souvenirs (1999), p. 262; Milford, pp. 17-18, 21.

[14] Alice Miller, The Drama of the Gifted Child (1981).

being abandoned is displeasing the parent. In Zelda's case, she never doubted her mother's love, but the Judge's affection was another matter. One of the reasons Judge Sayre lived near the streetcar stop was that he was so nearsighted he could never have driven a car; one can only wonder how responsive he was to his children, particularly if they were distant from his physical presence. As Miller describes the young child's dilemma, because the child is trying to please the parent, he or she learns to put on a "false" or an "as-if personality." Any child who fears both or one of the parents is therefore hindered from the necessary stage of individualization: long past the time for developing a true self, then, the child faces the emptiness of not knowing who or what he or she truly is.

For Zelda, part of her love of reading might have stemmed from her trying to attract her father's attention. The bookcases throughout 6 Pleasant Street were filled with matching sets of Henry Fielding, Shakespeare, Thackeray, Dickens, Sir Walter Scott, Mark Twain, Ouida, and the Greek and Latin classics. There were countless histories; there were dozens of children's books (and big sisters to read them to her); there were, of course, shelves of legal tomes. Throughout her life, Zelda read. She read popular novels and later in life she admired William Faulkner's *Sanctuary* and the work of the writers she knew in Paris; and she was pleased to find herself and Scott as characters in Carl Van Vechten's 1930 novel *Parties*.[15] She also knew from childhood that she had been named for the beautiful Gypsy woman in Robert Edward Francillon's 1874 novel, *Zelda's Fortune*. Her mother was also an avid reader.

---

[15] Carl Van Vechten, Parties: Scenes of Contemporary New York Life (1930).

Music was also important in the Sayre house. The Victrola stood in one corner of the library, the piano in the other. Buying the newest sheet music for the piano was more important than the newest record—people sang around the piano afternoons and evenings. When she had time from running the house, Minnie, too, played and sang. The Sayre sisters practiced new dance steps—the Maxie, the Turkey Trot. Records in the Sayre collection included those by Mary Garden, Geraldine Farrer, Caruso, and the orchestral and piano recordings of the music of Bach, Brahms, Schumann, Chopin, and others.

Most of the time, from the first few years of her life, Zelda played outside where she was fearless. Whether she was running (as fast as any of the boys she knew) or roller-skating down the hazardous Sayre Street hill or the Perry Street hill, she was intent on getting somewhere fast—largely for the sake of the speed itself. She saw nothing she could not take on—a friend quotes her saying, when she is a toddler playing in the sandbox, "I'm digging me an e-nor-mous river."[16] She would not be overshadowed just because her siblings were older and bigger. A child who was Zelda's neighbor, living just past the school that separated their houses, remembers Zelda racing after her on skates—the child had decided she too was old enough to skate down the curvy Sayre Street hill, and it took some fast skating on Zelda's part to catch her and slow her down.

For this neighbor, the Sayre house was a "mecca" for play-mates. Zelda and her sisters put on costume plays using the spacious back hall as a stage. More often, even in summer's

[16] Exiles, p. 12.

heat, they played out in the large back yard—more of an open field behind the house. There they found green moss to use in making shadow boxes. They built tree houses in the "low-limbed sugarberry trees," which usually had grape vines to swing on. After supper and before dark, the neighborhood children of all ages played I-spy, hide-and-seek, prisoner's base. Sometimes they all begged jars from home and caught fireflies. At intervals, Zelda remembered waiting for "workmen to put new carbons in the arc lights and give us the old ones."

Much of the time, Zelda was a leader, even among the boys in the Sayre Street area. She was going to be tall (something over five feet, four inches) and she was strong. Despite her slimness, she was athletic. She climbed trees and skated, went barefoot and fought in the chinaberry wars; later she became a champion swimmer and diver, and often helped younger children learn both skills. She traveled the town in order to swim every day—sometimes at the YMCA, sometimes at the Country Club pool, sometimes at the park swimming pool, sometimes at Catoma Creek. She rode her bike, she ran, she skated. And once she began dancing lessons, her strength increased as well from that training.

The Sayres lived near enough to the Capitol complex that Zelda was often seen in central Montgomery. She revered the romance of the Confederacy, and would muse over the gold star set in the marble flooring of the front entryway of the Capitol. She wandered among the cluster of stately white marble buildings, climbing the tiers of steps, envisioning herself a legislator of old; years later, with such girlfriends as Tallulah Bankhead and Sara Haardt, she danced up and down those austere stairs.[17] She would sit near the pyramids of cannon balls in front of the Capitol, dreaming of what she envisioned as brave battles (as most Montgomerians knew, there was usually a breeze on Capitol Hill). Again, Zelda would visit the small graveyard of the Confederacy, sometimes slyly moving flowers from one grave to another, designing an appropriate mourning ritual for the Southern men she had only imagined. The space, and the history, of Montgomery was important to Zelda.

She also found pleasure in surrounding herself with flowers and trees. She liked the japonica, the kiss-me-at-the-gate, honeysuckle, jasmine, wisteria; she liked seeing the shaggy outlines of pine trees from her bedroom window, and the shaded places under the large backyard trees: she might read there, or make a village out of bark, or try to redirect a trail of ants. In the heat of the Montgomery summer, her mother would take her and sometimes other of the children to a cool resort in the modest town of Saluda, North Carolina. Zelda remembered the change in atmosphere vividly; later, she wrote about the shadowy long roads which were bounded by trees that overhung so lushly that seeing the road was difficult. "Vines rust over the broken balconies; in the evening deep wells of shadow absorb the world."[18] Traveling by train from Montgomery, Minnie and her family would do little except sit on the shaded porch, walk down the hilly path to the post office and village, and enjoy well-cooked meals. Saluda was

[17] Exiles, pp. 18-19; Sara Haardt, "Dear Life," Southern Album (1936), pp. 284-5; Bankhead, Tallulah, p. 15.

[18] Zelda's journals, PUL.

the farthest stop north on the mountain railway. The Judge would come for weekends or a week during the summer, but most of the time belonged to Zelda and her mother. Even without playmates, Zelda was content in the quiet green world of North Carolina's Smoky Mountains.

Zelda as Adolescent

To chart Zelda's year-by-year development is impossible now. When she wrote about her girlhood, in stories as well as in the two novels—*Save Me the Waltz*, published in 1932, and "Caesar's Things," never published but written in the early 1940s, Zelda did not specify when events happened. (The reader also knows that her writing is fiction, and so there is slim reason to use material from it as if it were fact.) We know that Zelda taught Sara Mayfield to dive, but we do not know when. We know she tagged after her brother Anthony, but that he did not encourage her. We have no idea when her menstrual periods began, though in a household of sisters, the event may not have bothered her so much as it may a child who grows up alone. We know that she thought her ballet training important, and that her teacher gave her the sense that she could be a good dancer, a better-than-good dancer.[19] We know she didn't mind going to the Montgomery public schools, on which her father insisted because he served on the school board—even though most of her girlfriends went to nearby private schools, Miss Gussie Woodruff's Dames' School and the newer Margaret Booth School. Those schools were for girls only, so Zelda may have considered the coed student body at Sidney Lanier High School an advantage. We know

---

[19] Exiles, p. 18; Taylor, Sometimes Madness, p. 22; Milford, pp. 14-15.

that as her sisters married and left home, the struggles between her father and her mother over the children diminished, and once all four of the older Sayre children had married, life ran more smoothly.

There was more time for Minnie Sayre to make meals, and clothes, for Zelda. Always a difficult-to-please eater, Zelda had lived her life on the edges of mealtime, taking as her due the special treats her mother found for her in the pantry. She stayed slender in part because she didn't care for large meals. But she did care for the clothes her mother fashioned for her. Sometimes pretentious and just plain "too old," the dresses Minnie chose for Zelda were a way of recasting her own former beauty. Zelda too had learned to sew, and the concept of making clothes (or, later, of making draperies for the houses she lived in) came easily to her.

Zelda's party dresses were one of the reasons she found herself set apart from her beginning year at Lanier High School. Always more comfortable with boys than girls because of the kinds of games and sports they were likely to play, Zelda used the notion of difference to separate herself still further from the girls who would have been her likely companions— she did, however, have good girlfriends. In the segregated high school, located at the edge of Montgomery's Garden District, Zelda's courses were what would have been considered advanced track: chemistry, English literature, mathematics, geography, French, Latin, history, physiology. She carried a high B average. She liked history, mathematics, English; she could manage languages. But she remained interested in the pastimes of her childhood—she took up tennis and golf, when finances allowed; she continued to swim, and was named best swimmer and diver among the women of her class;[20] she continued to study dance and became known in the city for her ability. She read. She learned the newest ballroom dance steps. She watched the romances of Rosalind and Clotilde lead eventually to marriage, after she had earlier seen them take jobs and leave the house in the morning, sometimes walking with the Judge to the streetcar stop, and eventually go to work at the bank or the newspaper office without their face veils. Later, they began eating their lunches downtown, at a public restaurant. Even in Montgomery, times were changing.

All of these events were exciting to the young Zelda, who called herself an "excitement eater."[21] She watched the way life was changing, even for women. She overheard her parents discussing the Bankheads allowing their granddaughter, Tallulah, to move to New York City after she had won a photo contest in Photoplay. Only fifteen, Tallulah was cared for in the city by an aunt, so as to take advantage of the stage auditions that her prize entitled her to: within a few more years, she was acting on the London stage. Two years younger than Zelda, Tallulah and her sister Eugenia, who was a year older, had been occasional playmates of Zelda's—all were dancers, all were adventurous.[22]

Distinctively attractive as Tallulah Bankhead was, with her dramatic eyes and heavy makeup, Zelda Sayre knew that she was prettier, and that she was a better dancer. Even in her first year at Lanier, Zelda was exploring what her beauty and her

---

[20] PUL, scrapbook.

[21] Quoted from SMTW in Exiles, p. 20.

[22] Bankhead, Tallulah, pp. 54-5; Lee Israel, Miss Tallulah Bankhead (1972), pp. 26-7.

verve could achieve for her: she had more social freedom than most of her girlfriends.[23] Almost every day after school she went to the drugstore for a "dope," a Coke with an aspirin. In today's terms, Zelda "hung out." She was not above picking people up, or at least talking with them—she was not properly shy and reticent. She was less a Southern lady than her mother would have guessed.

When psychologist Jean Baker Miller discusses women's development, the various girls-becoming-women patterns, she emphasizes that women's lives are inherently filled with changes, and that women do much of their learning by what she terms "living change." With the varied decades of their lives—free from responsibility at first, then married and acting the role of wife, then becoming mothers and then grandmothers—Miller concludes that women's lives "are closer to change, real change." In every instance, according to this authority, "change requires learning. But the specific processes involved in women's learning are submerged and go unrecognized because the dominant culture describes learning only in accordance with its own interests and understanding."[24]

In accordance with this paradigm, biographical treatment of the years of Zelda Sayre's adolescence is comparatively vague: the most said by biographers is that she was not an exceptional student, that teachers thought she was bright and energetic. She was clearly a presence in the class, however: in the senior class yearbook honors, Zelda was chosen as prettiest, most energetic, and—in the senior girl composite—as having the most

---

[23] Andre LeVot, F. Scott Fitzgerald (1983), pp. 63-4.

[24] Jean Baker Miller, Toward a New Psychology of Women (1976), pp. 54-5.

desirable mouth. Given that Zelda was existing within the world of Montgomery, Alabama—except for partial summers in the tiny village of Saluda, North Carolina, with trips to Blowing Rock or Asheville, places that would hardly rate high for sophistication—she must as a teenager have been conscious of her feminine role in the coming years, to capture the attention of men, to be courted, and finally to marry.

She had watched this active drama play out in the Sayre household. She had seen the ways her mother helped her sisters; she had heard the arguments between Minnie and her father when beaux were considered unsuitable. In training herself to manage the stages of romance, Zelda took those experiences to heart. But as Miller continues, for a woman to become the submissive object of the courtship romance, her youthful independent personality must change. Zelda—as a headstrong and forthright child and adolescent—was in no way docile or submissive. As Miller states,

To be considered as an object can lead to a deep inner sense that there must be something wrong and bad about oneself … To be treated like an object is to be threatened with psychic annihilation … when one is an object, not a subject, all of one's own physical and sexual impulses and interests are presumed not to exist independently. They are to be brought into existence only by and for others—controlled, defined, and used. Any stirrings of physicality and sexuality in herself would only confirm for a girl or a woman her evil state.[25]

Few developing women had the possibility for conflict that Zelda did. Few young women were their family's babies,

[25] Ibid., p. 59; CT

22

and fewer still had been so healthily independent as to lead unrestricted lives. In Zelda's case, the members of the Sayre household lived in close enough quarters that she was able to observe closely her three sisters as they went through the courtship rituals, complete with arguments and, in at least one case, the replacement of the woman's desired prospective spouse with another, at her father's insistence. If Zelda had ever thought of the concept of modeling her life as a young woman after any of the lives of her three sisters, she would have realized that she was unlike Marjorie, Rosalind, or Clotilde. She had been given the privileges of the "baby" and she had pushed those privileges to the edge of propriety; she was an adolescent girl who was clearly occupying the subject position in life.

While Zelda occasionally went with Minnie to the Episcopalian church, where her mother sometimes sang in the choir, she was not interested in church doctrine. She was more likely to spend weekend afternoons in one of Montgomery's four movie theaters, seeing a film twice if time allowed. Zelda wanted to be the glamorous Hollywood blonde who captivated every man that saw her, and she thought she wanted to leave Montgomery in order to become that glamorous blonde[26]—but she loved her warm and comfortable Southern city. In Montgomery, most achievements came easy for Zelda Sayre: she was accustomed to daydreaming her way through difficulties.

Zelda might not appear to be the exceptional over-achiever her friends and family considered her to be. Unlike the achievements

[26]   Taylor, Sometimes Madness, pp. 5-6; and see Simone Weil Davis, Living Up to the Ads (2001).

of her scholarly father, Zelda's were not academic, nor were they the kinds of endeavors that parents of precocious daughters discussed. Did it matter how many kinds of dives she had learned to execute? To Zelda, it did. Did it matter that she often begged to go for drives in the autos of young men she did not know well, partly because she was intent on learning to drive herself? To Zelda, it did. Did it matter to her mother's circle of friends that she led the girls' revolt over the uniforms they were required to wear for physical education? Those women never heard of that activity, but even Minnie would have drawn a line at her daughter's being socially obstreperous. Being too visible was not a lady's way. Whether Minnie considered herself a Kentucky woman or one from Alabama, she was a lady.

Becoming a Belle

Added to the wealth of information Zelda had accrued from just living in the Sayre household, observing the lives of its older daughters, was the beginning of her own celebrity. Difficult as it is to envision, Zelda Sayre became a newsworthy personality when she was scarcely fifteen, for doing a dance—and in a town of 40,000 people. (Some of the news coverage may have occurred because her sister had been the society reporter before she married and moved to New York; more likely, the paper was experiencing a slow news day, and the Sayre's youngest child benefited.)

In the spring of 1916, Zelda danced a solo at the ballet recital in the stifling City Auditorium, a recital which was followed by community ballroom dancing.[27] In her pink tutu, her blonde

---

[27] PUL, scrapbook.

hair curled perfectly around her petal pink face, Zelda was clearly a talented young beauty. Though her face was round and innocent, she had the poise of a much older dancer. The audience was mesmerized. Once the recital finished and the general dancing began, the boy her mother had asked to dance with Zelda (not knowing how her tomboy daughter would fare with the ballroom crowd) had just begun his service when other boys and men cut in immediately. Her "date" did walk her home, but that was the first he had seen her again that evening. The chattering, nonplused young girl was as pleasant (and in a quiet way, as flirtatious) as a college-age woman; she was also as good a ballroom dancer as she was a ballerina. Zelda Sayre's popularity had begun.

Social life in Montgomery during the summer revolved around subscription dances. Privately organized, the bands paid for by the college men who sponsored them, the dances were usually held in the open air dance pavilion at Oak Park, close enough to residential areas that people could walk or take streetcars. Lists of girls the men wanted to see participate in the dances were posted in advance on the door of Harry's, the local ice cream parlor, and the custom was that a man signed up opposite the name of the girl he wanted to "take" to the dance. The girls and women who appeared on the lists had no choice in the matter—except choosing not to go. And if women went to the dance without having been listed, they were considered gauche.

Zelda would turn sixteen on July 24. She had been to a great many subscription dances before her birthday. It was for that breaking of the social code, which protects the innocence of the Southern girl of good family, for which her friends' families faulted Minnie. A few of Zelda's young friends also went to the dances, but none so regularly and none so vivaciously as Zelda. Her work for the summer had become these dances, along with the Saturday night dances at the Country Club—the dances and swimming. She wore a new one-piece Annette Kellerman suit in a beige-colored jersey, and laughed at rumors that she swam in the nude.[28] The form-fitting suit was thought to be shocking, unless one were an Olympic champion.

It was this summer that the Judge was said to have forbade Zelda's leaving the house. Nevertheless, from her bedroom window, which overlooked the front porch, she managed to get out of the house and go to most of the dances. Unfortunately, the Montgomery Advertiser added to the friction between Zelda and her father by running a feature that reproduced a silhouette of her profile, wearing a jaunty tam, with the description,

You may keep an eye open for the possessor of this classic profile about a year from now when she advances just a little further beyond the sweet-sixteen stage. Already she is in the crowd at the Country Club every Saturday night and at the script dances every other night of the week. She has the straightest nose, the most determined little chin and the bluest eyes in Montgomery. She might dance like Pavlowa if her nimble feet were not so busy keeping up with the pace a string of young but ardent admirers set for her.[29]

Zelda's junior year at Lanier High School passed quickly. Although her parents would not let her go to dances at colleges, she saw enough men on the weekends—and occasionally during the week, if she could figure out a way to cut her classes—to maintain the same fever pitch her life had reached during the

---

[28] Bankhead, Tallulah, p. 63; Exiles, p. 24.

[29] PUL scrapbook.

summer of 1916. The weather in Montgomery seldom kept college men who wanted to drive over from Auburn or Georgia Tech away—and the warmth of the climate kept the traffic at Boodler's Bend consistent all year long. Girls and women who would park at Boodler's were said to be "boodling"—and Zelda knew about that kind of necking and petting. While boodling might have been customary, it is also the fact that the real belles did not need to attract men through sex: being with Zelda, or any other belle, provided enough excitement. It would fit with Zelda's desire to break conventional norms that she go to Boodler's Bend, and that she be seen doing so; but she might not have been sexual once she got there.[30]

One consistent activity in Zelda's life was the ballet. She took lessons until she was seventeen, and during her junior year, she participated in the usual recitals and programs—always to high praise. One account in the Montgomery paper said that Miss Sayre "is an unusually talented and gifted dancer." Either that year or the next, she was chosen for lead roles in community performances: she was with the group of dancers who performed "The Dance of the Nile" in the Junior League vaudeville; she was chosen to enact the part of England in the Rotary Club Allied Nations pageant; and she was "War" in the Masque of War & Peace pageant. The news coverage once more singled her out for her excellence.

Zelda's junior and senior years blur in the scrapbook. It seems clear that the literal whirl of her social life kept her family on

---

[30] Durr, Magic Circle, p. 64; Bankhead, Tallulah, p. 73 (the actress remembered: "at seventeen, I was a virgin. I certainly didn't look like one ... . I was a technical virgin at twenty").

edge—even her loyal mother began to remonstrate that she was out too late, that she was smoking cigarettes, and (though Minnie did not make an issue of it at this time) that she was drinking. The United States had not yet passed the Volstead Act—Prohibition would begin in January, 1919—but gin and corn liquor, mixed with Coke, were the drinks of choice on campuses. College men carried flasks of some kind of alcohol, tucked in an inner pocket of their heavy-knit school sweaters.

According to Zelda's friends, she dated college men from the best Montgomery families. Sara Mayfield lists "Leon Ruth, Peyton Spottswood Mathis, John Allan Sellers, Dan Cody, Lloyd Hooper."[31] Some of these men had gone to private academies before college; it was rare that boys of Montgomery's elite families stayed in town for secondary education. Young as she was, Zelda would not have known most of them, then, in the public schools, at the local tennis courts, or at the swimming pools. They were, accordingly, as exotic to her as she in her sheer youth was to them.

Sara Haardt drew the picture of Montgomery's expanding industry at this time, an expansion which transformed the temperament of the usually sedate city.[32] Considering itself "the Paris of the South,"[33] Montgomery was proud that it could maintain taste, class distinctions, decorum. But as industrial and agricultural production increased from $3 million to $19 million, and the euphoria of technological expertise from the Wright

[31] Exiles, p. 23.

[32] Sara Haardt, The Making of a Lady (1931).

[33]   Marion Elizabeth Rodgers' Introduction to *Mencken* and Sara:A Life in Letters (1987), p. 24.

brothers' establishing their flying school in 1910, everyone was feeling "modern." Even jazz was becoming acceptable. As Zelda remembered growing up in Montgomery,

there was scarcely a ripple in our lives. Life itself seemed severe, almost smugly secure ... everything was changed. Life had suddenly become exciting, dangerous; a crazy vitality possessed us. I felt it as I leaned over to fasten the straps of my skates the moment before I went sailing wildly down the middle of Perry Street hill, screeeching at the top of my lungs and catching hold of the backs of automobiles as they dashed up the hill again.[34]

It was because of the Wright flying school and the airfields built for it that the "air depot" was located in Montgomery. Once the United States entered World War I in 1917, Camp Sheridan opened and soon 20,000 troops and flight personnel were located at the edge of Montgomery. Zelda talked about the release of energy once the military had arrived:

then the war came and we had the inescapable feeling that all this beauty and fun—everything—might be over in a minute. We couldn't wait, we couldn't afford to wait, for fear it would be gone forever; so we pitched in furiously, dancing every night and riding up and down the moonlit roads and even swimming in the gravel pools under the white Alabama moon that gives the world a strange, lovely touch of madness.[35]

Sara Haardt's description of these years in her novel, *The Making of a Lady*, parallels Zelda's recollections of this "violent mobilization of Meridian's [Montgomery's] war resources,"

Meridian was like an animated ballroom in its sudden whirlwind

[34] Zelda Fitzgerald's interview with Sara Haardt, quoted in ibid., p. 25.

[35] Ibid., p. 26.

of skirts. Women swarmed in the office buildings … they paraded the streets in Red Cross uniforms and khaki skirts, they raced back and forth to the camps in cars streaming with flags and bunting. All the vacant stores in the business district were turned into committee rooms for the Red Cross, the War Camp Community Service, the Girls' Patriotic League, with shifts of charming young women serving tea with their little information pamphlets. There were decorated booths at the intersections of the busiest streets filled with pretty girls selling tags and stamps and imitation Flanders Fields poppies. They clustered in excited groups, giggling at the idea of approaching men they had never seen before, arching the thin lines of their eyebrows …[36]

Men had begun arriving at Camp Sheridan in the fall of 1917, at the start of Zelda's senior year at Lanier High School. Many of the officers received passes and even memberships to the Montgomery Country Club: the town was open to them. Dances there and at the Exchange Hotel brought out patriotic young women, all intent on befriending the young soldiers who might soon be sent to Europe—to the front, and to their deaths. In the case of the already busy Montgomery belles, who had long since been involved in a phalanx of evening dates—a 6 p.m. date for supper, followed by a 9 p.m. date for dancing, followed in some cases by an 11 p.m. date for late supper—the influx of so many new men was mind-boggling. What the arrival of the military did in part was to erase the importance of family name and class standing; no one could know those details about the soldiers and fliers who came into Montgomery to see and dance with the beautiful Southern women.

---

[36] Haardt, The Making of a Lady, pp. 219-21.

The community dances, created to welcome the military men, were frequented by what Haardt describes as

a mixed crowd, soldiers and civilians and tawdry little girls from the side streets who posed as visitors from Atlanta and Birmingham—all the girls in town who had achieved a certain aura of popularity ... loafers from the pool rooms edged into the stage line.[37]

It was clear that "the Paris of the South" had lost all sense of boundaries, and that myriad unknown men were as acceptable to the city and its women as the college men of the town's most prestigious families had previously been.

Among the money-raising activities that Montgomery undertook during Zelda's last year in high school were benefit vaudeville shows, benefit bridge parties, and beauty balls with booths for girls and women to sell both dances and kisses. For several months, Zelda and her friends—about twenty boys and girls in all—put on variety shows for elements of the military camps: the "Jelly Beans" were singers, dancers, joke tellers, and all-round attractive people. Parades with patriotic floats moved through the streets to the strains of "The Stars and Stripes Forever," "The Good Old U.S.A.," "Maid of America"—and "Dixie."

Hysteria may not be too strong a word to describe the frenzy of social life in previously staid Montgomery. In the midst of it all, acclaimed to be one of the city's most beautiful and talented belles, was Zelda Sayre. And when she performed a solo dance in the summer of 1918, to begin a Country Club

---

[37]   Ibid., p. 229; Exiles, p. 21; Milfbrd, pp. 19-20; Taylor, Sometimes Madness, pp. 27-9.

dance to which, as was customary, the Camp Sheridan officers had been invited, it was F. Scott Fitzgerald who asked everyone around him who she was. Told that Zelda was too young for him, Scott only maneuvered his way to the dance floor and staked what was to become his permanent claim—even though Zelda Sayre was not yet eighteen.

TWO - The Courtship

When Fitzgerald became smitten with the young blonde with a face like a flower, he found his usually effective charm blunted. "I don't make late dates with fast-talkers," Zelda announced when lie pressed her for permission to come see her the following night.[38] True to the experiences she had had during the past two years, keeping a phalanx of desirable young men happy in their ardent courtship of her, Zelda had become a good judge of people. The somewhat fragile but handsome Irish officer, beautifully turned out in his Brooks Brothers uniform (far from standard issue for the 67th Infantry), seemed to be nothing special, though he was a good dancer.

Zelda was not eighteen, but her birthday was around the corner, and her high school graduation on May 31, behind her. She considered herself no longer a child. She had made her parents aware of this on several occasions earlier in the year; she was growing more difficult about their permissions,

---

[38] Kendall Taylor, Sometimes Madness (2001), p. 34.

often not telling them about her busy social calendar. Perhaps Minnie was complicit in Zelda's growing independence: classmates remember the flowing white silk dress, chiffon wrap, and hat that Zelda wore to graduation, after the girls of the class, partly in deference to the war effort, had agreed to wear simple dresses, spending no more than five dollars on fabric.[39] Clearly, Zelda's movie-star costume had cost more. So she was asked to sit in the audience, rather than on the stage with her classmates. A laughing Zelda complied.

When Lieutenant Fitzgerald had learned that he was being sent to Camp Sheridan from Fort Leavenworth in Kansas, he had contacted his Princeton classmate Ludlow Fowler to ask for the names of some of the prettiest and/or the fastest girls in Montgomery. Because Fowler was much older than Zelda, he did not mention her: he did not know her. Fitzgerald had found several of the women on Fowler's list and was dating them that summer. But he found Zelda on his own.

He found her because she had just danced the formal ballet solo, "The Dance of the Hours." Dance in America was a new art, a glamorous one.[40] It wasn't only the excitement of the highly original Isadora Duncan, moving her uncorseted

---

[39] Milford, p. 23.

[40] . Besides Anna Pavlova (or Pavlowa) and Isadora Duncan, the vogue for Irene and Vernon Castle had begun somewhat earlier, about the time of Owen Johnson's The Salamander (1914), the novel which was the start of the flapper mentality in 1914. As Robert McAlmon remembered, "none of us children considered ourselves grown up unless we could honton or turkey-walk over 200 miles a week of so-called dancing" (Robert McAlmon and Kay Boyle, Being Geniuses Together, 1920-1930 (1984) p. 308.

body beneath flowing Grecian robes, making her barefooted pilgrimage into the imaginations of all observers, worldwide; it was the news from Paris about the exodus of the Russian ballet to France—and the traveling companies that further popularized serious dance, with its amazingly deft toe dancing, throughout the States. The Montgomery Advertiser's reference to Zelda's becoming another Pavlowa indicates the place of serious dance in the American imagination: as much as becoming a movie star, girls in the States tried to become dancers. In her own sense of herself and her talents, Zelda was confident that she too could become an important dancer, or actress, or movie star. Her skittish happy life as someone's date was not only fun; it was a kind of subtle preparation for the life of fame to come. She could see in her mirror, as well as in the eyes of her many admirers, that she had an unusually arresting face and body: she was perfectly proportioned, she was in wonderful shape, she was slim but still sexy—and she had recently emphasized her body by having all her skirts shortened to the knee.

When Scott had been told that Zelda was too young for him, he demurred. Not yet twenty-two, he did not think of himself as old: he had been one of the youngest in his Princeton class, when he entered (not from passing entrance examinations or on the basis of decent grades at hic preparatory school; Newman in New Jersey, but from the persuasion of his oral interview); he had been one of the youngest writers for the Princeton Triangle shows. That he had not come close to graduating—because of his continual sitting out of terms, punishment for poor grades and missed classes—but had started his fifth year only as a way of passing time until his enlistment caught up with him seemed not to have tarnished his definition of himself as a "Princeton man."[41] He used that as capital in meeting women.

Scott Fitzgerald did, however, carry a recognizably Irish name, which implied possible Catholicism as well as a low position in class-conscious East coast society. Although his father was descended from several important Maryland families, Edward Fitzgerald had not been a business success.[42] After Scott's birth in 1896 in St. Paul, Minnesota, the family had lived for some years in both Buffalo and Syracuse, New York but then Procter & Gamble had fired Edward so the Fitzgeralds returned to St. Paul where his mother's family money insured them a social niche. Renting houses in the correct part of town, much of the time on Summit Avenue, the Fitzgeralds eked out a foothold within good society. Scott, however, was seldom popular—other boys found him whiny and conceited—and because he was getting bad grades in the public schools, his aunt volunteered to send him to Newman.

Living in the East, Fitzgerald traveled between St. Paul and the coast by train, and saw himself as one of the cosmopolitan Midwesterners who would rise to prominence through Eastern connections. He fell in love with Ginevra King, the

[41] Starting in 1951 with Arthur Mizener's The Far Side of Paradise: A Biography of F. Scott Fitzgerald, biographers of Fitzgerald have rehearsed these five years in great detail; see the Bibliography for information about books by LeVot, Mellow, Meyers, Piper, Sklar, Turnbull and SSEG. Scott Donaldson's Fool gives the most detailed account of Fitzgerald's Princeton academic record (pp. 20-5).

[42] See biographies above and Scottie Fitzgerald Smith, "The Colonial Ancestors of Francis Scott Key Fitzgerald" (1981) as "Afterword" in SSEG, and Broccoli's "Brief Life" in Life, pp. xix-xx.

beautiful daughter of a wealthy Chicago family;[43] and from the eventual end of that romance, developed his belief that rich girls did not marry poor boys. What seemed to be Scott's customary fate—that he was tolerated instead of liked, and that his dream of attaining a "top girl" to love was doomed to fail—began in his adolescence, and continued through his military career, where he described himself as being the worst aide-de-camp in history.

Zelda Sayre could not know any of this history, however. Fitzgerald was from a part of the country so remote to her (since she never left Montgomery except for those North Carolina summers) that what she heard—all that she heard—was East coast and Princeton. She knew of some of the older Montgomery men who had gone to Princeton; they seemed more sophisticated than her friends at nearby Southern schools. Mentally, she put Scott in their company, and she was doubly intrigued when he sent her a chapter from his rejected novel.

Between their meeting in July and Scott's being transferred north in late October, Zelda spent many hours with her Princeton suitor. On September 7, 1918, Scott noted in his *Ledger* that he had fallen in love with her. Even though Zelda did not stop seeing other men, she gave Scott priority—he called her from camp at least once a day, she told him her innermost dreams (to become famous in the arts, among other things), he sometimes took meals with the Sayre family. Fitzgerald obviously had the inside track: he was a regular on the shambles of a bus that came from Camp Sheridan to Montgomery, and then he came by cab the rest of the way. The girl who lived at

---

[43] See biographies above, SSEG, and Fool, especially pp. 46-52.

6 Pleasant Street had become Scott's "top girl," and he viewed her as essential to his future life.[44]

Because the October transfer from Montgomery meant that Fitzgerald would probably be sent to France, it is likely that he and Zelda consummated their relationship sometime that month.[45] The casualty count of the Allied forces was dinner table conversation at the Sayres': Zelda's married sister Clotilde was back living with the family because her husband was in France; his battalion had lost a great many men.

Scott's travels were circular, as it turned out. He never got to France. Instead, he left Camp Sheridan for an East coast destination, was then sent to Camp Mills on Long Island and then, after the Armistice on November 11, was sent back to Montgomery to await his discharge. It was during the first weeks of his return that he and Zelda argued bitterly.

Fitzgerald wrote a friend that he was determined not to marry, no matter how much he loved Zelda.[46] By December of 1918, however, he recorded in his *Ledger* only the word *LOVE*.[47] The next few months in Alabama, with his courtship moving toward engagement, Scott had to learn a great deal about the business of courting, and in this case, courting an immensely popular

---

[44] See biographies above; supplement with Milford, Exiles, SMTW, CT, DS, DZ and Taylor, Sometimes Madness.

[45] See biographies, especially Fool, pp. 62-3 and SSEG, p. 89.

[46] On December 4, 1918, he wrote Ruth Sturtevant, a woman he had casually dated at Princeton, saying that "my mind is firmly made up that I will not, shall not, can not, should not, must not marry" (SSEG, p. 91).

[47] Also *Ledger*, p. 73; earlier, on September 7, 1918, Fitzgerald had written "Fell in love [with Zelda] " (Fool, p. 51).

woman. Partly because of his parochial education, and partly because Fitzgerald had always fallen in love with the "top girls," his sexual experience had been limited.[48] Like Ginevra King, Zelda Sayre was so popular she seldom gave sexual favors; in Scott's case, however, she had. His dilemma was being able to tell how much Zelda had learned from her years as a "boodler" at Boodler's Bend—and how much of her behavior stemmed from her love for him. For much of the rest of their lives, Scott worried about how much Zelda had known about sex before she had met him.

When Fitzgerald received his discharge on February 14, 1919, and four days later left for New York, where he hoped to work as a journalist while continuing to revise his novel, he considered Zelda his mate. He asked his mother to welcome her to the family.[49] She promptly wrote that letter, and then Zelda worried about answering it,[50] because—as she reminded Scott—she customarily wrote only to men, and hers were flippant and teasing letters. Those were also the kind of letters she wrote to Scott.

---

[48] See Elizabeth Beckwith MacKie's account of the young college man Fitzgerald on the lookout for romantic conquests ("My Friend Scott Fitzgerald," 1973).

[49] Andre LeVot, F. Scott Fitzgerald, A Biography (1983), p. 68.

[50] Zelda's letters reprinted in DS, DZ, pp. 12-13, 16, 19. There are a number of her letters from this time period that are not included in the book. The tone of her writing is usually direct, vivacious, insightful — and sometimes comic. For instance, this paragraph from a letter dated simply "spring, 1919," evidently her response to Fitzgerald's hunting for an apartment for them. He has sent her a map of New York. She writes, "The map of New York might just as well be China—All I saw was the dot where we would live — I couldn't help wondering over the fact that two rooms and bath took up the same space as Washington Square and Statue of Liberty. You are so sweet, Scot [sic], and thoughtful ... Thank God I'm marrying you, and not New York ...".

Officially, Zelda had never stopped seeing other beaux, although she had made herself less available. She made no excuses to the barely-absent Scott when a few days later, on February 22, she went to Auburn University for a week of parties with the star football quarterback. In what is extant of the courtship correspondence (Scott saved what appear to be many of Zelda's letters, but of his, only an occasional letter and some telegrams pasted into her scrapbook remain), Zelda told him about new men that she and her good friend Eleanor had met, about visits to campuses, and about Montgomery dances. Predictably, Scott was distracted from his work. He had invested everything in his courtship of Zelda, and now he saw how easily he might lose her.

Repeatedly, he used the metaphor of princesses looked in towers.[51] Zelda reprimanded him for his overuse, and suggested that they needn't write to each other every day (which Scott was doing). Her solution to his repetition problem was that they should write to each other when they felt like doing so.

The spring of 1919 was Zelda's debut as an acknowledged star of Montgomery dance.[52] The Les Mysterieuses, the quasi-secret group of' sixty of Montgomery's socially prominent young matrons—a group to which Rosalind Sayre Newman belonged—sponsored a charity ball each April. For the 1919 occasion Rosalind and her mother, Minnie, wrote the playlet that prefaced the "Folly Ball" and featured Zelda's solo ballet number. Being fitted for the glamorous costume took Zelda

[51] In both letters and F. Scott Fitzgerald's *Ledger* (1972), p. 73.

[52] Milford, pp. 46-7.

back to her teenage dreams of becoming a dancer. She liked the immersion in practice, in routine: Zelda liked to work when it meant being admired. The event, and the way she looked in costume, was so important to her that she sent the Kodak photos to Scott.

The (Brief) Engagement

In March of 1919, Scott sent Zelda what she described as pajamas out of *Vogue*, and on March 22, he mailed her his mother's ring, which she had just sent on to him. Scott had already written to Zelda's mother Minnie about his intentions, but at this time he enclosed a letter to the Judge for Zelda to give him. She seemed to be afraid to do so, probably understanding, at least subconsciously, that her brilliant father—self-sufficient and unapproachable—was not going to be pleased that his youngest daughter had chosen for a husband a charming would-be writer, a man who had not graduated from college and had only limited financial prospects. Two men could hardly have been more different: the Judge, like many Americans before Prohibition, did not drink; that Scott did was a worry to both Zelda's parents.

It is unclear from Zelda's letters whether or not she gave Scott's letter to her father. She did, however, wear the diamond ring; she reported to Scott that her doing so caused a sensation at the Country Club dance.[53] Then her letter continued to describe her busy social calendar; her "engagement" seems to have changed her life very little. When the worried Scott came to Montgomery for an April weekend, he was not

---

[53] LeVot, F. Scott Fitzgerald, p. 69 and see DS, DZ, p. 22.

reassured. When he got back to New York, where he was unhappy in a low-paying advertising job, he sent Zelda a gray-blue feather fan, a flamboyant accessory suitable for a would-be starlet. She loved it. In May he sold his first story. *Smart Set* paid him $30, and with the money Fitzgerald bought a pair of white flannel trousers for himself and a soft pink sweater for her.

Then came Zelda's error in juggling her romances. Soon after Scott had left in April, she met a Georgian who was golfing at the Montgomery Country Club. He invited her to Atlanta for a party weekend; she went, and she returned home with his fraternity pin. Realizing, however, that she was engaged to Scott, she wrote this suitor a note of apology and returned his pin. The error came in that she sent his letter and pin to Scott, and sent him the letter intended for Fitzgerald.

Scott arrived in Montgomery on the next train, demanding that they marry at once. The argument was bitter, and Zelda returned his ring.[54]

Scott went back to New York, quit his job, and began a three-week drinking spree (he drank until enforcement of the Volstead Act closed most of the New York bars).[55] On July 4 he took a train for St. Paul, where he lived at home throughout the summer and fall, reconceiving and rewriting his rejected novel, with the aid of some of Zelda's letters and, possibly, her diary.

---

[54] SSEG, p. 96.

[55] To Ruth Sturtevant, on June 24, 1919, Fitzgerald wrote, "Unless someday she will marry me I will never marry" (Fool, p. 64).

The Narrative of Zelda and Scott

Rehearsing the ins and outs of the Zelda Sayre-Scott Fitzgerald engagement is of interest chiefly for characterization of the principals. From the start, during the summer and fall of 1918, Scott was jealous of Zelda and her friendships and dates. He had difficulty understanding that she was a good friend to a number of her would-be suitors[56]—that she had gone swimming with them for years, that they had played tennis together on all the Montgomery courts, that they had ridden bikes and, more recently, motorcycles together, that they had set up each other's buddies with dates, and that they had been sneaking drinks and cigarettes together in the comparatively safe milieu of their long-term friendships. Because Scott had led a different kind of adolescence, moving from school to school and finally out of St. Paul entirely, he didn't understand what these Montgoiuerians shared. He found it hard to believe that Zelda had heard stories about the Mayfield and Cody families from the time she was a schoolgirl in her own kitchen. (That he tried to comprehend these relationships gave him the first of his Tarleton stories, "The Ice Palace,"[57] which describes the casual friendships

---

[56] Exile, pp. 16-25, and see Livye Ridgeway Hart, "Profile of Zelda" (n.d., unpublished) (University of Alabama Library).

[57] Indicative of Fitzgerald's romanticization of the South, this story is one of the first he credits to being Zelda's idea (F. Scott Fitzgerald, "Fitzgerald on 'The Ice Palace': A Newly Discovered Letter" (1972)). See also C. Hugh Holman, "Fitzgerald's Changes on the Southern Belle" (1982), Scott Donaldson, "Scott Fitzgerald's Romance with the South" (1973), Tahita N. Fulkerson, "Ibsen in 'The Ice Palace'" (1979) , John Kuehl, "Psychic Geography in 'The Ice Palace'" (1982) , and Edwin Moses, "F. Scott Fitzgerald and the Quest to 'The Ice Palace'" (1974).

between Sally Carrol and the boys she goes swimming with.)

He also found Zelda's attitudes toward sex frightening. Perhaps as a result of her saturation in the film culture of the day (most of the silent movies were romances, with body language more important than print captions), and of her reading of such popular novels as Owen Johnson's *The Salamander*[58] and translations of the French novels her sisters read, Zelda talked a good game about open relationships. While Scott romanticited their courtship, Zelda insisted that neither of them needed to be sexually possessive. She played the role of the modern woman, the "New Woman" who would understand if Scott in New York found someone he wanted— temporarily—to make love to.

Even if Zelda's stance was largely rhetorical, her words shook the conventional Scott. Partly because of her youth, he had put her on a pedestal of sexual innocence; he would be her teacher, her guide. His Catholic education reinforced his attitudes, and he felt that he needed to marry Zelda quickly once they had begun a sexual relationship. This idealization of Scott's passion for Zelda surfaced repeatedly in his poems, and the fragments of them, that focus on the Montgomery summer and fall when Zelda did become his. For instance, this stanza from an unpublished Fitzgerald poem titled "One Southern Girl":

---

[58] Published in 1914 and made into a stage play and a film, both starring Ruth Findlay (one of George Jean Nathan's lady friends). The popular film cost over $100,000 to make, and was set in New York's Jungle Club in Harlem. The' rebellious protagonist, Dore Baxter, is a new woman, "audacious and reckless," who cries out against conformity: "No, no! I won't be commonplace ... we are different now. We can be free — we can live our own lives!" (Salamander, pp. 104, 139).

Still does your hair's gold light the ground
And dazzle the blind 'till their old ghosts rise;
Then, all you cared to find being found,
Are you yet kind to their hungry eyes?
Part of a song, a remembered glory—
Say there's one rose that lives and might
Whisper the fragments of our story:
Kisses, a lazy street—and night.[59]

Fitzgerald was a writer. He believed his and Zelda's love was unique, that it was—and would remain—"a remembered glory." One of Zelda's names for Scott was "The King of Roses"; the metaphoric identity of the rose as sexual description, Zelda's rose, comes into play here, but in Fitzgerald's imagination it is the "one rose," parallel to the title, "One Southern Girl," that gives meaning to all love. The closing line suggestively recaptures the moment in his memory of their kisses, the "lazy" Montgomery street, the darkness, and perhaps their new intimacy.

Like the more fragmentary poem, "Our April Letter,"[60] this one tries to place the couple in the South, a lush and therefore exotic place for the speaker, a place that also seems conducive to the erotic: "This is April again. Roller skates rain slowly down the street ... April evening spreads over everything, the purple blur left by a child who has used the whole paint-box." Trying to re-create Zelda's childhood, the roller skates on which she spent many summer days, the energy with which

---

[59] Scott Fitzgerald, Poems, 1911-1940, p. 113.

[60] Ibid., p. 114.

she used up her art supplies, Fitzgerald here speaks as the cautious observer, marveling at the difference between them and their places of origin.

Scott Fitzgerald as Character

Far from self-confident, Scott fit the pattern of the person who drinks to compensate—whether the compensation is for feelings of inferiority, or feelings of other kinds of inadequacy. One of the ways in which Fitzgerald differed from Zelda Sayre was in his formation of friendships. It is startling to read in a letter from John Peale Bishop, who had been one of his best Princeton friends, writing later to Allen Tate, who admired Scott's writing, about Scott's bifurcated personality. Bishop wrote that his only information about Zelda's health was from "Scott's drunken gossip and that depends upon whether he's trying to bolster himself up or make himself out a lowly Midwestern worm. As you know."[61] Inferiority of family status and finances, of national origin, of religious beliefs, of academic performance, of personality—Fitzgerald had a number of characteristics that he saw as troublesome in his life of becoming a famous writer, surrounding himself with men and women of the acknowledged social elite.

For Scott and Zelda to marry meant that he would be the first of his Princeton crowd to wed: he would, he assumed, be the envy of men he thought superior to himself Edmund Wilson, Alex McKaig, John Peale Bishop, John Biggs, Townsend Martin, Ludlow Fowler. He had raved to Biggs about Zelda's "figure," as

---

[61] John Peale Bishop to Allen Tate (John Peale Bishop, The Republic of Letters (1981) p. 15.

if that were reason enough to marry her.[62] In Scott's imagination, the Fitzgeralds would he the pair of beautiful people who made everyone else envious of their great love, the idealization of the very myth Fitzgerald was writing about—the flapper and her handsome escort.[63] Extravagant even within the showy culture of young collegians trying to earn their living in New York, the Fitzgeralds dressed the part, spent money as if they were heirs to fortunes, and created absurd events in their partying so that the media would repeat, and repeat, and repeat, the stories.

Surely Scott was himself surprised at the things he and Zelda did. Surely he was surprised at the amount they drank. From his 1917 letter to Edmund Wilson, who was already in the service, about his spending the summer in St. Paul with his "companions," gin and the philosophers Bergson, James, and Schopenhauer, the record of Fitzgerald's drinking was hardly disguised.[64] He drank at Princeton; he drank in Minnesota; he drank in the military; he drank in Montgomery—even though Zelda was very young.

Although his father also drank too much, the members of the extended Fitzgerald family were not drinkers. St. Paul society—like most upper-middle-class and middle-class people—did not imbibe, and their not drinking was the context for passing the Volstead Act: the rationale was that drinking, defined as a lower-class problem, was taking money the poor needed to live. By legislating morality in this way, the middle classes of the United States could protect the less well-educated and well-funded from

---

[62] John Biggs quoted by Rex Polier, "Fitzgerald in Wilmington," Philadelphia Sunday Bulletin (1974).

[63] SSEG, pp. 130-2, LeVot, F. Scott Fitzgerald, pp. 82-6.

[64] Scott Fitzgerald, Letters of F. Scott Fitzgerald (1963), p. 318.

the ravages and waste of alcoholism. When F. Scott Fitzgerald wrote about the wild drinking and smoking and petting college students that made his fiction famous, he knew that his readers, by and large, did not themselves participate in these exotic behaviors.

Whether or not Scott Fitzgerald could at that time in his life be considered an alcoholic, to John Crowley, Tom Dardis, and most of his biographers, the label would eventually be apt. As Crowley put it, "Fitzgerald's alcoholism was finally never in doubt, however, except to Fitzgerald himself."[65] If not alcoholic, Fitzgerald in his mid-twenties was surely addictive, and he had a number of characteristics that put him at risk in an unregulated social world. One striking quality was his tendency toward self-pity. Never content with the abilities he did have, he yearned to be more important, more talented, more handsome than he was. Psychiatrist Alice Miller connects this kind of "grandiosity" with the child who needs an extreme amount of admiration.[66] In the case of Fitzgerald, because his two sisters had died shortly before his birth, his mother worried about him, and was consistently over-protective. He was therefore what Miller terms "his mother's special son"[67] and whatever he did, or tried to do, was held up for high praise. Because he received so much admiration from his mother, he continued to need

---

[65] John W. Crowley, The White Logic, Alcoholism and Gender in American Modernist Fiction (1994), p. 66; in his chapter on Fitzgerald, "The Drunkard's Holiday: Tender Is the Night," Crowley rehearses some of the alcoholic's traits.

[66] Alice Miller, The Drama of the Gifted Child (1981).

[67] Ibid., p. 41 and see Jonathan Schiff, Ashes to Ashes: Mourning and Social Difference in F. Scott Fitzgerald's Fiction (2001).

that admiration in order to feel loved. Miller's theory is that grandiose types often try to pair themselves with others who are equally inclined toward exaggerated ambitions and unrealistic self-images—which may underlie Scott's fascination with both Ginevra and Zelda. One remembers his telling Edmund Wilson that if he could not marry Zelda, he would never marry. He later said that if Zelda did not marry him, he hoped she would die.[68]

Authorities on alcoholism describe the addictive personality's self-centeredness, coupled with a fear of intimacy. What results is a skewed view of any relationship: "Because alcoholics ... are likely to embellish their feelings of intimacy with crisis-driven emotions, any possibility for true intimacy may trigger illusions of selective dependence. None of these people seems to have any real understanding of the meaning of love or friendship."[69] Matts Djos locates inordinate fear within the alcoholic's personality:

a higher level of anxiety, dependence, and defensiveness. This is sometimes reflected in a remarkable degree of moodiness, impulsivity, hostility, and distrust ... alcoholics have lower self-esteem, are more goal-oriented, strive more for a superficial feeling of achievement, and consistently exhibit an intense need for personal power. Such

---

[68] "I wouldn't care if she died, but I couldn't stand to have anybody else marry her" (quoted in Fool, p. 65).

[69] Matts Djos, "Alcoholism in Ernest Hemingway's The Sun Also Rises: A Wine and Roses Perspective on the Lost Generation," Casebook on Ernest Hemingway's The Sun Also Rises, ed. Linda Wagner-Martin (2002), p. 145; see also Kenneth E. Eble, "Touches of Disaster: Alcoholism and Mental Illness in Fitzgerald's Short Stories," The Short Stories of F. Scott Fitzgerald, ed. Jackson R. Bryer (1982); Arthur Waldhorn, "The Cartoonist, the Nurse, and the Writer: 'An Alcoholic Case,'" New Essays on F. Scott Fitzgerald's *Neglected* Stories (1996); and Tom Dardis, The Thirsty Muse: Alcohol and the American Writer (1989).

problems may be manifested by the development of facades suggesting a great deal of uncertainty regarding sexual identity.[70]

Because Fitzgerald had lived his early life within a clearly-marked heterosexual culture, investing his emotions in his admiration for women, there was little reason for him to have been anxious about his sexuality—despite the photos of him dressed as a beautiful chorine for the Princeton musicals. His later life in the more openly bisexual cities of Europe, however, was to encourage various kinds of homophobia, if not paranoia about the possibilities of his being considered gay.[71]

Broken Engagement, and After

Even a brief glimpse into Fitzgerald's behavior during his courtship of Zelda, and his immediate acts once she had broken the engagement and returned his ring, shows a number of specific traits that might have given her pause. Clearly, Scott was a jealous man, who needed to control his partner. He also used poor judgment in his choices of gifts for Zelda—pajamas, a flamboyant feather fan, a sweater marking her as a sex object, at least in his eyes. His coercive trips back to Montgomery, and his insistence that she write to him every day, evince his need to be reassured. And the final sequence of actions: his impetuous behavior once he returns to New York and quits the only job he had been able to find, as if announcing to his parents that he will not be responsible for his own financial wellbeing, and

---

[70] Djos, "Alcoholism," p. 141.

[71] Biographers Andre LeVot and Jeffrey Meyers comment on the behavior of Fitzgerald and others (as "Princeton transvestites") (LeVot, F. Scott Fitzgerald, p. 52; Jeffrey Meyers, Scott Fitzgerald, A Biography (1994), p. 27).

his drinking spree, undertaken at considerable cost of health, safety, and money, behavior which echoes some of his college drunks when he threatened to jump from windows; followed by his moving back home, where it appeared that he thought it his parents' duty to support him while he rewrote his novel.

Zelda, however, was not warned. Yet she also did not try to reconcile with him. No letters exist from the five months of their separation, between the time she returned his ring until October, when Fitzgerald broke his silence, telling her that Scribner's had accepted his novel, *This Side of Paradise*. Once more successful, Scott felt that he could resume the courtship.

Zelda's letters then were responsive. Yet before he traveled back to Montgomery in November, he wrote dramatically to a friend as if the relationship were in limbo. He wrote that he was "going to try to settle it definitely one way or the other."[72]

The wedding appeared to be back on the calendar, though no date was set. Scott talked about a New York wedding; he talked about a New York apartment; he sent Zelda a telegram every time he had good news about selling a story (placing his work was much easier once Scribner's had taken the novel, and with Harold Ober working as his agent).[73] Because he could sell his stories, he was working on both short fiction and the next novel. He made two trips to Montgomery during January 1920, during the second bringing Zelda an expensive diamond and platinum watch,[74] which he had bought with money from

---

[72] Fitzgerald to Ludlow Fowler (Fool, p. 65).

[73] DS, DZ, p. 42 and PUL, correspondence and Zelda's scrapbook.

[74] SSEG, p. 108; Bruccoli estimates the watch cost $600.

the movie sale of his short story, "Head and Shoulders." The Montgomery gossips were busy: would the popular Zelda Sayre, still too young to debut, marry this Northern writer? Zelda was still seen at dances and parties; what did her social life imply? Her sister Rosalind, now living in New York with her husband, wrote her that they had seen Marilyn Miller in the New York Follies, and thought Zelda was both prettier and a better dancer.[75]

Then, in a February letter, Zelda thanked Scott for "the pills"[76] but said she could never take them—and the fear of pregnancy darkened their happiness. Had she been pregnant, she would have gone to New York and been married. Otherwise, in 1920, to abort meant that she risked her health and her future ability to bear children. The various emmenagogue pills ("Chickester's Diamond Brand," "Tansy and Pennyroyal Compound Pills") were often ineffective, but so were mustard plasters, cayenne pepper, cotton seed, and the desperate exercises.[77] Even though abortion was illegal, there were midwives and doctors who would perform surgical procedures, but the chances of Zelda's being allowed to have an abortion from Judge Sayre's house were slim. Had he known about her possible pregnancy, he might well have simply put her out of doors.

By March 1920, although Zelda's pregnancy had been a false alarm, she and Scott decided they would marry soon. It

[75] PUL; Milford, p. 57.

[76] DS, DZ, p. 44.

[77] Leslie J. Reagan, When Abortion Was a Crime (1997); see also Janet Farrell Brodie, Contraception and Abortion in Nineteenth Century America (1994), p. 208.

was agreed that the Judge would pay for Zelda's train ticket to New York, and that her oldest sister Marjorie would go with her. So on March 20, in the Montgomery paper, the Sayre family announced Zelda's engagement, a precisely written set of paragraphs that claimed that when they had met, Fitzgerald was a graduate of Princeton, and Zelda a Red Cross nurse.[78]

It sounded like a wartime romance, which it was not at all. And it also sounded much more romantic than it was ever to be.

---

[78] PUL; see DS, DZ, pp. 39-47 and PUL for the various stages of enthusiasm of both parties.

THREE - Celebrity Couple

In the last letter Zelda as an unmarried woman wrote Scott, she used the metaphors of the fairytale romance, as well as the princess in her tower: she was not afraid to marry, she said, because to fear, one must be either "a coward" or "very great and big. I am neither." She writes that she is coming to him to love and care for him. It is in some ways a very mature letter—and Zelda Sayre is not yet twenty. It begins, "Darling Heart, our fairy tale is almost ended, and we're going to marry and live happily ever afterward just like the princess in her tower who worried you so much—and made me so very cross by her constant recurrence."[79]

As if in answer to this letter is Scott's March 30 telegram to Zelda, which appears to be about her arrival and their wedding, but turns out to be about the great success of *This Side of Paradise*, his novel which was officially published on March 26: "We will be awfully nervous until it is over and would get no rest by

---

[79] DS, DZ, pp. 42-3.

waiting until Monday First edition of the book is sold out."[80] From his suite in the Biltmore hotel, Fitzgerald was tracking sales, reading reviews, making sure people knew he was the newest writer in the city's literary galaxy. While Zelda spent her last night in Montgomery talking and giggling with her best friend, Eleanor Browder, Fitzgerald was out drinking with Princeton friends—and announcing how famous he was becoming, much to the chagrin of his former classmates.

On the Saturday before Easter, then, April 3, 1920, Scott and Zelda were married by the Reverend Bernard McQuade in the rectory of St. Patrick's Cathedral.[81] Because they were not married in the church itself, Zelda did not have to take instructions in the Catholic doctrine. While her parents were no doubt saying little to their Montgomery friends about the fact that Scott was Catholic, given the Southern religious hierarchy that privileged the Episcopalian church, which Minnie and her children attended, they were probably relieved that Zelda was no longer their responsibility. In their sixth decade, the Judge and Minnie had felt the strain of Zelda's high-spirited life, at least the past few years of it; even her tolerant mother had written her a note of rebuke the previous year, telling her she could barely tolerate her smoking, but that she would never accept her drinking.

The Sayre parents did not attend the wedding, nor did the Fitzgeralds. Zelda was, however, well-supported by her three older sisters. Marjorie had traveled to New York with her; she was her attendant. Both Clotilde and Rosalind and their husbands

---

[80] Ibid., p. 47.

[81] See Milford, p. 62; Arthur Mizener, The Far Side of Paradise (1951), p. 119.

were to attend. Once people had begun to gather, however, Scott—attended by Ludlow Fowler, his Princeton friend who was from Montgomery—decided the ceremony should begin before its twelve o'clock time. So Zelda and he were married before Clotilde and John Palmer arrived. And since Scott had not thought to have a luncheon planned, people then simply left (no doubt complaining to themselves about his gaucherie) while Zelda and Scott went to their suite in the Biltmore.

Zelda wore a midnight blue suit with a fashionably long skirt and a matching leather-trimmed hat. Scott brought her a bouquet of orchids and small white flowers, reminiscent of the first orchid he had sent her, the first she had ever received. Orchids, like the champagne cocktails she loved, were for her the mark of urban sophistication, and Scott never missed the chance to remind Zelda that he was cosmopolitan. But the critical Scott soon felt that his new bride's sense of fashion was more suitable to Montgomery than to New York, so he asked his friend from Minnesota—Marie Hersey—to take Zelda shopping.[82] Zelda never recovered from the sting, and noted years later that she rarely wore the Patou suit which they had bought on that shopping trip. (She accepted Scott's tutelage graciously, but she knew what she was going to do with her body, and she remained comfortable with her own sense of style.)

It was not the first time Scott was wrong about Zelda. Because she was so much younger than he, Scott assumed he could instruct her in the ways of city life, sex, and social roles. Zelda, however, saw herself as the stronger personality of the couple: she had, in some ways, proved that when she had broken their

---

[82] Milford, pp. 65-6; Mizener, Far Side of Paradise, pp. 118-19.

engagement the year before. Her behavior then suggested that she could do without Scott's return. Romantic as he was about any woman that he loved—for the past two years obsessed with loving Zelda Sayre—Scott had erased from his mind the sight of Zelda riding behind another officer on his motorcycle, Zelda with cigarette in hand—too drunk to make her way up the Pleasant Street porch steps, a laughing Zelda with one of the Montgomery boys shining the spotlight of his Stutz Bearcat on the boodlers at the Bend … and had replaced the woman he was to marry with some *Saturday Evening Post* image of the smiling, modest housewife. He needed instead to remember one of the last times he had taken Zelda to the Beauvoir Club, to hear the jazz that was looked down upon by the better classes of both whites and blacks in Montgomery, only to find her intent on shocking everyone there with her Shimmy.

What was really set in motion on April 3, 1920, was a battle for the control of the Fitzgeralds' lives as a couple. When Zelda succumbed to Scott's insistence that they marry, she was near the end of a four-year period of being the belle of Montgomery. She still had the box of military and fraternity ribbons, pins, and medals; she had the memories of long nights of dancing, drinking, and flirting; she was still surrounded by the Southern college men who wanted to party—but she was tired. Her sisters were married; many of her friends were getting engaged. Of the men who pressed her to marry, and there was at least one suitor who was sure he could convince her to marry him rather than Fitzgerald, Scott was the most glamorous in that he could take her away from her history and her home.[83] There was no

[83] SSEG, pp. 131-3; Milford, p. 72.

question that she loved him, but she had loved other men. Marrying Scott had another advantage: he might also provide a route to some kind of fame and career for her. She had a better chance of being discovered, of finding a way to the stage or to film, living in New York than she did in sleepy Montgomery. And she had no idea how much she would miss her home place.

Stories about the Fitzgeralds while they honeymooned at the Biltmore, and then at the Commodore, are legion.[84] Yet they resided at both those hotels for fewer than three weeks. Surrounded by Scott's Princeton friends, they spent much of that time out "on the town"—Zelda hungry to explore the city that had so long fascinated her, and Scott eager to show off his fascinating bride. According to Alex McKaig's journal from these months, the Fitzgeralds were seldom alone. The Princeton crowd came for cocktails, or during the evening, or late at night. None of Scott's friends was married, most had never been in an intimate relationship, and to a person they were attracted to Zelda. They saw her as a sharp, modern sister; they told her stories about their own romances and asked her advice; but they also flirted with her whenever they could.

The Princeton snobbery was clear from McKaig's first journal entry, when he described Zelda as "temperamental small town, Southern Belle" who "Chews gum—shows knees." He noted as well: "Both [Scott and Zelda] drinking heavily" and predicted (on the ninth day of their honeymoon), "I do not think the marriage can survive."[85] But after spending a great deal of time with them, during the summer in their rented Connecticut

---

[84] SSEG, pp. 131-4; Andrew Turnbull, Scott Fitzgerald (1962), pp. 109-12.

[85] Alexander McKaig journal for April 12, 1920, in Turnbull, Scott Fitzgerald, p. 112.

house and at various New York parties, McKaig also succumbs to Zelda's charms. In a November entry, "I spent an evening shaving Zelda's neck to make her bobbed hair look better. She is lovely—wonderful hair—eyes and mouth."[86] A few weeks after that, as he was squiring her around New York because Scott was working, McKaig wrote that Zelda asked him to kiss her, but he didn't: "I couldn't. I couldn't forget Scott—he's so damn pitiful."[87] By the next April, McKaig's entry praises both her beauty and her mind:

Fitz confessed this evening at dinner that Zelda's ideas entirely responsible for "Jelly Bean" and "Ice Palace." Her ideas largely in this new novel. Had a long talk with her this evening about way fool women can rout intelligent women with men. She is without doubt the most brilliant and most beautiful young woman I've ever known.[88]

Regardless of McKaig's change of opinion about Zelda and her intellectual substance, Zelda from the start had seen herself as Scott's literary partner. She had read drafts, she had discussed story ideas, and she had progressed to creating dialogue, supplementing character and doing general editing. Whenever Scott was writing in the New York hotel, Zelda wanted to be available—even though he seemed to prefer that she leave the room.

For both Fitzgeralds, however, their honeymoon days gave them the indelible labels of both "partier" and "drunk." When they dressed to go out, which was a lengthy process in itself, the Princeton men were often in their rooms: there are stories

---

[86] Ibid., p. 114, for November 27, 1920.

[87] Alexander McKaig journal for December 4, 1920, in Milford, p. 80.

[88] Alexander McKaig journal for April 17, 1921, in Turnbull, Scott Fitzgerald, p. 115.

of Zelda's calling to them from the bathtub, and telling long and sometimes funny stories from the bedroom. Despite her seeming flirtatiousness, she must have tired of their presence, even if they were admirers. Scarcely a night passed that the group didn't go out, and when they did, they drank—and then their drinking led to more invitations to other friends, and sometimes to people no one knew, and to the pranks for which they quickly became notorious.[89] How many New Yorkers, in fact, could have seen them riding on the hood and the roof of a taxi, as they were when they met Dorothy Parker? Surely, Parker spread that story. And who would have cared that the two Fitzgeralds spun through the Commodore's revolving door for nearly half an hour?

Publicity followed them: Zelda's diving into the fountain at Union Square was commemorated by Reginald Marsh's drawings for the drop curtain of the Greenwich Village Follies—Zelda in the fountain and Scott "riding down Seventh Avenue with a group of young literary celebrities."[90] Then there was Scott's attempted disrobing at a performance of the Scandals, a more serious breech of decorum. Most of the events, however, were far from newsworthy in these early Prohibition days—when

[89] SSEG, pp. 130-4; Milford (pp. 67-70) quotes Dorothy Parker saying of her early meeting with Zelda, "I never thought she was beautiful. She was very blond with a candy box face and a little bow mouth, very much on a small scale and there was something petulant about her" (p. 68). The net result of their notoriety, however, was the kind of judgmental criticism Elizabeth Hardwick voiced in her review of Milford's Zelda, "As persons, the Fitzgeralds were not, in my view, especially appealing. Their story has a sort of corruption clinging to it, the quality of a decadent fairy tale ..." (Seduction and Betrayal (1974), p. 87).

[90] Ruth Prigozy, Introduction, Cambridge Companion to F. Scott Fitzgerald (2000) p. 10.

the consumption of various kinds and qualities of alcohol made all behavior less and less predictable. What was newsworthy was the fact that the two people performing were themselves gorgeously young. As John Dos Passos admitted, even though both of the Fitzgeralds made him nervous, there was no couple so perfectly matched, none more breathtaking than they.[91] In New York, which like any American city in this postwar period was rigidly classed, filled with an older generation who could afford to stay at its best hotels, the presence of the beautiful Southern belle and her dashing husband, whose novel a great many people had at least heard of, was the stuff of gossip.

Part of the Fitzgeralds' agenda in New York was to attend as much theater as they could. They saw musical reviews, serious stage plays, films: they saw Ina Claire, Theda Bara, Marilyn Miller, the Barrymores; they liked Constance Talmadge, Chaplin, and Lloyd, and anything directed by D. W Griffith. They each wanted to be in movies. Scott had yearned for a stage career ever since he wrote and acted in his own play, *The Coward*; he was then thirteen. Part of his motivation for writing for the Princeton stage was to participate in the touring productions of those plays, but his low grades made him ineligible. As Ruth Prigozy notes, "Zelda's love of the theatre was as intense as Scott's."[92] Most of the men Zelda met complimented her by saying she should be in films; she had heard that comment from

---

[91] John Dos Passos, The Best Times (1968), recounts "lunching at the Plaza with Scott and Zelda marks the beginning of an epoch" (p. 144). Dos Passos admitted that Scott "didn't look at landscape, he had no taste for food or wine or painting, little ear for music except the most rudimentary popular songs, but ... there was a golden innocence about them and they were both so hopelessly good looking" (pp. 146, 144)

[92] Prigozy, Introduction, Cambridge Companion, p. 11.

early adolescence. It was one of the reasons she was attracted to knowledgable New York types like George Jean Nathan,[93] theater critic and editor, and Carl Van Vechten,[94] dance critic. And when she and Scott were approached as possible leads for the film treatment of *This Side of Paradise*, they were neither coy nor embarrassed by the prospect: they both wanted to act.

In short, both Fitzgeralds were happy to entertain, and if outrageous behavior was one of the ways they could make a mark in New York, they would behave outrageously. They considered the month of April their honeymoon, but as Scott came to realize their life in New York was expensive, he became nervous, at times reverting to his college boy behavior and leaving the table checks for his friends to pay.

After the Honeymoon: Into the Woods

For financial reasons but, more charitably, so that Scott could have time and privacy to write, the Fitzgeralds rented the Wakeman cottage in Westport, Connecticut, and moved in early May. They bought a car, a used Marmon sports coupe which—according to Montgomery friend Leon Ruth, who had helped them buy it—neither of them could drive well.[95]

---

[93] Both Scott Donaldson's biography and Andre LeVot's convey the sense that George Jean Nathan's attraction for Zelda, and hers for him as a powerful, well-connected intellectual and theater maven, might have been more passionate than innocent (Fool, p. 68; Andre LeVot, F. Scott Fitzgerald (1983), p. 88). The plot of Fitzgerald's story "One of My Oldest Friends" may support this contention. See letters between Nathan and Zelda, PUL.

[94] PUL, correspondence between Zelda and Van Vechten; see Bruce Kellner, Carl Van echten and the De Luiln (1968)

[95] PUL; Milford, p. 69.

But they could get to Connecticut to look for rentals, and once settled there, could drive back into New York for parties. Besides the parties Scott and Zelda gave, those of George Jean Nathan's—equipped as they were with cases of bootleg gin—were the most talked-about.[96] Zelda wrote to Ludlow Fowler that the country was nice; they had joined a swim club, Scott was writing, and she liked to sit under the trees ("the needles tickle so where you sit").[97]

Taking their honeymoon in the heart of New York, a city Zelda had never visited but had long anticipated, may have been a mistake. The culture of the prosperous city only fed her exaggerated lust for experience: hungry for excitement, she found staying in the hotel difficult. Her extravagant and perhaps fanciful sense of what was available clashed repeatedly with the kind of days and nights Scott had envisioned for them. And there was the easy availability of liquor—if not in the clubs that Scott liked, then through purchases from the hotel staff.

Their honeymoon, then, was a festival of evenings out with friends, rather than an increasingly intimate experience. Both she and Scott had thought that making love would take up

---

[96] PUL, correspondence between Zelda and Nathan; in his letter of July 28, 1920, he tells her he has "laid in three more cases of gin; September 13, 1920, he has bought five more cases. Intermittently, he calls his letters "love letters," suggests that she get a post office box so that their correspondence can be private, and refers to the fact that their relationship is "all very Scandalabra like." Years later, Zelda titles her play Scandalabra. In Nathan's 1958 Esquire essay about the Fitzgeralds, he says that he and Scott never had a falling out over his attentions to Zelda, even though "Zelda and I were accustomed to engage publicly in obviously exaggerated endearing terms which Scott appreciated and which were in the accepted vein of Dixie chivalry" (p. 157, A George Jean Nathan Reader (1990)).

[97] Zelda to Ludlow Fowler, May 9, 1920, p. 6, PUL.

much of their time; before their wedding, they had never spent a night alone. It was, after all, Zelda's sexuality—or at least the appearance of it—that had captivated Scott.[98] When Zelda wrote from Connecticut to Ludlow Fowler, saying that she had gained so much weight he was not to mention her appearance when he visited, she was suggesting that she was already pregnant.[99]

In the midst of Zelda's news about who they knew and what they were doing in the East, a recurring theme is Scott's avid attention to his writing. Only a few weeks married, Zelda is complaining about his routine: he kept to an elaborate schedule, which no one could interrupt. He cut back on his drinking. He tried to stay celibate. Later, when Scott complained that Zelda interfered with his writing, it echoed Alex McKaig's analysis from that first year, "If she's there Fitz can't work—she bothers him—if she's not there he can't work—worried what she might do."[100]

McKaig reassured himself that none of Scott's friends would take on Zelda as a mistress. But he continued to record one of the frequent conversations he had with Zelda about what she was to do with herself, her life: "Discussed her relations with other men. I told her she would have to make up her mind whether she wanted to go in movies or get in with young married set. To do that would require a little effort & Zelda

---

[98] Scott's later references to "gold-hatted" Gatsby, as he worked on his 1925 novel, may suggest his preference for the expensive "goldbeater's skins" condoms, imported from France, which were gold leaf lined with cattle membranes (Janet Farrell Brodie, Contraception and Abortion (1994), p. 208).

[99] Zelda to Ludlow Fowler, May 9, 1920, PUL, p. 5.

[100] McKaig journal, October 12, 1920, in Turnbull, Scott Fitzgerald, p. 113.

will never make an effort."[101] McKaig's reference to "that" is ambiguous—would going into the movies take more effort than getting in with the young married set? That Zelda would talk so openly about her dreams of stardom makes clear the kind of ambition she had, whether or not she was willing to implement those dreams.

By July, only three months married, Zelda was homesick. Her yearning for Montgomery increased when she read a telegram from a group of her old beaux. They told her the town was dying without her—"No pep. No fun ... The Country Club is intending firing their chaperone as there is no further need for her. Knitting parties prevail."[102] So she and Scott drove the Marmon south and finally, after a week and 1200 miles, arrived in Montgomery.[103]

In the mode of Scott's using whatever experience he had, he wrote a three-part story about the trip ("The Cruise of the Rolling Junk") although Ober could sell it only to *Motor* magazine, for a paltry $300. To open, he makes their costumes funny; their pair of driving goggles has no glass in one eye. The two of them embody youth: "To be young, to be bound for the far hills, to be going where happiness hung from a tree ..."[104] and when their car has breakdowns (and in one case, loses a wheel), Fitzgerald uses comic dialogue. This kind of travel being expensive, once they reach Montgomery, he wires for money and notes that

---

[101] McKaig journal, quoted in Taylor Kendall, Sometimes Madness (2001), p. 98.

[102] PUL.

[103] Scott Fitzgerald, "The Cruise of the Rolling Junk" in Motor (three issues), 1924; in book form, The Cruise of the Rolling Junk (1976).

[104] Cruise of the Rolling Junk, Part I, p. 58.

"Zelda, who is astonishingly naive, was amazed and cheered at the notion of money being wired about so cavalierly."[105]

The sentiment of the impractical, and uncomfortable, trip—a token to please his homesick bride—accrues in the last of the three episodes, where Fitzgerald changes the narrative line and has the Sayres absent from home, having taken the train to Connecticut to surprise their daughter. But the return to Montgomery is happy nevertheless:

the word blew around that Zelda was home and in a few minutes automobiles began to drive up to the door and familiar faces clustered around us—faces amused, astonished, sympathetic, but all animated by a sincere pleasure at her return.[106]

The tone of nostalgic good humor carries this admittedly slight set of essays, but neither the writing about the trip, nor the trip itself, was high comedy.

The white knickerbocker suit Zelda had had made to match Scott's was a scandal on the drive; at one North Carolina hotel it kept them from being given a room. And some jealousy surfaces when Scott recounts that once they had crossed the state line into Alabama, Zelda listed each of the men she had dated from each town they drove through: she was having some severe growing pains as she acclimatized to life in the North as a married woman.

They stayed in Montgomery for nearly two weeks. They were able to sell the car, at a loss, so that they could take the train back to New York. And they got the Sayres to promise that they would visit in New York and Connecticut (it would

---

[105] Ibid., Part II, p. 43.

[106] Ibid., Part III, p. 70.

be the Judge's first trip to the city since 1882). Zelda's need, for much of her life, to return home was a sign of her often unexpressed devotion to her father, as well as her obvious love for her mother. At repeated intervals, almost predictably, Zelda came home to Montgomery and, as long as her parents lived there, to 6 Pleasant Street.

Zelda had not yet grown out of the adolescence that kept her bound to her parents and to their opinions of her. They loved her for her promise as well as her beauty. Had she understood how much promise Minnie saw in her, she might have escaped becoming only Scott Fitzgerald's wife: her husband defined her as a "mental baby vamp,"[107] and when he defended that type of woman, saying that he would not have married any other type, he reinforced the role Zelda knew she was supposed to be playing. Her often outrageous behavior reflected on her husband, and made him the notable man about town that his years at Princeton and then in New York as a single person had denied him. Zelda was Fitzgerald's success. Even as he pretended that his new assurance came from *This Side of Paradise* having sold 33,000 copies, it came more directly from having a stunning wife on his arm.

Filling that clearly-defined role, however, restricted Zelda. She was almost seventy years ahead of the positive woman-centered philosophies, such as those of Carol Gilligan[108] or

---

[107] Scott Fitzgerald's phrase from his 1921 Shadowland interview, quoted in Milford, p. 77.

[108] Gilligan's groundbreaking study of women's development, In a Different Voice (1982), changed much thinking about girls' and women's behaviour.

Martha Nussbaum; she had few sources of information that could have helped her counter the influence of Scott's beliefs about women in general, and Zelda in particular. As Nussbaum wrote in 1990,

the need for women to overcome alienation from self and self-contempt in order to overcome the demoralization, self-effacement, and frustration of aspirations ... women need to achieve self-love. Not love for oneself as an individual, but rather love of other women and love for oneself as a woman.[109]

Instead of hearing this kind of language, Zelda read a steady diet of *Modern Screen* and slick women's magazines.

One of the competitive rites the Fitzgeralds had established during their courtship was the setting up of flirtations with other members of the opposite sex. That first summer, Zelda's relationship with George Jean Nathan balanced Scott's with Eugenia Bankhead, Zelda's former Montgomery playmate, Tallulah's sister who was now living in Connecticut.[110] Zelda's having given lip service to sexual freedom did not mean she was sanguine about his possible infidelities; the roles had been set early in their relationship: she was the sexual woman, she was the goddess of Scott's love.

George Jean Nathan knew from his first meeting with Zelda how to impress her. Often relegated to the outside of New York society because he was Jewish, Nathan co-edited Smart Set with H. L. Mencken. More importantly, in Zelda's view, Nathan was the companion of stage and screen actress Ruth Sullivan, whose performance of Owen Johnson's "salamander" character

---

[109] Martha C. Nussbaum, Love's Knowledge (1990), p. 103.

[110] Jean Bankhead, Tallulah's older sister; see Fool, p. 53.

Zelda had seen repeatedly in the film version at a Montgomery theater. Besides this personal link, Nathan knew many other actors, as well as producers, directors, and financial backers: he appeared to be one way for Zelda to meet such influential people. Never married, Nathan was living a life that combined the sensual with the aesthetic; he was at every opening night, his parties were filled with people from the arts world, and he gave off an aura of a knowing, sexual sophistication. While Scott was pleased when Smart Set took his first story, and he admired both Mencken and Nathan as intellectuals, he was surprised that a man such as Nathan would be interested in Zelda—or would pretend an interest in Zelda.[111]

Nathan's charm was his wit, his aggression, and his parties stocked with anywhere from three to five cases of gin. His letters to Zelda once the Fitzgeralds moved to Connecticut are flirtatious, though he always mentions Scott in them; but they are clearly letters designed to attract her interest. (In the Fitzgerald papers, they are among the few files that Zelda kept, from all the letters she received before or after her marriage.) It is in the Connecticut cottage that Nathan read Zelda's diary, and offered to buy it for publication in Smart Set.[112] Scott, however, refused his offer, saying that he needed the diary for its use in his own writing. Nathan's offer may have been part of his quasi-courtship of Zelda, a move that made her realize he saw the mind that she sometimes hid. Or it might have been a way for him to irritate Scott. His offer, in fact, may have prompted the Fitzgeralds'

---

[111] Nathan finally married at age 79.

[112] Several versions of Nathan's offering to publish Zelda's diaries exist: see Milford, P. 71 as well as Nathan's "Profiles of Other Writers," Reader (1990), p. 158.

trip to Montgomery—making their absence from the New York party scene legitimate without offending the powerful Nathan. They were back at those parties after their return, however, according to Zelda's August 16 letter to Ludlow Fowler about her having "cut" her "tail" in a bathtub during one of Nathan's parties, a cut which required three stitches: "the bottle was bath salts—I was boiled—The place was a tub somewhere—none of us remember the exact locality."[113]

One can imagine the scene, particularly the blood, the alarm, and the need to get Zelda to emergency care somewhere in the city. The hyperbolic nature of the Fitzgeralds' daily lives was becoming uninteresting to even their closest friends. Characteristic of the hazy memories of hard drinkers, both Scott and Zelda recounted their exploits with more and more refurbishing, until events became unrecognizable—even to people who had been there. Their storytelling was also part of their drinkers' syndrome: such people

talk about talking; they talk about "other" people and "other" circumstances; they talk about liquor, about affairs, and travel— zealously avoiding personal references which might unhinge the charade of emotional stability which they have barely managed to erect … words don't match actions; actions don't match claims; and fantasies and hopes are totally out of sync with what is possible.[114]

Yet during these summer months, which appear to hover at the edge of a precipice of emotional disaster for both Fitzgeralds,

---

[113] Zelda to Ludlow Fowler, August 16, 1920, PUL.

[114] Matts Djos, "Alcoholism in Ernest Hemingway's The Sun Also Rises: A Wine and Roses Perspective on the Lost Generation," A Casebook on Hemingway's The Sun Also Rises, ed. Linda Wagner-Martin (2002), p. 145.

Scott was working hard on his second novel, *The Beautiful and Damned*. As a writer, he had already proved that hopes that were unrealizable might, in fact, be realized; from his inordinate success, Zelda drew the message that her hopes, too, were not wide of the mark. For in the strange psychological cauldron of the creative process, the debacle of their summer had provided Scott's material for much of his new novel: a number of his and Zelda's exploits were turned into the fictional life of the young marrieds: there is also the character of Bloeckman, an elegant Jew, who rises within the film industry while Anthony fails, and then uses his position of importance to attract Rosalind. A few years later, in his story "One of My Oldest Friends," Fitzgerald describes again the possible Zelda-Nathan liaison, this time casting Nathan as Charley Hart, a man who "had a faculty for noticing things—noticing dresses and hats and the new ways I'd do my hair. He was good company. He could always make me feel important, somehow, and attractive."[115]

The uses to which Scott put his real life experiences in the summer of 1920 were no different than the uses to which he had put his and Zelda's experiences, as well as her letters and excerpts from her diary, in his earlier work. Living with F. Scott Fitzgerald was never meant to be reassuring; even hours of intimacy were fodder for his literary imagination. By the time Zelda wrote the review of *The Beautiful and Damned* for the *New York Tribune*, saying coyly that "plagiarism begins at home," [116]her husband's use of their experiences was well known. What

[115] Scott Fitzgerald, "One of My Oldest Friends," The Price Was High (1979) p. 117.

[116] . Zelda's first published review, "Friend Husband's Latest" (New York Tribune, April 2, 1922), CW, p. 388.

surfaces less frequently, and often years past the event, is fiction that reflects Scott's own separate life experiences—his love affairs during the 1930s, for example, and what must have been, then, his own self-disgust.

For Scott the writer, life existed as life but it also existed as a sourcebook for his fiction. In some ways, the pain of his fights with Zelda could be transmuted into his work. But for Zelda, who still identified herself primarily as a sexual being, changes in her sex life with Scott mattered immensely to her. There was nowhere to put the pain of her realization that only a few months after their wedding, Scott's desire for her could so easily be transferred to other women. Zelda, barely twenty, had nothing to shape her day around except attending to Scott, attention from Scott, and sex with Scott. She had no profession; she did not need to find a quiet place to write the fiction that paid their bills. In Westport, she took care of the household, went swimming and sunning, made social plans, ordered the bootleg liquor, and looked forward to the parties and the trips to New York that brightened her life. But as the months in Connecticut proved, Zelda's life needed to be lived with its flame turned to high: if there was nothing to do that was fun, she would create fun. That she and Scott were drinking inordinately, at every meal, every night—with or without other people—meant that their minds were seldom clear, their judgment seldom stable.

Several of the summer and fall episodes from 1920 prove how quickly Zelda had fallen into a life of heavy drinking. These stories, usually told by friends rather than by either of the Fitzgeralds, are frightening. One was Zelda's walking down the railroad track to flag the train when she had decided to leave Scott.[117] Writing busily, he was paying no attention to her. When he realized that she had gone, he ran after the train, chasing it down the tracks. Although he had no money with him, the conductor allowed him to ride to New York. When Alex McKaig wrote about the event, he said both Fitzgeralds were so distraught that they could have been killed; both came to his apartment and continued their fight, with Zelda still refusing to give Scott any of their money.

Another is the same kind of "running" story, reminding the reader of the heavy drinker's habit of evading and denying unpleasantries—or the accusations about drinking habits. People who drink to excess become "accomplished runners,"[118] and they spend much of their lives trying to keep their friends from knowing what equally accomplished liars they are.

After the Fitzgeralds had moved back to New York in the autumn of 1920, to a small apartment on West 59th Street, Zelda would sometimes leave home without Scott's knowledge. They would fight, she would stay in the bathroom with the water running and he would eventually turn to something else, only to discover later that she had left the apartment. Once when this happened, according to Alex McKaig's diary,[119] Scott did not go out in search of her but instead called all their friends with the desperate but vague message that something horrible had happened, asking them to come immediately. They did. Some of them did. Then Zelda phoned and someone picked her up. Scott's own response was only helplessness.

---

[117] McKaig in Milford, p. 75; Turnbull, Scott Fitzgerald, pp. 111-12.

[118] Djos, "Alcoholism," p. 147.

[119] December 4, 1920, quoted in Milford, p. 80.

Pregnancy

Sometime that October Scott and Zelda began talking about having a child. They had been married six months, Zelda was now twenty and Scott twenty-four, and it would be, for them, a new kind of experience. No one they knew had children. They didn't understand about sleepless nights and feeding problems, but they were fascinated with the idea that a baby that looked like its attractive parents would be fun. Perhaps Zelda was still smarting from the fact that when her parents had visited in August, they had stayed only one night in Connecticut and then had spent the rest of their visit with Clotilde and John, and their first grandchild.[120] Everyone involved also knew that the Sayres were offended by the drinking the Fitzgeralds and their friends were doing.

Undoubtedly, too, becoming a "family" rather than just a warring couple had some attraction for Zelda. So little was known about prenatal care, however, that she had no idea that in pregnancy she would need to stop the drinking and smoking that so pleasured her.

There was much about pregnancy that Zelda did not know, but she might have guessed that having a child would not be any solution to her problems with Scott. Just a few months before their wedding, she had run into the stone wall of his control in that pregnancy scare—there was no discussion: there was only Scott's order that she get rid of it. His assumption about any possible pregnancy then was that Zelda would choose to preserve their image as the glamorous engaged couple.

She may have thought that becoming a father would make

---

[120] SSEG, p. 143; Zelda to Ludlow Fowler, August 16, 1920, PUL.

Scott a more thoughtful husband. She may have thought their having a child would put herself and the baby back inside Minnie's good graces—she had not liked the judgments she saw on her mother's face during the August visit; perhaps she thought that having a child would make her seem as mature as Clotilde.

By becoming a mother, Zelda would in some ways replace her own mother—or her own need for that figure. This psychological identification among the women of a family is a major attraction of the birth process, according to Marilyn Yalom. She writes,

Where is the woman who could say that she has never been awed by the thought of herself as a mother, never worried about the pains of childbirth, never wondered whether children would prove to be unbearable or, conversely, confer a privileged status? ... Women's sense of self, derived from a myriad of biological, existential, interpersonal, and social factors such as one's gender, family, class, and race, is so fundamentally bound up with the idea of motherhood that any theory of mental health or mental illness that does not take it into account must be seen as a defective theory.[121]

So the Fitzgeralds continued to live the party life, now operating from the New York base, and they experienced lonely Christmas holidays—bereft of any family. They claimed, however, to be creating their own family unit. Then on Valentine's Day, February 14, 1921, Zelda's belief that she had conceived was confirmed. Both she and Scott were happy.

Zelda immediately went by train to Montgomery. She wanted to share this part of her life with her mother and her girlfriends; she was looking for her own "women's community."[122]

---

[121] Marilyn Yalom, Maternity, Mortality, and the Literature of Madness (1985), p. 108.

[122] Ibid., p. 106.

Her stay in Alabama was short, however, because Scott had decided that, to be truly cosmopolitan, they should travel to Europe before their child was born, or before Zelda would not be allowed to travel. So Zelda came back to New York and began packing for London.

Contrary to everything they had heard from friends, the Fitzgeralds did not find England or France or Italy amusing. Because they were in such demand in New York, even a moderate level of social life abroad seemed insultingly plebian to them. Few people there knew who F. Scott Fitzgerald was—after all, his first book had been out scarcely a year—and the two good-looking Americans were not so striking set in the midst of the moneyed crowds of European cities. They did visit and take meals with Lady Randolph Spencer Churchill, with novelist Shane Leslie (a man instrumental in getting Fitzgerald's early novel to Scribner's, a friend of Father Fay's), and with the venerable John Galsworthy. That Zelda, always a difficult eater to please, was sickened by much of the food they were served was an unforeseen difficulty. Traveling, living in strange countries, and being faced with handling luggage were all realities they had avoided in the States.

There was also the problem for the usually slim Zelda that she was gaining weight, that her tiny waist was disappearing into the rounded midriff of early-term pregnancy. In Europe, Zelda had only a limited wardrobe; as a pregnant woman, she did not want to buy new clothes that she would have no use for after the child was born. Her physical discomfort did not improve her temperament as they went to the cathedrals, the museums, and the sites that they knew they should see. Zelda's recollections of their time in London are less dour than are

Scott's; she recalled that they "were respectful in the Cecil in London: disciplined by the long majestuous twilights on the river and we were young but we were impressed anyway by the Hindus and the royal processions."[123]

They spent only a few days in Paris, meeting no one: Zelda recalled slyly that "there were dirty postcards, but we were pregnant."[124] They then went to Venice, Florence, and Rome. In Venice, "We had fun in a gondola feeling like a soft Italian song,"[125] whereas in Rome, comically, "it was the flea season [and] men from the British embassy scratched behind the palms."[126] Staying in London as they waited for their return ship, they both felt an intense loneliness. In Zelda's cryptic prose, "the room was an inside room and gray all day, and the waiter didn't care whether we left or not, and he was our only contact."[127]

United in her pregnancy ("we were pregnant"), she and Scott had shared the reactions to their grand world tour (on which they had traveled by ship, first class). Although disappointing in terms of new literary and social contacts, the trip may have been one of the few times husband and wife spent their time almost exclusively with each other. It may have been a good sojourn, emotionally, even though Scott wrote to Edmund

---

[123] Zelda Fitzgerald, "Show Mr. and Mrs. F. to Number," *CW*, p. 420, see Zelda's letter to Scott about her desired slimness: "I'd so love to be 5 ft. 4" x 2"-Maybe I'll accomplish it swimming" (DS, DZ, p. 12).

[124] Ibid.

[125] Ibid.

[126] Ibid.

[127] Ibid.

Wilson that he found Europe of only "antiquarian interest"[128] and planned not to return.

Where they did return, however, was to 6 Pleasant Street in Montgomery. A year after her glamorous New York marriage, Zelda Sayre was home—and very unglamorous in her mid-term pregnancy. Catching prenatal care wherever she happened to be, she was still relatively uninformed about the rest of the birth process.

Zelda was miserable in Montgomery's summer. The humid heat which she had always loved and the lush environs of almost-tropical foliage and trees (magnolias, pines, tulip trees, anything with overarching boughs to scrape the carefully tended side-walks); flowerbeds burgeoning with summer hibiscus, gladiolus, marigolds, roses, coleus, and zinnias; and the eternally blue Alabama skies were for the first time in her memory oppressive. She could not play tennis. She could barely walk the distances she wanted to cover. And when she did attempt to go to swimming pools, formerly her summer sanctuary, the one-piece bathing suit she was able to fit into was horribly disfiguring. Or, rather, it was not disfiguring at all—it revealed her pregnancy without any possibility of disguise. Friends told the story that Zelda's condition was so visible that when she did attempt to go swim-ming, she was asked to leave the local pool.[129]

A furious Zelda was not a happy one. Even though her moth-er's household provided more good food than she had thought possible, food that tasted to her like "home"; even though Scott was, somewhat surprisingly, willing to stay on in the heat, Zelda

---

[128] Scott Fitzgerald to Edmund Wilson, July, 1921, Life, pp. 46-7.

[129] Milford, p. 84

decided that settling in Minnesota might be a wise substitute for a Montgomery that had turned unwelcoming. She had not yet met Scott's parents or his sister. The relationship between Scott and his family puzzled her; romantically, Zelda thought that living in St. Paul and having the child there would be a way of bridging what she perceived as the differences among the Fitzgeralds.

Making their first appearance in St. Paul when Zelda was seven months pregnant did little for her morale. She had clothes that were suitable for the cooler climate, but she did not fit into them; otherwise, she had hot-weather maternity clothes. She was alternately too cold or too uncomfortable. She gained so much weight in those last months of pregnancy that even moving was difficult, so the weeks went by and she did little shopping for the baby.[130] She read, she helped Scott with his writing, and she complained about his new stationery: its letterhead was "F. Scott Fitzgerald/ Hack Writer and Plagiarist/ St. Paul Minnesota."[131] She could hardly leave the Commodore Hotel where they were living. She wore an unbecoming red jersey dress when she did meet Scott's friends; few people thought she looked interesting enough to learn to know. Scott had reconnected with some of his college friends so the socializing that was done became boys' nights out: the only woman friend Zelda made was Xandra Kalman, a good-humored person who did most of the caring for the sometimes frightened, and always apparently bored, Zelda. Xandra and her husband Oscar were the Fitzgeralds' best friends—in some respects, their only St. Paul friends.

---

[130] Milford, p. 84; Exiles, pp. 69-73.

[131] PUL.

Because much of the social activity in the St. Paul—Minneapolis area seemed to center on White Bear Lake, Zelda and Scott eventually—through Kalman's contacts—rented a summer house there. (When Scott and his sister grew up in St. Paul, even though the Fitzgeralds had joined the club they had not lived there, so they would take the bus out only when friends who did live at the lake had invited them. It was therefore, in Scott's memory, a highly desirable location.[132]) Meanwhile, in order to be near the city hospital, they remained at the Commodore and Zelda watched as "leaves blew up the streets [and] we waited for our child to be born."[133]

By the time of Patricia's birth on October 26, most of the leaves were off the Minnesota trees. The pines stood out clearly against the empty branches of the deciduous trees. It was already cold; Zelda noticed the cold much more in what seemed to be the emptiness of the Northern climate than she had the year before when they had lived in New York City.

She was also bothered by her fears of giving birth. Uncomfortable as she was, her feet swelling so much that she could not wear most of her shoes, the prospect of having the child—and therefore no longer being so heavy—still gave her nightmares. She was surprised at women's competitive spirit about giving birth—no one complained about the pain of labor; everyone said she would do it over and over, because her children were so precious. Unpleasant details were no part of

---

[132] See Dave Page and John Koblas, F. Scott Fitzgerald in Minnesota: Toward the Summit (1996) and Lloyd C. Hackl, F Scott Fitzgerald and St. Paul: "Still Home to Me" (1996).

[133] Zelda Fitzgerald, "Show Mr. and Mrs. F. to Number," CW, p. 420.

any of these conversations.

Biographical accounts of the Fitzgeralds are largely silent about the birth of Patricia.[134] It is suggested that Zelda's labor was long and painful, and that Scott was absent for some of it. Like many first-time fathers, Scott may have felt that the birth experience was Zelda's, and he may have feared what changes would result from the whole somewhat terrifying process. Psychiatrists link the transformative experience of childbirth with other

existential facts of life ... aging and death ... and the philo-sophical constructs of isolation, freedom, and responsibility. Such existential givens often lie dormant within an individual until they are evoked by a boundary experience, such as sickness or war or childbirth.[135]

In Scott's life, having missed the war by only weeks, being at this time of his life reasonably healthy, and keeping himself somewhat distant from childbirth, he had not yet crossed any of those experiential thresholds that might have changed his sometimes immature behavior.

With typical irony, one must acknowledge that Fitzgerald did borrow from Zelda's statements under the anesthesia at the time of Patricia's birth, to create Daisy's lines in *The Great Gatsby*—that the best thing for a woman to he was "a beautiful little fool."[136] While he may have felt outside the process of giving birth, Scott was still an expert writer. He knew a good line when he heard it.

---

[134] SSEG, p. 156; S, pp. 21-2; Exiles, pp. 73-4; Jeffrey Meyers, Scott Fitzgerald (1994), p. 176; LeVot, F. Scott Fitzgerald, p. 112.

[135] Yalom, Maternity, Mortality, p. 6.

[136] Scott Fitzgerald, The Great Gatsby (1969), p. 17.

FOUR - Travels

Some of the most haunting paintings in the Zelda Sayre Fitzgerald oeuvre are two gouaches of a mother and child, the mother nursing the baby. Figures are disproportionate. Done largely in shades of blue, each painting features a slash of what might be seen as either a blanket or a stream of breast milk— one done in red ("Nursing Mother with Red Blanket"), the other in a different shade of blue ("Nursing Mother with Blue Blanket").[137] Each gouache is approximately 26 inches by 20. In the more frightening red blanket picture, only the lower part of the mother's head is visible; in the blue painting, the mother's entire head appears. As with all of Zelda's paintings from the early 1930s, these also surprise with both their grotesque figuration and their arrangements of color.

Given the evident passion—even if ambivalent—inscribed in these paintings, Zelda's relationship with her child is clearly much more important than most biographical accounts make

---

[137] See Zelda, p. 45.

it. From Minnesota, she wrote to Ludlow Fowler that the baby was "AWFULLY cute and I am very devoted to her,"[138] and that her only disappointment was that Patricia was not a boy.

By spring, she was sending photographs of herself and the baby to friends. George Jean Nathan replied on May 29, 1922, "The picture proves to me that you are getting more beautiful every day. But whose baby is it? It looks very much like Mencken."[139] H. L. Mencken was far from a handsome man; his heavy-jowled face and irascible expression had made him one of the New York intelligentsia likely to be caricatured. The Fitzgeralds' round-faced child was a typical, pretty baby, and like most babies, looked like a somber-faced adult. Luckily, Patricia seemed to be healthy and happy, although little about the baby comes through in Zelda's letters to friends, most of whom were not yet married and so hardly interested in the secrets of childcare.

There were days—there were entire weeks—when Zelda could not believe that taking care of a baby, even with a nurse, was so time-consuming. The worrying about what she was eating, in order not to spoil her breast milk, was a frustrating constant for a woman who was never a robust eater; and was now particularly dismayed because she had not lost all of the weight she found abhorrent. The conflict between trying to diet and trying to nourish her child made her sulky. Sleeplessness as Patricia cried to be nursed or changed added to Zelda's cross winter; she wrote, in seeming amazement, to Fowler,

This damn place is 18 below zero and I go around thanking

---

138 Zelda to Ludlow Fowler, December 22, 1921, PUL.

139 George Jean Nathan to Zelda, May 29, 1922, PUL.

*God that, anatomically and proverbially speaking, I am safe from
the awful fate of the monkey ... We are both simply mad to get
back to New York.*

They must stay in Minnesota till the lease on the house
runs out, she said, but added that Fowler should come for a
visit before then. With a glimmer of her old teasing sexuality,
Zelda noted, "I have a luscious bed that I could easily get in
and maybe we could keep warm that way."[140]

For Scott too, who had spent summers in St. Paul but had
not been there for the winter since he was a teenager, being
trapped in the cold was not pleasant. They arranged to have
Patricia baptized in the Catholic church; they spent time with
the Kalmans and a few others of the White Bear Lake crowd.
They went to the Yacht Club dances and contributed to the social
revelry—though Zelda vetoed entertaining at home because
the noise always woke up the baby.[141] Generally, the year after
their daugher's birth was one of silence. Scott finished *The
Beautiful and Damned* and it was serialized in the high-paying
Metropolitan Magazine. Zelda wrote little, even in retrospect
noting only, "We didn't travel much in those years" [1922-23].[142]

Winter in Minnesota was relentless. The winds were harsh,
the roads and sidewalks often impassable. The inside air was dry
with heat that seemed inadequate. For Zelda, who had never
seen such quantities of snow, the landscape was pretty to look
at but she did not care to be out in it. Athletic as she was, snow

---

[140] Zelda to Ludlow Fowler, December 22, 1921, PUL.

[141] SSEG, p. 157; Arthur Mizener, The Far Side of Paradise (1951), p. 151.

[142] "We didn't travel ..." Zelda Fitzgerald, "Show Mr. and Mrs. F. to Number" CW,
p. 420.

skiing might have appealed to her, but there is no mention of that pastime in any of their records.

The winter of 1922 was, of necessity, a tune of attention to the body, to the health of both mother and child: continual worries over chapped faces and diaper rash, coping with the inexplicable crying from the child that—sometimes—no one could please. The bright spot sexually was the fact that because Zelda was breast-feeding, and because lactation was supposedly one way to avoid conception, they didn't use condoms. The old wives' tale was misleading: within a few months, Zelda was pregnant again.[143]

The bleak winter reflected her mood. She had just spent a year devoting herself to pregnancy, and she was still carrying the weight of childbirth. To settle back into that process, and perhaps to stay on in St. Paul—since Scott was pleased with how cheaply they lived there—was, for her, unthinkable. She could not do it. She would not do it. She could not envision her life with two small children.

The Beautiful and Damned was to be published in March of 1922, so Zelda and Scott made what had become a long-anticipated trip to New York, leaving Patricia in the charge of a nanny, overseen by the senior Fitzgeralds. Although Scott and Zelda drank in St. Paul, their systems were no longer accustomed to the quantities of illegal spirits available in New York, especially with Scott being feted for his second novel. They drank and drank. They saw their Princeton friends, their Connecticut friends, and friends of the Scribner company. They fell into bed early in the morning, and recovered enough to start out again

---

[143] SSEG, p. 159; Milford, pp. 87-8.

that evening. And because getting an abortion in New York was easier than doing so in Minnesota, Zelda underwent that procedure. As Scott noted cryptically in his *Ledger* for March 1922, "Zelda and her abortionist."[144]

Zelda was probably lucky that she came through the process in reasonably good health. Hundreds of American women—over 20,000 in each year of the 1920s—died from abortions or post-operation infections. The standard procedure was done in a doctor's or midwife's office, the pregnant woman lying in a surgical chair, allowing her uterus to be probed with a "womb opener,"[145] a "nickel-plated, sliver-like [instrument] ten or twelve inches long." Returning home, she would then go into labor and abort the fetus. Another method was packing the cervix with gauze or a rubber catheter, to bring on contractions. The most effective procedure but perhaps the most dangerous because of the risk of perforation of the cervix—was the D & C. the dilation of the cervix followed by the use of the curette, a spoon-shaped instrument. In 1921 the Sheppard-Towner Act had been passed, which provided federal matching funds to states to improve maternal and infant health. Though it was abolished in 1929, it did a great deal to increase both options for care and a favorable public reaction to the need for abortions, even though they remained illegal in every state.

The tone of Scott's note, "Zelda and her abortionist," however, suggested his impatience with—or his psychological separation

---

[144] Fitzgerald, F Scott Fitzgerald's *Ledger* (1972), March 19, 1922, p. 176; from Fitzgerald, Notebooks, No. 1564, PUL, "His son went down the toilet of the XXXX hotel after Dr. X-Pills" (p. 244).

[145] See Leslie J. Reagan, When Abortion Was a Crime (1997), p. 72ff.

from—the process. Perhaps his Catholic rearing and beliefs had come to the fore and he reacted by seeing abortion as the act of selfishness on the woman's part (characterizations in an early draft of *The Beautiful and Damned* support this attitude). Or perhaps he had come to enjoy having Patricia—now called "Scottie"—as part of their lives and was eager to add a son to the family. Worried as he was about finances, Scott might well have been complicit in the abortion decision: even with months of good writing under his belt, he saw that he would either have to sell everything he wrote to Hollywood, or he would need to become as prolific—and as popular—as Booth Tarkington in order to pay for their usual standard of living.

That both Scott and Zelda had been ill during the winter added to the grimness of their lives in St. Paul. Spring came so late in Minnesota, compared with the Alabama spring as Zelda remembered it, that it seemed to mock her: in the North the long winter continued until it ran into early summer. Even as they moved out to White Bear Lake into the summer cottage that Xandra had found for them, Zelda promised herself that they would be back in New York before the next winter began.

Perhaps part of her resolve led to the frantic partying that went on early in the summer; in fact, the Fitzgeralds were asked to leave the rental.[146] They moved into another rental house not far from the Club area, and Zelda and Xandra played golf nearly every day. Zelda was a reasonably good golfer, in contrast to Scott who could play—and did—but had less natural athleticism. By mid-summer, Zelda was doing well in the women's

---

[146] SSEG, p. 169; Milford, p. 192; S, p. 23.

golf tournament.[147] She also tried water-skiing but the large lakes were obviously more dangerous than her Montgomery quarries and lakes. Not yet a year old, Patricia was no stranger to the beach.

Zelda wanted to return to New York in part because she had published a few pieces of her writing; *McCall's* had paid her $300 for an essay that they did not print until 1925. Tired of hearing Scott's complaints about money, feeling deprived of the means to shop for clothes now that she had lost some of the "baby weight," Zelda saw that she could also earn—even if not so much as Scott did. Like him, she wrote by hand and then used a typist to make fair copies of her work.

Her writing career proper began when Burton Rascoe asked her to review Scott's new novel. Rascoe was starting a book section for the *New York Tribune*, and he undoubtedly saw the humor in having the wife who was the iconic flapper dissect *The Beautiful and Damned*—particularly if she could write a piece that got in "a rub here and there." Zelda's "Friend Husband's Latest" did that, along with conveying a strong personal voice. She began the review with a personal touch: "I note on the table beside my bed this morning a new book with an orange jacket." After playing down what she termed her "brilliant critical insight, my tremendous erudition, and my vast impressive partiality," she created a segue into the reasons she wanted *The Beautiful and Damned* to sell—she wanted to buy a $300 dress, a platinum ring, and a new overcoat for Scott. She praised the book as "a manual of etiquette" because it "tells exactly, and with compelling lucidity, just what to do when cast off by a grandfather …

---

[147] PUL, scrapbook.

or when told that one is too old for the movies."[148] She claims it is also a housekeeping manual, suggesting a meal of tomato sandwiches and lemonade for dieting.

This is the piece that comments on her having recognized "a portion of an old diary of mine which mysteriously disappeared shortly after my marriage, and also scraps of letters which, though considerably edited, sound to me vaguely familiar."[149]

Critic Zelda also dissects the novel's heroine, points out inconsistencies in her appearance and her age, and then contrasts her with other women characters from other modern novels (Dreiser's Jenny Gerhardt, Cather's Antonia, and Hardy's Tess), characters that Zelda finds boring in their collective tragedies.

One of her most interesting paragraphs is her criticism of Scott's literary pretentiousness:

The other things that I didn't like in the book … were the literary references and the attempt to convey a profound air of erudition. It reminds me in its more soggy moments of the essays I used to get up in school at the last minute by looking up strange names in the Encyclopaedia Britannica.[150]

She makes several deft literary references, comparing the ending of the novel—in which Gloria chooses to buy the wrong kind of fur—to the tragedies of Hardy. She also aligns the progression of Gloria's "deterioration" with Henry James' charting of a character's taste. Meant to be comic, Zelda's own literary allusions work.

During this spring, she also wrote "Where Do Flappers Go?"

---

[148] Zelda Fitzgerald, "Friend Husband's Latest," CW, p. 387.

[149] Ibid., p. 388.

[150] Ibid., pp. 388-9.

at the request of *McCall's*, an essay which was retitled "What Became of the Flappers?" when it appeared in October 1925. Zelda noted that no one had planned for the "flapper" to exist; rather,

The flapper springs full-grown, like Minerva, from the head of her once-declasse father, Jazz, upon whom she lavishes affection and reverence, and deepest filial regard. She is not a "condition arisen from war unrest".

Setting such a misconception straight, Zelda instead spoke about the courage of the woman who saw life differently—and would lead it differently. "The best flapper is reticent emotionally and courageous morally ... she does all her feeling alone."[151]

Her essay "Eulogy on the Flapper" appeared in the June issue of *Metropolitan Magazine*, accompanied by the now-famous Gordon Bryant sketch of her profile and her glorious hair. In this more conventional piece, Zelda's style takes over her content. She focuses her writing with short emphatic sentences: "The Flapper is deceased." "I am assuming that the Flapper will live by her accomplishments and not by her Flapping."[152] In the rest of the essay, she creates the casual run-on voice of a speaker not above the well-directed quip, the intent hilarity of the cocktail party circuit. But within her mildly humorous defense of the flapper—who cannot have aged to thirty, because she was created only a few years past—there is one paragraph of a different tone. Here Zelda says, in effect, that a woman has the right to

experiment with herself as a transient, poignant figure who will be dead tomorrow. Women, despite the fact that nine out of ten of

---

[151] Zelda Fitzgerald, "What Became of the Flappers?" CW, p. 39.

[152] Zelda Fitzgerald, "Eulogy on the Flapper," CW, p. 391.

them go through life with a deathbed air either of snatching-the-last-moment or with martyr-resignation, do not die tomorrow—or the next day. They have to live on to any one of many bitter ends, and I should think the sooner they learned that things weren't going to be over until they were too tired to care, the quicker the divorce court's popularity would decline.[153]

Taken from the context of the essay entire, this section is far from comic. It instead emphasizes a woman's tiredness, and her lack of real choices—"any one of many bitter ends." It works with her earlier description of the need to puncture the illusions of the young: better they learn cynicism at twenty, when they can more easily stand it, than to wait until they are forty or beyond. Accordingly, Zelda defends the impetuous: if a woman runs away and elopes with some man she only slightly knows, then when the marriage is annulled and years later she remarries, what has been the harm? After their flings, women can marry—"or go into the movies or become social service 'workers' or something." At that time in their lives, there are likely to be choices. Flapperdom, says Zelda, is only making young people "intelligent and teaching them to capitalize their natural resources and get their money's worth."

Great Neck, New York: The Return to Partying

It was not in any particular plan that the Fitzgeralds would move to Great Neck. They didn't even know what, or where, Great Neck was. But as fate would have it, once the summer was over in Minnesota and before Scottie's first birthday, when they returned to New York to house-hunt, everyone was talking about that

[153] Ibid.

area. Scott had spent much of the summer in St. Paul working on the play that he hoped would bring them $100,000. Eventually titled *The Vegetable*, it was to be his way into the world of show business; many of his contacts in New York, accordingly, were people interested in Broadway production and in film. Many of them either lived in Great Neck or had friends who did. Ring Lardner, one of the writers Scott had met during his spring New York visit, also had a home in Great Neck.

Finding a house to rent there in early October, 1922, Scott moved in and sent Zelda back to St. Paul to retrieve Scottie. When she and the child returned by train, Scott met them with a nurse that Zelda thought was entirely wrong; for some weeks, she took care of her daughter herself.

What was to happen to the Fitzgeralds' lives in Great Neck was an intensification of the drinking that had—despite Zelda's pregnancy and Scottie's birth—never really abated.[154] But here in Great Neck, once again driving a second-hand coupe, this time a Rolls, Fitzgerald found it easy to go into New York, drink himself into unconsciousness, and arrive several days later back in Great Neck with no memory of where he had been, or with whom. Nor was it a time to make peace with Zelda, who had felt so confined in Minnesota that she looked forward to whatever parties existed. As she wrote Xandra Kalman the month they moved into the "Babbitt-like" house,

We have been gotten drunk with three times by the Ring Lardners and various others. He is a typical newspaper man whom I didn't find particularly amusing. His wife is common but I like her.[155]

---

[154] SSEG, pp. 172-3; Milford, p. 99.

[155] Zelda to Xandra Kalman, October, 1933, PUL.

The letter continues, reinforcing Xandra's observations that when Zelda lived in St. Paul, she was generally critical about the people there. She had few friends; her demeanor suggested that she wanted few. But as this section of her letter to Xandra, who was her very good friend, shows, Zelda was also conscious of class and of class markers, especially spoken English. "Ring plays the saxophone and takes us to Mr. Gene Buck's house." Buck was one of the originators, and angels, of the Ziegfeld Follies, so Zelda was happy to know him and to move in that crowd. She was always aware of her own qualifications for being in show business. She told Xandra that Buck

lives in a house designed by Joseph Urban. It looks like a lot of old scenery glued together and Mr. Buck says "seen" when he should say "saw" and is probably a millionaire. He discovered Olive Thomas and tells me I look like her. I like Mr. Buck. He married a Dulcey-type chorus girl who has lovely legs and consequently a baby.[156]

The social drinking the Fitzgeralds and their friends did, which put the same people—the same husbands and the same wives, sometimes in different configurations—in intimate proximity over time led to the flirtations that marked Scott's life. In the year and a half that they lived in Greak Neck, rumors about Scott and Helen Buck surfaced repeatedly.[157] As Scott Donaldson wrote in his biography of Fitzgerald,

Through the years there was almost always someone besides Zelda. Jean Bankhead in Westport, Helen Buck in Great Neck, Olive Burgess in Paris, Sara Murphy and Marice Hamilton on the

---

[156] Ibid.

[157] Fool, p. 53.

Riviera, Dorothy Parker there and in New York—these names like many others found their way into Fitzgerald's Ledger of significant encounters during the 1920s. Just how significant these encounters were is difficult to determine ... If no fires were set, Fitzgerald certainly provided his share of smoke.[158]

Zelda's championing open attitudes toward sexuality came back to haunt her, often when she was herself not strong enough to accept the thought of losing Scott. Their life in Great Neck appeared to be a melange of Scott's trips to New York, sometimes with Zelda but more often alone; going to parties in both Great Neck and New York (parties which lasted several days); entertaining in their own comparatively small house; and going to the Princeton football games. Zelda did little writing. Unfortunately, neither did Scott, except to continue work on his play.

Biographers of the Fitzgeralds tend to date Scott's turn to alcoholism somewhat later than 1922, but the pattern was already clear.[159] He had been drinking for ten years. Always difficult when drunk, Scott spent much of his adolescence apologizing to friends for his behavior. But what tipped his behavior into alcoholism was the quantity of his drinking. It is misleading, several years later, when he has met Ernest Hemingway and that young American thinks that Scott cannot hold his liquor. What Hemingway did not know, and what many of the Fitzgeralds' friends did not realize, was that their drinking was nearly constant. By the time evening came, Scott and Zelda were already drunk. Then if they had another drink or two, they were

[158] Ibid.

[159] SSEG, pp. 177, 180-2; Peter Kurth, "A Portrait of Zelda Fitzgerald" in Zelda, p. 24.

well past social politeness—they played imbecile tricks, went to bed (in whoever's house they were), behaved dangerously, passed out, and often had to be taken home.

On occasion, Scott would announce that he was on the wagon. As he defined "drinking," however, it was only hard liquor that he was limiting; Zelda and he considered wine a beverage that all educated people drank with meals. When he was "not drinking," he often consumed many bottles of beer—or sometimes even greater quantities of Coke. Perhaps he was hypoglycemic, because throughout his life he relished ice cream and fudge, which he often made for himself in his kitchen. But even if he was cutting down on alcohol, he insisted that there be a supply in the house. One of Zelda's responsibilities in each of their locations was to find and befriend a local bootlegger,[160] and to keep a stock of good alcohol in their cellar. Like most heavy drinkers, Scott built his day around the next drink, the next social occasion, and the rituals of expectation—assembling the bottles, setting out the glasses.

Fitzgerald's friendship with Ring Lardner was a link with disaster.[161] Lardner would drink for days and even weeks at a time; his disappearances were legendary. Because he and Scott loved to talk about writing, and because each admired the other's work, they spent much time together. But as they talked—often all night—they also drank. To have a companion for his drinking was the worst possible situation for Scott; at least when he and Zelda drank, she urged him to come home

---

[160] As her address book attests, Zelda had located bootleggers in New York, Baltimore, and Los Angeles. PUL

[161] Andrew Turnbull, Scott Fitzgerald (1962), pp. 36-7; SSEG, pp. 172-3.

at the close of an evening. If he did not, she left on her own. Later, when he arrived by a cab that some friend had put him into, she made the situation difficult. With Lardner, all such behavior became a source of comedy.

Lardner also provided for Scott, in Scott's words, his own drunkard. As Fitzgerald wrote, everybody needs his own drunk—to feel pity for, to compare himself with, to worry over. So long as Lardner drank too much and behaved objectionably, the charming Fitzgerald seemed to maintain his innocent profile. For those who knew Scott when he was drinking consistently, however, as did Morrill Cody, the opinion was that Scott wasn't bad when he was sober, but "drunk, he could be unbearable, abusive, cruel, and vile-mouthed." Cody thought Scott's behavior might have been a reaction to the fact that Zelda had class: she was a lady. In contrast, Scott "had no family tradition to point to."[162] His friendship with Lardner, then, and the people in Lardner's circle, was a way to make himself a leader of a group, to allow him to show off Zelda (which was always effective, both in Great Neck society and with his Princeton friends), and to allow him to keep drinking.

There are indications in the Fitzgerald archive at Princeton that Zelda, too, tried to cut back on both her drinking and her smoking. One random list, for example, begins with the mention of "ten cigarettes a day." The next item is "1 aperatif [sic] before breakfast// white wine, champagne." The next is "aperatif [sic] before lunch // 2 water glasses of red wine." The final item is "cocktail before supper // white wine." Her spacing suggests that the first line—whether aperitif or cocktail—is

---

[162] Morrill Cody, Women of Montparnasse (1984), p. 58.

separate from the second, that she will drink an aperitif before lunch and then two water glasses of red wine with lunch. Even considering that a "water glass" in the 1920s would be smaller than a modern water tumbler, this list about her smoking and drinking would suggest a quantity beyond social drinking. Years later, when Scott looked back on the Great Neck period, he claimed that Zelda didn't drink much unless she was on a party. Her list suggests otherwise.[163]

In another October letter to Xandra Kalman, Zelda tells about their month of house-hunting, while they lived in New York and partied with the Princeton crowd. She begins by patting herself on the back for their having behaved "so long" in Minnesota, but admits now that they "have had the most terrible time— very alcoholic and chaotic … getting drunk with Zoe Akins and George Nathan and hiring Swedish servants—having come all the way from Minnesota to avoid them."[164] She invites the Kalmans to come east for the Princeton-Yale game. They didn't. Then in her January 5, 1923, letter, she thanked Xandra for the black nightgown, commenting that it was "just what I needed,"[165] a phrase that implied some need for a boost in her spirits. She then recounted what she called their "astounding holidays," which ran

from about a week before Xmas to this afternoon at the Famous Players studio. We went out with Julian Johnson … and saw "Glimpses of the Moon" [Edith Wharton's novel, for which Fitzgerald had written captions] *being filmed. We met Bebe*

[163] Zelda, list in her essays and miscellaneous, PUL.

[164] Zelda to Xandra Kalman, October 13, 1922, PUL.

[165] Zelda to Xandra Kalman, January (misdated June in collection) 5, 1923, PUL.

Danials and Rubye De Reever and Nita Noldi and they are just about like what I thought which isn't much.

Nita is sort of a bulging vamp whose shape is full of lumps and whose head is full of ozone and whose mouth is exceeding full of teeth. Bebe is better, but horribly HEBRAIC … she's positively racial. Rubye can best be judged by her name and by the nature of her best girlfriend, Miss Rose Mints.[166]

Zelda wrote about a dull New Year's Eve party, which she livened up by throwing "everybody's hat into a center bowl-shaped light." In closing, she said that her New Year's resolution—or did she mean hers and Scott's?—was "no drinks for 3 months."[167]

Judging from Scott's writing, the abstinence was also his. Complaining of insomnia and recurring bad dreams, he noted in his *Ledger* in February, however, that he was "still drunk." The armistice with alcohol was not working, though at the time of the Fitzgeralds' third wedding anniversary, in early April, they may have been dry. But after an argument with Zelda at about that time, Scott noted that he became "Tearing drunk" and then he resumed the two- and three-day binges in New York.

By June, Zelda's letter to Xandra does not mention whether or not there was any successful drying out period during the spring. She instead describes what she calls the "razzle-dazzling" Great Neck, "now that hot weather has arrived. All the pools and even the Sound reek of gin, whiskey and beer to say nothing of light wines. I am afraid we have moved to a place of very ill repute." She has concocted a new drink which is "3 parts

---

[166] Ibid.

[167] Ibid.

gin, 1 part water and the juice of a lemon."[168] Biggs recalled visiting the Fitzgeralds there and by 3 a.m., with Zelda "very tight," she drove the car "right off a pier into the Great Neck Bay. Fortunately the tide was out but the car sank in up to its hubcaps and we had a terrible time getting out of the sticky, mucky stuff."[169] Zelda writes that she is surrounded with "some nifty polo-ists," and that "I have unearthed some of the choicest boot leggers (including Fleischman)."[170]

Zelda's big news, however, is that they cannot return to Minnesota to visit the Kalmans because Scott's play may go into production at any time (it did not do so until the fall). In the meantime, he has begun a new novel [The Great Gatsby], about which he is very serious. As Zelda wrote, Scott has "retired into strict seclusion and celibacy. He's horribly intent on it and has built up a beautiful legend about himself"[171] and the ways in which Zelda disturbs his writing process. While Scott's demand for celibacy can be seen as more of a power play than a health requirement, an insistence calculated to make Zelda uncomfortable, it did get her attention about his being hard at work. As Morrill Cody was later to say,

Zelda did not stop Scott from working, really. What stopped him was his inability to recover from drinking. He'd lose several days, or a week. Also, Zelda went out on her own. Then Scott's jealousy drove him crazy.[172]

---

[168] Zelda to Xandra Kalman, June 21, 1923, PUL.

[169] John Biggs in Seymour Toll, A Judge Uncommon (1993), pp. 62-3.

[170] Zelda to Xandra Kalman, June 21, 1923, PUL.

[171] Zelda to Xandra Kalman, June 21, 1923, PUL.

[172] Cody, Women of Montparnasse, p. 57.

Partly because of Scott's new writing project and partly because she was lonely for family, Zelda invited Rosalind to spend parts of July and August with her and the baby in Great Neck. The sister most like her, Rosalind was nearly nine years older, and had a stable and happy relationship with her spouse, Newman Smith. That Scott liked Smith was a bonus; otherwise, he often spun out the fantasy that Zelda's family did not like him and was therefore trying to set Zelda against him. During this "razzle-dazzling" summer, however, Scott drank enough to put his standing with his in-laws in jeopardy. One of the less-than-memorable scenes from that summer was Scott's keeping Zelda and Rosalind at a party all night and into the next morning. When the women finally left without him, Zelda admitted to Rosalind, "I never did want to marry Scott."[173] Loyal to her husband as Zelda customarily was, her comment was indelibly etched in her sister's mind.

The Fitzgeralds' personal situation brightened once *The Vegetable* went into production: the play kept Scott at the center of people's attention. Unfortunately, it flopped so badly on opening night in Atlantic City that people walked out during the second act.[174] Scott tried to work on it during the following week, but he finally gave up. In a November 1923 letter to Xandra, Zelda said he had returned to the novel. What she mourned in the letter was that she had bought an expensive dress for the opening, and it couldn't

---

[173] Quoted in Milford, p. 100.

[174] As John Biggs described the opening night, for what he called the "perfectly terrible" play: "We stood together in the hack of the theater and as the play went on, more and more people left, until we finally found ourselves practically in the front row" (Seymour I. Toll, A Judge Uncommon (1993), p. 62).

be exchanged or returned. Clearly, finances were tight in the Fitzgerald household. She also told Xandra about Ring Lardner's recent disappearance in the saga of what she called "his drinking himself into an embalmed state." He was finally found "carousing at Evelyn Nesbitt's cafe." The snide Zelda added, "[Nesbitt] is attractive and she doesn't take dope anymore. Isn't that too sweet of her?"[175]

Drinking, to whatever extent, still remained the socially-acceptable pastime; educated people did not do drugs—here, dope. Given that the United States was now three years into Prohibition, with enforcement supposedly in place, the amount of purchasing and consuming of illegal alcohol was hardly believable. In Fitzgerald's accounting, he found their expenses as well hardly believable—1923 was a year in which he had made $36,000. Yet he and Zelda were still in debt to Scribner's, and there was no end in sight of their continuing indebtedness. Sobered in mood if not in fact, he and Zelda began planning for a move to France, where the exchange rate might enable them to maintain a lifestyle that was acceptable and also to live within their means. In mid-April, 1924, the three Fitzgeralds sailed for France.

---

[175] Zelda to Xandra Kalman, November, 1923, PUL.

FIVE - Europe Once More

One of the reasons Zelda agreed with Scott that their life might be more pleasant—cheaper, healthier, closer—abroad than in Great Neck was the fact that she was becoming increasingly ambitious. The small successes she had had in 1922 and 1923 with her own writing, and her own celebrity, had encouraged her to think about finding some way to do her own work. As she had said in a 1923 interview—which was with her and not Fitzgerald—she was investigating possibilities for her own development: "I've studied ballet. I'd try to get a place in the follies. Or the movies. If I wasn't successful, I'd try to write."[176]

Even as the Fitzgeralds moved to France, with the clear purpose of allowing Scott to complete what he was sure would be his best novel, the story of James Gatz (Gatsby), Zelda also saw Paris as a scene for her endeavors in both dance and writing. In the spring of 1924, the Diaghileff ballet was the talk of the town, as it had been—along with the Swedish ballet—for the

---

[176] Zelda Fitzgerald's Baltimore Sun interview, October 7, 1923, in Scott Fitzgerald, F. Scott Fitzgerald: In His Own Time (1971), p. 262.

past several years. With Diaghileff managing Les Ballets Russes, he had implemented his belief that ballet was seldom just dance. It instead combined "the three essential elements of ballet: music, painting, and choreography."[177] The sensational characteristics of any Diaghileff production were the comparative shortness of the ballet and, more visibly, the brilliance of the decor and the music—Alexandre Benois and Leon Bakst were painters often involved in the productions, as had been Gerald and Sara Murphy on several occasions. Picasso had long been involved with the Russian ballet and Fokine choreographed regularly. The ballets of the 1920s were set to scores by Stravinsky, Debussy, Prokofiev, Florent Schmitt, and other contemporary composers.

The last event of the 1924 spring season was Le Train Bleu, the most modern ballet to be staged. The scene was by Picasso and Laurens, the music by Darius Milhaud, the language by Jean Cocteau. While the production was criticized as being too dramatic and literary, involving too little dance, it dominated conversation: "Mme Nijinsky chiefly made use of the music-hall, the cinema (with slow-motion effects), and every possible sport."[178] Before that production, others in the spring season had included Les Facheux, with Braque as designer, and Les Tentations de la Bergerel, with Juan Gris as painter. Financially, Diaghileff realized that he could no longer afford to mount

[177] Quoted in Serge Lifar, A History of the Russian Ballet (1954), p. 207.

[178] Ibid., p. 263; see also Calvin Tomkins' Living Well Is the Best Revenge (1962) which attributes much of Gerald and Sara Murphy's social connection to the fact that they worked as unpaid apprentices on the scenery for several ballets, particularly for the 1923 Stravinsky ballet Les Noces (pp. 8, 30). John Dos Passos, too, recalled, "We were all mad for Diaghilev's Ballet Russe" (John Dos Passos, The Best Times (1968), p. 165).

productions in Paris, even with Balanchine joining his troup; therefore, many of his dancers had moved to the Ballets de Monte-Carlo under the direction of Rene Blue and de Basic.

The aura of excitement about dance in Paris was more noticeable than it had been when Zelda and Scott spent their brief time there en route to Italy in the spring of 1921. (Had they known where to look, they might have caught Diaghileff's Sleeping Beauty, with Mme. Egorova sharing the role of Aurora with other Russian dancers Spessivtzeva, Trefilona, and Nemtchinova.) As it was, in 1924, the young literati had learned that experimentation in the ballet paralleled experimentation in the other arts—music, painting, literature.

During their first visit to Paris, Scott and Zelda had not found Montparnasse. Now they headed straight for its nightclubs, hoping to hear Kiki at the Jockey, and to see Man Ray's photographs and some of his experimental films.[179]

That Scott was also on the lookout for books he could praise for their modernity is clear from his letters to a young American writer who had written him fan letters. In his correspondence with Patsy McCormick of St. Louis, he wrote: "The best books of the fall [1923] are The Lost Lady, first and foremost, and then Beer's Life of Stephen Crane."[180] He earlier had recommended MacKenzie and Tarkington, saying that "he [MacKenzie] and Tarkington together taught me all I know about the English

---

[179] See Billy Kluver and Julia Martin, Kiki's Paris (1989), pp. 11, 126, 134.

[180] F. Scott Fitzgerald to (Hazel) Patsy McCormick, PUL; while he does not emphasize James Joyce to her, in his 1923 "10 Best Books I have Read," he lists A Portrait [of the Artist] because "James Joyce is to be the most profound literary influence in the next fifty years." He also lists Joseph Conrad's Nostromo, saying that it is "the great novel of the past fifty years, as Ulysses is the great novel of the future" (p. 86).

language."[181] Clearly, one of Fitzgerald's enthusiasms about the books he liked was the author's control of point of view (here, Cather's Jim foreshadows his own Nick Carraway in *Gatsby*), as well as the use of realistic subject matter—the lives of the mixed-class Foresters in *Lost Lady* were presented without any discomforting pretension—and in a language that was true American English. The idioms of the day and of his country peppered Scott's own work and he responded positively to other writers' uses of what H. L. Mencken had in 1919 called "the American language."

Scott's praise for Zelda's writing was based in part on her ability to achieve a natural voice. For him, knowing how idiosyncratic her speech was, in its hybrid form of educated colloquialism and distinctive Southern patois, that she could write so as to capture that language, without effort, was impressive. While still in Great Neck, she had finished the long story "Our Own Movie Queen," which drew in some part from the audacity that Tallulah Bankhead had shown in entering the Photoplay contest and setting herself up for stardom, even if her early fame was largely British. The spoof of the possibility of an uneducated and unsophisticated girl becoming a "star"—in the convoluted and mechanical plot that has the stereotypical shop girl winning the prize—was intended to be the kind of comedy women's magazines would buy.

Dependent on racial and class stereotypes, the story might have been offensive to some readers: protagonist Gracie Axelrod lives in the wrong part of New Heidelberg, a section of

---

[181] Scott Fitzgerald to Patsy McCormick, June 26, 1922, PUL.

immigrants who are satisfied with the "incompetent whiskey"[182] they made and the fried chicken they perpetually ate. Gracie's family lives from the proceeds of a chicken shack restaurant. Above this backwater, separated from the poorer classes by the Mississippi River, lived the "ladies and gentlemen of the town" who liked being distanced from "their laundresses and their butchers and their charioteers of the ash can."

"Gracie's neighbors were fat Italians and cheerless Poles and Swedes who conducted themselves as though they were conversant with the Nordic theory." With a slam at Scott's interests in theories of race and nationalism, Zelda depicts countless incidents of class prejudice. As the plot becomes increasingly absurd, and Gracie is chosen beauty queen of the department store that controls the town, and is filmed to be included in the city's movie, the reader almost loses interest. Gracie's speeches are pat, her grammar bad, her mispronunciation phonetically spelled: as she says about the floorwalker in the Blue Ribbon department store, "He's a swell-looking fella ... B'lieve me, I'd just as soon marry a man like that. Then you could just walk in the store and say gimme this or gimme that and you wouldn't have to pay nothing for 'em."

As the story unrolls, the unlikely script is punctuated with class-defined descriptions. Gracie's coat is "of some indeterminate fur that in damp weather smelled like a live animal" and in it she "minced over the ice and crusted snow to the trolley stop."

In the denouement, once the upper-class characters' plot to replace Gracie with the daughter of the department store's

---

[182] Zelda Fitzgerald, "Our Own Movie Queen," CW, p. 273.

owner is foiled, Gracie starred in a remake of the film, she married the assistant director of the movie, and she became so prosperous (from her chicken shack) that she "buys all the movie magazines, *Screen Sobs*, *Photo Passion*, and *Motion Picture Scandal*, and she winks a cynical eye when a new opportunity contest is announced in Wichita, Kansas."

Bad as the story is, a year later Scott sold it as his to the *Chicago Sunday Tribune* for $1000. It appeared on June 7, 1925, under only his name, the first of Zelda's stories to be so marketed. He noted in his *Ledger* that he split the money with Zelda, and that the story was two-thirds Zelda's; only the climax and the revision were his. Judging from the consistency of the dialogue and the coherence of the plot, however, it seems plausible that it was Zelda's story entirely.[183]

She had also written a carefully acerbic response to "Does a Moment of Revolt Come Sometime to Every Married Man?" Along with the answers of seventeen other authors, including Scott, Zelda's piece appeared in the March 1924 issue of *McCall's*. After her comic opening, in which she presents herself as a spendthrift wife who is unable to wash her spouse's socks or sew on his buttons, she makes the point that all men are in a continual state of incipient revolt.

Finding a nurse for Scottie and meeting Gerald and Sara Murphy,[184] and through them Ada and Archibald MacLeish,

---

[183] See Scott Fitzgerald, F. Scott Fitzgerald's *Ledger* (which continues through 1937); see also Stephen W. Potts, The Price of Paradise, The Magazine Career of F. Scott Fitzgerald (1993).

[184] SSEG, pp. 193, 197-8. Not only early in their friendship but throughout, the Murphys worried about both Fitzgeralds. As John Dos Passos describes the "quandary"

as well as reconnecting with John Dos Passos, took several weeks. Zelda was not so harassed as the stories about their stay in Paris suggest (their bathing Scottie in the bidet may have been more an expedient move than an error; Scottie's drinking gin and tonic, and becoming ill at lunch, appeared to be sheer accident, not necessarily carelessness on her mother's part). Zelda knew perfectly well how to care for her two-year-old. They were close, they were loving. Zelda often designed and made mother-daughter dresses for them to wear together.

At the Murphys' urging,[185] the Fitzgeralds left Paris after only a few weeks and travelled in the south of France, staying first at the Grimm's Park Hotel in Hyeres. There they were surrounded with older people taking one kind of cure or another. In June they came to St. Raphael, to be near Gerald and Sara—who had captivated both Scott and Zelda. The Murphys were so elated at the cheapness of the Riviera off-season that they were building a house, named the following year "The Villa America." Besides the Murphys' presence, and their circle of friends which included Picasso, Miro, Bakst, Braque and others, renting the spacious Villa Marie, an estate designed around lemon, palm, and olive trees, satisfied the Fitzgeralds' need for warmth and beauty. Zelda felt as if she were summering in Montgomery, but a Montgomery replete with gorgeous views and azure waters.

Fitzgerald's friends experienced: "They were fond of him. They admired his talent. They were concerned about him. They wanted to be helpful but friendship had its limits" (Dos Passos, Best Times, p. 171).

[185] John Dos Passos recalled the Murphys' influence: "Scott, with his capacity for hero worship, began to worship Gerald and Sara. The golden couple that he and Zelda dreamed of becoming actually existed" (Dos Passos, Best Times, p. 170). See Amanda Vaill, Everybody Was So Young (1998) and Linda Patterson Miller (ed.) Letters from the Lost Generation, Gerald and Sara Murphy and Friends (1991).

To stay out of Scott's way as he worked on what was to become *Gatsby*, Zelda spent much of the day on the beach, where she not only sunned but swam long distances. She was often alone, or with her daughter. Gerald Murphy, for one, saw how little attention Scott gave Zelda while he was writing.

Traveling to the south of France had apparently not stabilized the Fitzgeralds. Archie MacLeish remembered meeting them and concluding that no one would take either Scott or Zelda seriously because of their "reckless drinking."[186] Ada and he liked Scott "very much" when he wasn't tight, "but when his eyes took on that Irish blur, no!"[187] Relationships with the Fitzgeralds, however, were not the reason Americans came to France—as MacLeish added, "Scott doesn't exist when you're talking at the level of Picasso and Stravinsky."[188]

Into the idyllic summer, with Zelda admittedly at loose ends, came a group of French aviators, leading a life as casual and sun-drenched as the Americans were. Meeting them changed the texture of the Fitzgeralds' next month: they all dined and drank together in the evenings, and they danced. During the afternoons, they swam. Sometimes when Scott would appear in the late afternoon, tired from a day of writing, the group would hardly notice him. More and more often, instead of the group, Zelda would be sunning on the canvas mat with the most handsome of the officers, Edouard Jozan.

According to Nancy Milford's interview with Jozan in the 1960s, he recalled the glamour of both Fitzgeralds—Zelda

---

[186] Quoted in Scott Donaldson, Archibald MacLeish (1992), p. 144.

[187] Archibald MacLeish, Archibald MacLeish: Reflections (1986), p. 61.

[188] Ibid.

was everyone's "shining beauty,"[189] but Scott attracted their attention because of his intellectualism. Remembering years later the summer of 1924, Jozan pointed out, "Zelda and Scott were brimming over with life. Rich and free, they brought into our little provincial circle brilliance, imagination and familiarity with a Parisian and international world to which we had no access."[190]

The Murphys saw Zelda and Jozan in the villages together; everyone watched with interest the progression of the friend-ship-cum-affair. Scott, however, seemed not to notice. Both Leos astrologically, Zelda and Jozan were about to turn twenty-four and twenty-five, respectively; they were beau-tiful and young, intent on dancing longer, swimming farther, being happier than Zelda had been since her belle days in Montgomery—when she was as remarkable for her stamina as she was for her beauty and wit. The relationship with Jozan—who sometimes flew so close over the villa that he frightened them, a trick reminiscent of the young fliers in Montgomery in 1918—took Zelda back to girlhood. Feeling young and desirable was itself enticing.

The silence that surrounds the end of the Zelda-Jozan friend-ship is impenetrable. One likely scenario is that Zelda told Scott she wanted a divorce because she was in love with Jozan and she wanted to be happy with him.[191] What Scott apparently did,

---

[189] Edouard Jozan's description of Zelda, from Nancy Milford's interview, in Milford, p. 108; see Exiles, pp. 95-8.

[190] Jozan's words from interview, Milford, p. 109.

[191] Fool, pp. 10-1; NAG, pp. 195-6; Andre LeVot, F. Scott Fitzgerald (1 983), p. 175; Milford, pp. 110-11; SMTW; S, p. 27.

quickly and with no discussion of the situation with anyone, was to lock Zelda into the villa. Mysterious as her disappearance from the beach was, by the time of Milford's interview with the much-decorated Jozan, he could not remember any break. He knew only that he did not find Zelda any longer in their usual places. And so he continued his life at the base and eventually transferred out.

Even though Zelda refers in several of her writings to having been locked away (there is extensive detail in her unfinished novel *Caesar's Things*, which she began writing only after Scott's death),[192] and to her broken heart at the end of the relationship with Jozan, few people in France noticed any problems. The Fitzgeralds had, in fact, invited Gilbert Seldes and his bride[193] to stay with them on part of their honeymoon trip, so in early August (when Zelda was supposedly locked in the villa) they arrived. The two thought Scott and Zelda were fine, compatible, cheerful. Seldes said that the only darkening of Scott's mood occurred on August 3, when Joseph Conrad's death was reported in the international papers. (In response to his death, Fitzgerald wrote a paragraph in the *Gatsby* preface about his just having read Conrad's preface to *The Nigger of the Narcissus*.)

According to Scott's *Ledger*, however, his entry for July 13 noted "The Big Crisis ... Zelda swimming every day." Then in August, after the Seldeses had gone, he noted his closeness to Zelda. But in the middle of a night later that month, Scott appeared at the Murphys' door in the Hotel du Cap asking

[192] CT; Exiles, p. 98.

[193] LeVot, F. Scott Fitzgerald, p. 175; Milford, pp. 110-11.

for help because Zelda had overdosed on sleeping pills.[194] Sara and Gerald immediately went to the villa where Sara walked Zelda "up and down, up and down, to keep her from going to sleep." It was clearly a suicide attempt. Strangely, it was never mentioned again among the four of them, even though the Murphys remained friends with Scott and Zelda for the next decade. This is one of the important events in the Fitzgeralds' lives that is not recorded in Scott's *Ledger*.

Still only twenty-four, still beautiful and vivacious but with an increasing sense of her inferiority to the woman Scott had thought he was marrying in 1920, Zelda was suffering in part from the loss of what she had assumed to be the great love of her life. She was also suffering from her own sense of anomie: for a girl who thought life had such promise, in so many exciting areas, she had ended up as she had warned in the "flapper" essay, with an increasingly bitter life. More than ever, she saw that she was in the control of her husband: Scott had the money, he had the power, he had the reputation. What would she do if she tried to leave him? How would she and Scottie live? And would she be emotionally strong enough to make a break?

By November, nearly everyone had left the Riviera and Scott had sent off the *Gatsby* manuscript (he wrote to Max Perkins that he and Zelda had spent a week going over it thoroughly together). Reading Henry James' early novel *Roderick Hudson*, Zelda suggested that the family go to Rome. None of them spoke Italian; it was not a good choice, and they were lonely. After the New Year they traveled on to Capri. Scott had corrected the proofs for *Gatsby*, he was eager for its publication. He assumed

---

[194] Honoria Murphy Donnelly, Sara and Gerald (1982), pp. 148-9; Milford, pp. 111-2.

that his earlier readers would see the improvement over his first and second books, and that the serious literary world would praise his work as that of a mature writer. From his continuous study of fiction, from his earnest application of the principles of good writing to his own work, Scott knew what he had done with this third novel. As he later wrote to Patsy McCormick,

Gatsby was far from perfect in many ways but all in all it contains such prose as has never been written in America before. From that I take heart. From that I take heart and hope that some day I can combine the verve of Paradise, the unity of The Beautiful and Damned and the lyric quality of Gatsby, its aesthetic soundness, into something worthy of the admiration of those few.[195]

Both the Fitzgeralds liked Capri, and Zelda started to paint.[196] She had begun sketching again when Scott was puzzling over the character of Gatsby; she drew her image of that figure over and over for him. With increasing interest in the art world that surrounded them in Europe, and with a hint of her previous excitement about drawing, she found she could occupy herself in painting. But she was bothered, as she was to be intermittently that year and the next several, with colitis; and the Fitzgeralds' normal patterns of drinking and eating were disrupted. There was little food that Zelda could eat, and her abdominal pain sent her frequently to Dial and other sleep medications for relief.

Although Scott had written in his *Ledger* in September of 1924 that he knew their marriage would never be the same, Zelda was trying to erase the fact of her seemingly great love for

---

[195] F. Scott Fitzgerald to Patsy McCormick, May 15, 1925, PUL.

[196] Jane S. Livingston, "On the Art of Zelda Fitzgerald," in Zelda, pp. 77-85; Peter Kurth, "A Portrait of Zelda Fitzgerald," Ibid., p. 26

Jozan. She read to Scott; she was solicitous about his comfort and his feelings. She tended to Scottie so that he would not need to be bothered with the inquisitive three-year-old, at least no more than he wanted to be. She helped with the proofs and with the fiction he was writing. For his part, Scott wrote to John Peale Bishop, "Zelda and I sometimes indulge in terrible four-day rows that always start with a drinking party but we're still enormously in love and about the only truly happily married people I know."[197] His confident tone in this letter differed from his morose statement to Perkins a few months before as he was preparing the manuscript; then he said "I've been unhappy but my work hasn't suffered from it. I am grown at last."[198]

The fact that Fitzgerald's important novel, *The Great Gatsby*, ended with the death of his romantically naive title character—and with the hateful characterization of Gatsby's great love, Daisy Fay, as she failed to accept her responsibility for either her affair or the death of Myrtle—was a comment on Scott's state of mind. In his view, the woman in whom he had invested his own great love—Zelda Sayre, whose name sounded something like Daisy Fay's—had betrayed him, and his clearly superior love. Perhaps some part of Fitzgerald felt deadened and angry over the situation. But once more, Scott had a means of transforming his personal anguish into writing.

A November letter from Zelda to Scott, accusing him of bestial behavior during their love-making, suggested that his

---

[197] Fitzgerald to John Peale Bishop, in Milford, p. 113.

[198] Fitzgerald to Maxwell Perkins, August 25, 1924 (Letters, p. 166).

personal anguish had not been entirely relieved through writing.[199] Zelda's charge, that his act brought on a severe asthma attack, suggests that Scott was making the most intimate act into punishment. According to contemporary philosopher Jessica Benjamin, at the root of the concepts of feminism and masculinity lie masochism and sadism. In truly egalitarian relationships, each partner plays a double role, "acting on the need to assert oneself by negating the other while also fulfilling the responsibility to recognize the other as an independent subject and agent." In sadomasochistic situations, however, the responsibilities are divided: "the sadist only negates; the masochist only recognizes." In the resulting tyranny of the sadist, what Benjamin calls "the demands of dominance" escalate. But even then, the masochist does not object but rather "continues to make the choice to submit, to want what the dominant partner wants her to want."[200]

When Zelda spoke out for herself, desiring a man other than Scott, she infringed on the pattern they had together developed. It was more than likely her change in role that disturbed Scott, and led to his own personal escalation of his desires. Then, frightened by the violence she had provoked in her husband, Zelda returned to her masochistic position, almost meekly.

To observers, if Zelda was ill with a broken heart, her daily

---

[199] LeVot's summary of her statement is that they had intercourse at the Hotel Miramore in November of 1924, where Fitzgerald performed a "most humiliating" act; then Zelda "almost died" from an asthma attack (LeVot, F. Scott Fitzgerald, p. 199).

[200] Diane Tietgens Meyers, Subjection and Subjectivity, Psychoanalytic Feminism and Moral Philosophy (1994), p. 74, drawing in part from Jessica Benjamin, The Bonds of Love (1988).

behavior was much more normal than might have been expected. But her August overdose seems not to have been an accident. Perhaps she was trying to convey to Scott, who had now become her literal jailer, that she was in steady pain. When the suicide attempt was apparently not repeated, it was as if Zelda had relinquished her right to have the kind of love she thought she had known with Jozan. She instead put on the face of responsibility. Perhaps she reminded herself daily, even hourly, that she was a mother, a woman married to a needy and temperamental writer, a woman whose own talents were not developed enough to let her create a separate identity. In Benjamin's terms, Zelda assumed the position of the masochist. And in that paradigm, the longer she and Scott maintained that precarious balance, the longer they played their sadomasochistic roles, the more quickly they headed for what Benjamin terms "rational violence."[201] Perhaps they had already arrived.

To France Once More

In early spring, the Fitzgeralds drove their Renault to the south of France and when the car broke down in Lyon, trained the rest of the way to Paris. There they recaptured in part some of the aura they had enjoyed each time they were in New York. Suntanned and still beautiful, Zelda was as eye-catching as she had ever been. As one young American said, there were women in Paris then who made an art of being watched[202]—Zelda, the model and singer Kiki, Lady Duff Twysden, and Flossie Martin, the New York chorus girl. But Zelda, Morrill Cody wrote, "was

[201] Meyers, Subjection and Subjectivity, p. 75.

[202] Morrill Cody, The Women of Montparnasse (1984), p. 14.

undoubtedly the most attractive woman in Montparnasse."[203] He admired her wide blue eyes, her soft Southern voice, her animation. Because she was flirtatious, he observed, Scott didn't understand that her interaction with men was seldom sexual.

Cody recounted a scene in the Dingo bar when Scott was arguing with Zelda over what he called her "carrying on" with some man, and, in the process, called her a "bitch." Sitting there with his wife, Cody told Scott he couldn't say that. Then Cody slugged the hostile Fitzgerald on the jaw and Scott slid to the floor. The bartender helped Fitzgerald up, seated him at a vacant table, got him a new drink and after a while, Zelda went over to him. Soon the two of them left, without saying anything to the Codys. Later, during another of their arguments at the Dingo, Zelda turned to Cody and said, "I wish you would hit him again. He needs it."[204] Scott looked startled. Zelda and Cody laughed, and then he joined in.

When *The Great Gatsby* was published to generally good reviews (but smaller sales than either Fitzgerald or Scribner's had hoped), Scott felt that once again he had something to offer Paris and its broadly-based American expatriate colony. He re-established friendships with Dos Passos, the Murphys, the MacLeishes, and Townsend Martin; and for the first time, Scott and Zelda met Ernest and Hadley Hemingway. Hemingway, always on the lookout for friendships with writers whose work he admired, was genuine in his appreciation of *Gatsby*. He shared Scott's admiration for the writing of Cather, Wharton, and—in 1925—Dreiser's *An American Tragedy*. In

---

[203] Ibid., p. 57.

[204] Ibid., p. 62.

fact, he and Scott found that they liked the same kinds of writing, most of the same writers, and each other: they were enthusiastic about their new friendship.[205]

Neither of them cared much for the other's wife. Scott assumed that Hadley was less sophisticated about modern writing than she was; the perceptive Hemingway saw an instinctive dislike within Zelda's wide blue eyes. Whether Zelda was wary of anyone that Scott admired so readily, or whether she was growing impatient with Scott's finding yet another drinking buddy, or whether she just didn't like the aggressive young Midwesterner—which was a definite possibility, since many Americans thought Hemingway made too much of his provincialism—Zelda made clear her suspicions of him from the first. The word she used was "bogus."[206]

In her weekly letters to her parents, Zelda wrote mostly about Scottie and the progress of Scott's writing. This season she wrote about the reviews *Gatsby* was receiving. Had they been able to return to the States as easily as they could move from Italy to France, Zelda would have done so—during the summer of 1924 Minnie had written to her from their summer vacation spot in North Carolina (this year, Waynesville) that she had been "too lightheaded to write."[207] Zelda worried about her mother's health: she was approaching sixty-five; the Judge

[205] See Scott Donaldson, Hemingway vs. Fitzgerald, The Rise and Fall of a Literary Friendship (1999); Linda Wagner-Martin, "Favored Strangers": Gertrude Stein and Her Family (1995); Ernest Hemingway, A Moveable Feast (1964); Ernest Hemingway: Selected Letters, 1917-1961, ed. Carlos Baker (1981); Life; and Exiles, pp. 105-8 and 112-13.

[206] Quoted in Donaldson, Hemingway vs. Fitzgerald, p. 156.

[207] Minnie Sayre to Zelda, July 19,1924, PUL.

was two years older than she. But she wrote often to Scottie, usually sending her a dollar bill for her to "shop."[208] They heard much less often from Scott's parents, who had moved from St. Paul to Washington, D.C.

Zelda wrote less about her own physical problems. Calling her digestive ailment "colitis," Zelda knew that she suffered from several ailments. There was the breathing paralysis: she called that asthma, and while it was frightening, it may have been less asthma than hyperventilation. Either condition could be triggered emotionally; either could be a reaction to fear as well as to anger. There was the problem of malfunctioning ovaries, abdominal pains that were accompanied by irregular menses, spotting, faintness. When Zelda referred in a letter to her having been sick in Rome, she describes her condition as "horribly sick, from trying to have a baby and you [Scott] didn't care much."[209] If part of the reconciliation between the two was the plan to have another child, Zelda's inability to conceive—for whatever reason—would have become yet another trigger for Scott's anger. Without a thorough physiological assessment, where to place the blame for infertility became a matter of name-calling: Fitzgerald's years of heavy drinking would not have enhanced the quality of his sperm.[210]

---

[208] Minnie Sayre to Scottie, 1925, PUL.

[209] Zelda to Fitzgerald, September (?) 1930, DS, DZ, p. 68

[210] There is also the possibility of Scott's having been infected with an asymptomatic sexually transmitted disease, which could have caused infertility in both or either of them. See Robert C. Brunham and Joanne E. Embree, "Sexually Transmitted Diseases: Current and Future Dimensions of the Problem in the Third World," pp. 35-58 in Reproductive Tract Infections: Global Impact & Priorities for Women's Reproductive Health, ed. Adrienne Germain, King K. Holmes, Pete Piui, amid

Their struggle to become pregnant continued throughout the next years. So did Zelda's painful illnesses, seemingly undiagnosed and unmedicated to any useful extent. As she wrote in a later stream-of-consciousness paragraph:

We went to Antibes [late in the summer of 1925] *and I was sick always and took too much Dial. The Murphys were at the Hotel du Cap and we saw them constantly. Back in Paris I began dancing lessons because I had nothing to do. I was sick again at Christmas when the MacLeishes came and Doctor Gros said there was no use trying to save my ovaries. I was always sick and having picqures* [sic] *and things and you were naturally more and more away.*[211]

Zelda's pariah-like status in the marriage and the social circle left her as miserable as her pain. When Dr. Gros sent her to Salies de Bearn for a two-week rest cure in January, 1926, she could sense Scott's impatience with the trip. Later, in the summer, she had her appendix removed.

The possibility of Zelda's regaining her health is dim once her appendix—and only that organ—is removed. Scott told friends that her doctor had said that Zelda's ovaries seemed healthy, so he was evidently still planning to have another child.

While Zelda did not write about her descent into what could have easily been labeled serious invalidism, other writers have. For Virginia Woolf, who struggled with the periodic illnesses that were both physical and mental, illness was the process in which "the body smashes itself to smithereens."[212] In 1930 Woolf

Judith N. Vvrasserheit (1992).

[211] Zelda to Fitzgerald, September (?) 1930, DS, DZ, pp. 68-9.

[212] Virginia Woolf, On Being Ill ([1930] 2002), p. 5.

wrote about "Those great wars which the body wages with the mind a slave to it, in the solitude of the bedroom against the assault of fever or the oncome of melancholia" or in Zelda's case, the relentless pain. Whereas Woolf was given chloral, Zelda was injected with morphine. Woolf made an eloquent, and relevant, complaint, about the sick needing a new language, one with words to describe illness:

it is not only a new language that we need, more primitive, more sensual, more obscene, but a new hierarchy of the passions: love must be deposed in favor of a temperature of 104; jealousy give place to the pangs of sciatica; sleeplessness play the part of villain, and the hero become a white liquid with a sweet taste—... chloral.[213]

In the biographies of both Scott and Zelda, the years immediately after the publication of *The Great Gatsby* are blurred.[214] They were living abroad, and even people who wrote about Antibes in 1925 and 1926 had difficulty remembering which event occurred when. What was a clear pattern was Scott's drinking. Already jailed once in Rome during the fall of 1924, he repeated his pugilistic behavior at increasingly closer intervals. In MacLeish's account, Scott was "almost always tight" whenever he and Ada were in Paris. Biographer Scott Donaldson recalled MacLeish's telling the story which he set in Antibes in 1926 of Fitzgerald's tossing ripe figs into the glasses of women who were attending the Murphys' party "so that champagne splashed on their gowns." Gerald Murphy asked Archie to take Scott outside for a while, so he then tried to talk sense to

---

[213] Ibid., p. 7.

[214] SSEG, Milford, LeVot, F. Scott Fitzgerald, Kendall Taylor, Sometimes Madness Is Wisdom (2001), etc.

him, telling him that his behavior was ruining the party. Scott replied, "You mean like this?" and slugged him. "The next day the Murphys banned Scott and Zelda from the premises of the Villa America for three weeks."[215]

Gerald Murphy recounted a more serious episode, dating it the late summer of 1925. With the Fitzgeralds, he and Sara were having dinner at an inn near St. Paul de Vence in the mountains above Nice. The dining room on a terrace stood at an elevation of several hundred feet above the valley. Gerald took the seat that was at the edge of the parapet and a series of ten stone steps: the drop into the valley was sheer. As the couples were eating, Murphy told Scott that Isadora Duncan (one of Zelda's idols) was sitting not far from them. Scott went to her table and sat at her feet. The aging Isadora, garishly made up, was flattered and called him her centurion.

At that moment, Zelda stood on her chair, jumped across the table and Gerald, and into the dark stairwell. As Murphy remembered, "I was sure she was dead. We were all stunned and motionless."[216] Within seconds Zelda appeared, bloodied, at the top of the stairs, and Sara ran to her and tried to clean the blood from her legs and dress. Clearly a cry to evoke some sense of her own importance out of her play-acting husband, who was foolishly pretending obeisance to a dancer he had never seen, Zelda's act was warning enough to the Murphys that something serious was wrong with both the Fitzgeralds' marriage

---

[215] Donaldson, Archibald MacLeish, p. 159.

[216] Gerald Murphy quoted in Milford, pp. 117-18; among the numerous sources for "stories" about the Fitzgeralds, see William Wiser, The Great Good Place (1991) where he recounts the diving competition at Corniche Grande, p. 147; see also Peter Kurth, "A Portrait of Zelda Fitzgerald," in Zelda, p. 25.

and probably Zelda. Yet in 1925, none of their friends made any effort to find help. If Scott were already offensive because of his constant drinking, then Zelda might well have become an object of sympathy. Why she did not was probably because she appeared to go along with Scott's unseemly manners: she was considered a co-conspirator. As John Peale Bishop wrote several years later to Allen Tate,

One must always remember that the life of the Fitzgeralds was a common creation. They collaborated, even on Scott's drunkenness. And either, I think, might have emerged from their difficulties alone, but never together.[217]

Such a fatalistic attitude from a person like Bishop, more influenced by his stable family and its fortune than by his understanding of his friends, indicated the boundaries of class. People drank, but they did not drink the way Scott and Zelda did. People had fun, but they did not cross the line of good taste as Scott and Zelda did. Children of Prohibition that these expatriates were, the age-old class markers still shaped the way their friends regarded them.

The powerful member of the Fitzgerald marriage was Scott; the friends were his, the reputation was his. As an important writer, he held opinions about literature that were both solid and prescient. His foolishness angered many of his friends, and warned others away from even attempting friendship with him. But what was happening to the Fitzgeralds might also be a case of misogyny in that the woman, the beautiful and intelligent woman, who behaved inexplicably, was less likely

---

[217] John Peale Bishop to Allen Tate, December 23,1930 (John Peale Bishop, The Republic of Letters in America (1981), p. 17).

to be salvaged. To call Zelda Sayre "crazy," as Hemingway supposedly did early in his friendship with Scott, was to echo social solutions enacted through time. As psychologist Jane Ussher notes,

"Madness" acts as a signifies which positions women as ill, as outside, as pathological, as somehow second rate—the second sex. The scientific and cultural practices which produce the meanings and "truths" about madness adopt the signifier "madness" as the means of regulating and positioning women within the social order.[218]

Particularly during the 1920s, a decade in which people's consciousness was shaped in part by the experimental psychologies of the early century as well as by the work of that new science, sexology, women were subject to many harsh judgments. Havelock Ellis in 1897 wrote that "woman is a temple built over a sewer";[219] Baudelaire called woman "that obscene and infected horror."[220] Society was still patriarchal; male privilege was seldom restricted but women were often considered problematic. As Ussher continues,

Rather than being a biological or genetic phenomenon, behavior is deemed mad because it breaks social rules; and the classification and diagnosis of the behavior results in the individual's being scapegoated by an oppressive society.[221]

Bishop's judgment made clear that he not only saw Zelda as part of the couple's difficulty, but that he gave her credit for being the instigator of Scott's drinking. Lulled into thinking that

---

[218] Jane M. Ussher, Women's Madness: Misogyny or Mental Illness? (1991), p. 11.

[219] Havelock Ellis, quoted in ibid., p. 19.

[220] Baudelaire, quoted in ibid.

[221] Ussher, Women's Madness, p. 165.

she was a classic temptress (probably because of Scott's explanation, that Zelda "interfered with" his writing), his friends had little sympathy for her because she appeared to be destroying their friend. It was a stereotypical narrative, the troublesome woman wreaking havoc with the sensitive, educated, talented man. This interpretation helps to support the contemporary belief that, often, "madness is a social construction." It also suggests that "blaming the woman effectively controls her. She is denied her anger."[222]

That Zelda was angry was clear to almost everyone who knew the Fitzgeralds. As she had said so clearly in that 1923 interview, she had career options: she had studied ballet, she was interested in acting, she could always turn to writing. What she did once they returned to Paris from the south of France, living this time in a fifth-floor walkup on the Rue de Tilsit, was to look into taking ballet lessons. But she became ill with colitis almost at once, and they stayed in Paris only a few months. In early March, 1926, they rented the Villa Paquita in Juan-les-Pins. Zelda continued to be ill, in considerable pain from sources no one could isolate or treat.[223]

Archie and Ada MacLeish arrived, followed by the Hemingways and their son Bumby. The colony of American expatriates created a unit that neither Scott nor Zelda felt comfortable with.[224] Zelda's illness gave her an excuse not to

---

[222] Ibid., p. 166.

[223] Exiles, pp. 103-4; SSEG, p. 225.

[224] See Nancy R. Comley, "Madwoman on the Riviera: The Fitzgeralds, Hemingway, and the Matter of Modernism," French Connections: Hemingway and Fitzgerald Abroad, ed. J. Gerald Kennedy and Jackson R. Bryer (1998), pp. 277-96, for a view of the intertwined emotional complexities through the works written by the

participate in the customary social life: she spent her time taking care of Scottie (though she often skipped going to her beloved beach and let the nanny take the child) and battling her pain. The summer was studded with occasions their friends later recalled as strange. One was Zelda's luxurious tabletop dance,[225] when the responsive orchestra began accompanying her silent movements and everyone in the restaurant watched. Another was Scott's throwing several of the Murphys' exquisite venetian glasses over a wall, breaking them and thereby asking Gerald to punish him.[226] Another was Scott's discomfort writing in the Villa Paquita,[227] so he used the excuse that Bumby was ill and offered Hadley, Ernest, and the child the Fitzgeralds' villa—while he rented yet another, the more expensive Villa St. Louis. It was a chaotic summer of imprudent and inexplicable behavior, financial misjudgements, and drinking.

Finally, in June, Zelda returned to Paris for the appendectomy that her doctors hoped would alleviate her abdominal pain.[228] Usually drunk, Scott was of little use during her convalescence. Eventually he brought her back to the Villa St. Louis and, in better health, she felt more sociable—though her pain continued at intervals. But as her letters to Scottie, written from a golfing hotel in Hyeres, suggested, she and Scott were taking some time

participants. As she says about the Riviera, "As a scene of writing, its function is one of origination, its promise is Edenic" (p. 278).

[225] Wiser, The Great Good Place, p. 246.

[226] As J. Gerald Kennedy phrases it in Imagining Paris (1993), Scott's "obsession" with the Murphys led to unpredictable behavior on his part (p. 194).

[227] See, among others, Donaldson, Hemingway vs. Fitzgerald, pp. 88-96.

[228] Milford, pp. 121-2; see Exiles for a comprehensive narration of Scott's behavior during Zelda's hospitalization (pp. 109-12).

together.[229] They had decided to stay out their Villa St. Louis lease, and to remain in Juan-les-Pins through the end of the year. Zelda's loving tone in these letters to her daughter suggested that everything had come right. Without her illness, and without the continual presence of Hemingway, the Fitzgeralds were once more a unit that would, with some luck, survive.

[229] Zelda to Scottie, undated, PUL.

SIX - Hollywood and Ellerslie

Back in the States after two and a half years abroad, the Fitzgeralds needed money. When an offer came from United Artists that Scott write a screenplay for Constance Talmadge, he was happy to take it. So, after a trip to Montgomery, Scottie stayed in Washington, D.C., with her nanny, living in the same hotel as the grandparents Fitzgerald, and Scott and Zelda went by train to Los Angeles. In Zelda's letters to her daughter, she describes the long train ride: "Crossing the desert was simply awful awful, and in spite of how much I missed you I was glad you were not making such a tiresome journey."[230]

Living in the Ambassador Hotel, with John Barrymore next door and actress Pola Negri across the way, Zelda and Scott were surprised that there was little nightlife. She wrote Scottie that movie stars went to bed early, and all the restaurants closed at midnight. Typical of her attentiveness to what a five-year-old might like to read, Zelda wrote about a "lovely red and blue

---

[230] Zelda to Scottie, undated, as are all the letters from their eight-week stay in Los Angeles. PUL.

parrot on the terrace of the hotel. He sits all day on the back of a chair and whenever a girl passes he calls out very loud, 'Think you're cute, don't you?' or 'Goodbye, Dearie', and the girls all think it's a person talking until they see the bird." That letter opened with, "Mummy is sitting out here without a coat in the most glorious sunshine I have ever seen wishing you were here" and closed with "I am crazy to get back East in spite of all this gorgeous weather and trees and flowers. For one thing, I want so badly to see my Boo-Boo. Give Nannie my love and write to me, you old lazy bones."[231]

Another of Zelda's letters to Scottie described their visiting a movie set.

They have built a whole French village up in the mountains and there were hundreds and hundreds of people dressed like soldiers and peasants. I could hardly believe we were still in America—it looked just like the war. There were even goats on the hillside and we almost drove our car over a bridge it looked so real.[232]

The Fitzgeralds had not been in Los Angeles long before Scott decided to form his own social circle. Determining the home address of popular film star Lillian Gish, he and Zelda drove unannounced to her house and rang the doorbell. When the maid answered the door, Scott spoke engagingly about Miss Gish being his favorite actress, and the Fitzgeralds were invited in.[233] One of Gish's Ohio friends was Jim Tully, a Ring Lardner kind of knock-about journalist and novelist.

---

[231] Ibid.

[232] Zelda to Scottie, n.d., PUL.

[233] See Lillian Gish, The Movies, Mr. Griffith, and Me (1969), pp. 282-3. Gish also recalls hiding because she feared the attentions of George Jean Nathan (p. 274).

The Fitzgeralds quickly became intimates of Tully as well as Gish, and they met other people through Tallulah Bankhead, and through the studio.

Judging from Zelda's letters, there was other socializing. She described meeting Lady Diana Manners, but told Scottie she is "very cold and hard to talk to." Zelda had bought a "very very pretty black suit that makes me look very proud and prosperous,"[234] but she missed Scottie:

You are a silly and I am as cross as a bear and two elephants, a crocodile, a lizard and a kangaroo with you for never writing to me—I do not believe you know how to write and I shall tell everybody that I have a little girl five who cannot write. It is very sad.[235]

Soon, however, Zelda received two letters from Scottie, with one for Scott: "It was more fun to read them than eating or diving or having a new dress or making sand-castles."

Tired of California after a month, Zelda wanted to come back East without Scott but he said "NO" so she was threatening to "hobo." She made a scrapbook about houses and asked Scottie to send her a picture of the kind of house she would like. Implications that their social life had picked up—that they were partying with both actors and the polo playing set—were juxtaposed with her news that Scott was invited to "be leading man in a picture with Lois Moran!!"[236]

---

[234] Zelda to Scottie, n.d., PUL.

[235] Ibid.

[236] Ibid. Scott's affair with actress Lois Moran, then seventeen, was obviously both visible and heart-wrenching to Zelda; see Fool, pp. 53-5 and Andre LeVot, F. Scott Fitzgerald (1983), pp. 223-5.

Zelda, however, told Scottie that he refused. He had, in fact, taken a screen test, but the test was not impressive. Part of Zelda's anxiety over staying in Los Angeles stemmed from Scott's fascination with the seventeen-year-old Lois Moran, a girl as beautiful and unspoiled as Zelda Sayre had been almost a decade earlier.

One of Zelda's last letters home began with a drawing of Scottie as a ballerina; she wrote: "This is Boo-Boo at dancing school—and just as soon as we get back I am going to go with you to see what kind of a noise you make when you fall." Their departure was again put off, however, while Scott waited to see whether or not the studio would use his script. In her next letter, Zelda described the tea party which had been given for them—to which Douglas Fairbanks, Ronald Colman, and Mary Pickford came. She told Scottie about the Sunday tea-party circuit, the fact that

people go from one house to another eating till by night time you almost have to carry your tummy on a wheelbarrow it is so full of cake and chicken salad. I am getting to be very fat, and you know how I hate that.[237]

That Lois Moran had given the party to which Zelda referred did not improve her humor. What she was most bothered by was Scott's comment to her that even though Lois was only seventeen, she was working hard, she had a skill, and she was making money. Zelda concluded that, in contrast, Scott saw her as only a society woman. In a disturbing scene, on a night when Scott was dining out with Lois, Zelda gathered into the bathtub all the clothes she had designed and made for herself,

---

[237] Zelda to Scottie, n.d., PUL; see S, p. 31.

and burned them.[238] Scott told her she was being childish. Then on the train going home, Scott told her that he had invited Lois to come visit them once they were settled. In a rage, Zelda threw the platinum and diamond watch which Scott had given her from a train window.[239]

What were to have been two weeks in Califbrnia had grown to eight. After these weeks, Scott too was eager to have a home and a place to write. With the help of John Biggs and the cooperation of Max Perkins, who thought that living away from New York might encourage Scott to finish the novel he had been promising Scribner's for the past years, the Fitzgeralds rented Ellerslie, a large mansion near Wilmington, Delaware.[240] Because its ceilings were so high and its rooms so spacious, Zelda ordered oversized furniture made in Philadelphia; she designed and sewed the window treatments herself. But settling in was costly, and United Artists had, in the end, not bought Scott's screenplay. For his work, he was paid the writer's fee ($3500) but not the higher fee ($12,000) which he had counted on receiving.

Zelda put off taking ballet lessons until summer, but she

---

[238] LeVot, Fitzgerald, p. 225. Part of the affront of Scott's claiming he admired Lois Moran because she was earning money, she was achieving her dream, denigrating the accomplishments of his wife. Zelda had found one of her talents in making her own clothes and, later at Ellerslie, making draperies. She had also published, and was soon to take up writing again. She felt that her life work had been helping her husband and caring for Scottie; she did not like the sense that she "did nothing." See her sister Rosalind's explanation in Kendall Taylor, Sometimes Madness Is Wisdom (2001) , p. 193.

[239] LeVot, Fitzgerald, p. 225; Milford, p. 131.

[240] Biggs, now married to Anna Rupert, consistently worried about the Fitzgeralds. With Max Perkins' support, Biggs arranged for a two-year lease of Ellerslie (from March, 1927); supposedly, away from New York, Scott would write (Seymour I. Toll, "Biggs and Fitzgerald," Newsletter, 1998, p. 12); S, p. 32.

had found a very good teacher, Catherine Littlefield[241] who directed the Philadelphia Opera Ballet Corps and had studied in Paris with Madame Egorova of the Diaghileff ballet. For the present, Zelda worked on Ellerslie and entertained, and tried to write seriously herself. Aside from the explosive May weekend when Lois Moran visited, more frequently the Fitzgeralds were united in their entertaining forays.[242] Soon, as John Dos Passos, Edmund Wilson, and Carl Van Vechten wrote, the weekend parties at Ellerslie were customarily sleepless, painful, and filled with very drunk people. Scott was making no progress on the novel that would—years later—become *Tender Is the Night*.

Entertaining may have been the only thing Scott and Zelda were of similar minds about: their arguments seemed to be constant. Still frequently ill despite having had the appendectomy, Zelda tried to keep up her end of the alcoholic hilarity, but

[241] Zelda's address book, PUL, shows that on occasion other members of the Russian ballet were in Philadelphia—sometimes Gavrilov, again Legate. The Cortissoz School, 1520 Chestnut Street, was one important address; Catherine and Caroline Littlefield's address was 10 South Eight Street.

[242] LeVot, Fitzgerald, p. 225; Exiles, p. 123; correspondence between Zelda and Carl Van Vechten, PUL. In Exiles, Sara Mayfield lists people who attended the Ellerslie weekends—Van Vechten, Thornton Wilder, Joseph Hergesheimer, Emily Clark Balch, New York lawyer Richard Knight (who admired Zelda and whose presence irritated Scott), John Dos Passos, Ernest Boyd, Townsend Martin, Ludlow Fowler, Gilbert and Amanda Seldes, Esther Murphy Strachey, Zoe Akins, Edmund Wilson, and others. For Boyd, just being near the Fitzgeralds was exciting: he recalled that Zelda was "a doll-like, feminine replica of himself [Scott] (Ernest Boyd, Portraits (1924), p. 217). In Edmund Wilson's essay, "A Weekend at Ellerslie," he describes "the atmosphere of exhilaration" (Edmund Wilson, The Shores of Light (1952), p. 378) but also the fall out from the party, even if held in what Wilson called "a magnificent setting" (ibid., p. 376). In Wilson's words, "The aftermath of a Fitzgerald evening was notoriously a painful experience," though it confirmed his earlier judgment that the literati of the 1920s gave rise to events in which "nonsense and inspiration, reckless idealism and childish irresponsibility, were mingled in so queer a way" (ibid., pp. 382-3).

once again the combination of heavy drinking and arguing with Scott led to hysteria and she had to be given a morphine injection, as she had in the south of France. Not above prescribing for herself, and understanding that she had to have something of her own that Scott could not belittle, she planned for the ballet lessons.

On July 24, Zelda turned twenty-seven. Scott knew that she had danced as a child and a teenager; he had seen her dance, and he had seen the acclaim she had received in Montgomery. He had no objections to her going into Philadelphia a few afternoons each week for lessons, and before long, Scottie sometimes accompanied her.

Getting her long-unused muscles back into shape was hard. Zelda was discouraged. She had bought a lovely nineteenth century mirror in Philadelphia, which she hung above the balance bar she had had installed in one of the living rooms—and she seemed to practice constantly. Friends remember their having to go into that room in order to talk with her in the midst of her exercises. They thought her behavior rude; Zelda thought it practical; Scott found it more and more aggravating, and called the glass their "whorehouse mirror."[243]

For a respite from her ballet practice—an activity which was more practice than it was ballet—Zelda wrote. That she finished four essays during 1927, in the midst of their social life and her dance regime, may have bothered Scott, who was writing little. He admitted years later that it was at Ellerslie

[243] Taylor, Sometimes Madness, pp. 197-9. The insulting phrase suggests Scott's antagonism toward Zelda's dance lessons and serious, time-consuming practice, which clearly begins during the Ellerslie years, not in Paris. Committed to dancing, Zelda also tried to curtail her drinking.

that he began using alcohol to aid his writing, rather than only after he had finished work. The water glass of clear gin was his frequent companion.

Zelda's 1927 essays continued some of the themes from her earlier writing. "Who Can Fall in Love After Thirty?" (published in *College Humor*, October 1928) recreated the voice of the understanding yet cynical wife, for whom being in love has become a habit. Romance needs to be exactly that—a habit; otherwise one (especially the mature male) "is likely to approach the mating impulse with [only] self-control and suspicion." For the older lover, his daily life remains paramount and, eventually, because she disrupts that life, "The lady loses." In contrast, for the habitual lover, "Passion is no less real for the fact that it is repetition."[244]

In the same vein and tone is "Paint and Powder," the essay Zelda wrote for *Photoplay*, which was later published in *Smart Set* (May 1929). In her paean to the beautiful girls and women of the States—"all America becomes like Hollywood where Venus shows you your seat in the theatre and Salome checks your hat and coat"—she contends that their presence is a mark of cultural well-being. "With prosperity and power, comes art, the desire for beauty, the taste for the decorative."[245]

Showing in these somewhat longer pieces the skill to embroider ideas with illustrations that seem unusual, Zelda writes the colloquial essay with more than adequate finesse to be published. Her other 1927 essays have more substance. In "The Changing Beauty of Park Avenue," which appeared in *Harper's*

---

[244] Zelda Fitzgerald, "Who Can Fall in Love After Thirty?" CW, p. 411.

[245] Zelda Fitzgerald, "Paint and Powder," CW, p. 415.

Bazaar, she wrote a gracious, even melodious, commentary on taste and class. Through her focus on detail, she moves far from the didactic. It opens lyrically:

Beginning in the pool of glass that covers the Grand Central tracks, Park Avenue flows quietly and smoothly up Manhattan. Windows and prim greenery and tall, graceful, white facades rise up from either side of the asphalt stream, while in the center floats, impermanently, a thin series of watercolor squares of grass— suggesting the Queen's Croquet Ground in Alice in Wonderland.

It is a street for satisfied eyes. A street of unity where one may walk and brood without being distracted by one's own curiosity. Through the arches and open gates one sees paved courtyards big enough to convey a cloistered, feudal feeling. It is the guarantee made by realty barons that people under their protection will always have enough air—and always morning air ...[246]

One of the expert qualities of this prose is its sonority (the o's and a's in the first sentence, with the accents of the g's and q's). Another is the contrasting length of sentences—the first short statement followed by the longer, more fanciful, descriptor. Then the second paragraph begins with the short, emphatic statement, working like a poem through its five s sounds. Once Zelda breaks out of conventional syntax with the fragment that continues the s pattern ("A street of unity"), she moves into references that are linked by the tonal pattern. Here she begins the statements that isolate this street of beauty and privilege for the exclusive use of the wealthy.

Polishing her descriptions into metaphors, Zelda succeeds here in giving the effect of a prose poem. "For Park Avenue has

---

[246] Zelda Fitzgerald "The Changing Beauty of Park Avenue," cw, p. 103

the essence of a pen-and-ink drawing of Paris." "There has never been a faded orchid on Park Avenue." "There is a lightness about these mornings." "It is a street for strutting."[247] In this piece she has moved beyond the merely startling effects that she earlier achieved, because these embedded sentences are integral parts of paragraphs that are themselves exactly right.

Zelda writes a pointed and meaningful class study through her inclusion of elements of money—purchasing real estate, purchasing non-essentials—and of meeting friends for lunch, experiencing the "gilded concierges," "crystalline shops," and "disciplined, cool smells," and noting the drawbridge in the Grand Central runway that creates the "emotion of entering a stronghold—the stronghold of easy wealth." Yet she has never drifted away from the euphoria of describing the beautiful avenue, "this long, blond, immaculate route."[248]

In contrast to this remarkable achievement, Zelda's other 1927 essay, "Looking Back Eight Years," which was intended to be published over both her name and Scott's, has a more abstract, perhaps male, inflection. One of its points is that "It has always surprised us that whether there is a war or not we will always be of the war generation."[249] The eight years in the title bring the reader to the effects of World War I on this often dissatisfied generation (described as being between twenty-five years of age and forty); Zelda suggests that the malaise of war created a sense of tragedy that has not been experienced since.

---

[247] Ibid.

[248] Ibid., p. 404.

[249] Zelda Fitzgerald, "Looking Back Eight Years," CW, p. 410.

Ventriloquism is not easy for any writer. The source of at least some of these ideas is Scott's characteristic thinking about race, patriotism, class. For Zelda to try to spin magical prose around these ideas is a tough, perhaps thankless, task. One of the more interesting elements of this publication was the illustration—sketches of both Scott and Zelda by James Montgomery Flagg.

Disintigration

The catastrophe which both Scott and Zelda remembered and wrote about from their year of living at Ellerslie occurred during a February 1928 weekend, when Rosalind and Newman Smith had come for a visit. Because Scott was invited to speak at Princeton's Cottage Club, he was gone. He returned late that night, very drunk. Mumbling that Zelda had called his father an Irish policeman, which she had never either said or implied, he threw a favorite blue vase into the fireplace. When she remonstrated, he hit her in the nose and, whether broken or not, it bled. Rosalind was horrified and told Zelda she had to leave Scott; she herself left the house early the next morning. Zelda, however, defended Scott and told her older sister that the Sayre family needed to stay out of her life, that she had made her choice and was happy.[250]

That spring, even with more than a year of their two-year lease at Ellerslie to run, the Fitzgeralds returned to Paris. Their apartment was in the Rue Vaugirard near the Luxembourg Gardens, so that Scottie could play there, and Scott resumed work on *Tender Is the Night*. At Zelda's urging, Gerald Murphy

---

[250] Exiles, pp. 123-4; Milford, p. 140; Taylor, Sometimes Madness, p. 200.

introduced her to Madame Lubov Egorova, the Princess Troubetskoy, and she continued serious ballet lessons. With her body in the best shape it had been in for a decade, Zelda was able to at least work toward the easy execution of the steps that the younger studio students achieved—but it took her entire store of physical and psychic energy.

Madame Egorova was so heartily admired that Zelda felt privileged to study with her. Having been one of Cecchetti's star pupils in St. Petersburg, Egorova aimed for faultless technique—particularly with toe work. As Serge Lifar, one of the stars of Russian ballet, wrote in his history of the dance,

Under Cecchetti's direction the new school kept on producing the finest dancers, so that at the beginning of the twentieth century the future of Russian ballet seemed firmly established; the year 1898 was marked by the first appearances of Mmes Egorova and Sedova; in 1899 it was Anna Pavlova.[251]

He continued that both Egorova and Sedova had

attracted a lot of attention both with the public and the press. They were both made premieres danseuses in 1903; both later left the Maryinsky Theatre and emigrated together to France, where they each have a ballet school.[252]

For anyone who knew ballet, Zelda's work in this studio would have been impressive. Unfortunately, the people who saw her practice—at her invitation—such as Scott and the Murphys, knew too little to appreciate the progress she was making. Gerald Murphy arbitrarily decided that Zelda was only trying to stay young. In reality, she was using up so

---

[251] Serge Lifar, A History of the Russian Ballet (1954), p. 161

[252] Ibid., p. 184.

much strength that her dance would have the opposite effect. She lived to practice, making the movements and correcting them, correcting them and repeating them—throwing her energy into what appeared to be tedium. She drank water during her practice hours, but she ate very little. She smoked cigarettes once in a while, and she tried to avoid alcohol, but Scott took umbrage when she didn't want to go out with him. Contrastingly, Scott saw her absorption in ballet as an affront; he remembered only the poor quarters of the studio, the poverty of the other dancers, and the smell of old sweat in garments that were seldom cleaned.[253]

Several years after she had begun studying with Egorova, Zelda attempted to write the story of her passionate study. The second half of her novel, *Save Me the Waltz*, describes the days and weeks of practice better than any other American fiction about ballet.[254] Max Perkins liked the novel particularly because of the way Zelda caught both the agony and the exhilaration.[255] In the novel, Alabama, the Zelda figure, loses herself in the dance:

Pulling the skeleton of herself over a loom of attitude and arabesque, she tried to weave the strength of her father and the young beauty of her first love with David, the happy oblivion of

---

[253] Indicative of his hostility toward her ambition, Fitzgerald not only criticized her performance and appearance (she lost much weight during this phase of her career) but belittled the quality of her choices. See Sara Mayfield's description of Zelda's telling her that she couldn't believe in herself because "Scott won't let me. He doesn't want me to believe in anything but him ...." (Exiles, pp. 126-9); Taylor, Sometimes Madness, pp. 203-7.

[254] SMTW, CW, pp. 112-96.

[255] Perkins to Zelda, August 2,1933, in Milford, p. 264.

her teens and her warm protected childhood into a magic cloak. She was much alone.[256]

Her description of the sheer work of learning steps is memorable:

"My foot hurts," said Alabama petulantly. "The nail has come off." "Then you must grow a harder one. Will you begin? ... "

Miles and miles of pas de bourrée, her toes picking the floor like the beaks of many feeding hens, and after ten thousand miles you got to advance without shaking your breasts. Arienna smelled of wet wool. Over and over she tried. Her ankles turned; her comprehension moved faster than her feet and threw her out of balance. She invented a trick: you must pull with your spirit against the forward motions of the body, and that gave you the tenebrous dignity and economy of effort known as style.

"But you are a bête, an impossible!" screeched Arienna. "You wish to understand it before you can do it."[257]

By the end of a season of study in Paris, Alabama

was gladly, savagely proud of the strength of her Negroid hips, convex as boats in a wood carving. The complete control of her body freed her from all fetid consciousness of it ... Alabama was promoted to Beethoven.[258]

Despite the excellence of Zelda's training with Egorova, she might have made faster progress—and been as well trained— had she studied with a less traditional teacher. Egorova taught according to the traditions of the Imperial School, which meant much emphasis on technique and particularly on toe

---

[256] SMTW, CW, p. 122.

[257] Ibid., p. 120.

[258] Ibid., p. 127.

skills. Egorova paid little attention to the fact that once Isadora Duncan had taken over the popular imagination, toe work was considered less and less essential—in another decade, dancers would be wearing heel shoes rather than ballet or toe slippers.

For Scott, Zelda's dance was only an interference. He complained that she slept all day Sunday; it was the only day Egorova did not teach. Clearly, Zelda was exhausted. Further and further alone in her work, she was not intentionally paying him back for his coldness, his trips to New York to be with Lois Moran, his interest in Marice Hamilton on the Riviera.[259] Rather, Zelda's focus was strangely impersonal. On the one hand, it was entirely on herself—her desires, her ambition, her body, her skill—but on the other, it was never meant to devastate him. It was that she had only so much life to give, and for once in their marriage she was giving it to herself instead of to him. Her resentment that what she had had to give had not been enough for him—or so his attraction to other women implied—necessarily colored all their interaction. But if Scott had expected Zelda to become his victim, to sulk around after him like one of their usually untrained dogs (which neither of them could bear to correct), he did not know Zelda very well. In her psyche, what she saw as her justified resentment at his treatment of her had been transfigured into a challenge that she become as good as Lois Moran, that she learn to do something well, that she become her own person—or actress—or dancer.

The conflict was more deeply rooted within Zelda herself than it was in her anger with Scott. His emotional withdrawal

[259] Fool, pp. 53,142.

gave her a focus to complain about, but according to developmentalists Phyllis Greenacre, D. Winnicott, and Elizabeth A. Waites, Zelda as a creative person was struggling with the Zelda who had been so perfectly socialized to be the beauty, the lover, the "Baby."[260] In Waites' terms, "both Zelda's intense idealization of Scott and her explosive battles with him can be viewed as an externalization of her ambivalent relationship to herself as an artist." Waites lists as considerations, Zelda's difficulties in separating from a doting mother, her narcissistic as well as oedipal disappointment in an idealized but emotionally remote father, and her defensive attempts to cope with conflict through splitting, projection, and identification with an idealized partner.[261]

Zelda had become a daredevil to cut the ties with her overprotective mother; she had married Scott to show her distant father, whose entire identity seemed to repose in his "work" as a judge—but she also married Scott so that she had someone, like her father, to attach herself to. She had married Fitzgerald, according to this analysis, so that she could "remain simultaneously the rebellious exhibitionist and the dependent child, while enjoying, without serious creative effort, the fruits of artistic fame."[262]

Because of her dependence on Fitzgerald, she became an acquiescent accomplice in Scott's uses of her. Ambitious but ambivalent and unsure of her talents, she subordinated both

---

[260] Elizabeth A. Waites, "The Princess in the Tower: Zelda Fitzgerald's Creative Impasse," Journal of the American Psychoanalytic Association, 34:3 (1986), p. 641.

[261] Ibid.

[262] Ibid., p. 648.

her public image and her private artistic ventures to her role as femme inspiratrice.[263]

As Zelda aged, however, as she lost her vitality as Scott's preferred sex partner, and when she could not conceive another child, she was forced to relinquish the role she had previously played in the marriage.

Feeling insecure about her writing and hesitant to announce that she was a serious painter, Zelda turned to the dance. From the psycho-dynamic perspective, her compulsive dancing was an attempt to hold together a fragmenting self. At the same time, it was an effort to correct a character flaw which had always been a creative liability, her lack of self-discipline. Lacking internal controls, she had married a controlling man who provided sonic external ones; but he was now becoming increasingly erratic and disorganized.[264]

What both Zelda and Scott remembered about these years of their frantic moving from place to place—Paris to the Riviera, Rome, the Riviera, Paris, the Riviera, Hollywood, Ellerslie, Paris, Ellerslie—is one long torrid argument about his drinking. Set into this psychological frame, Zelda's panic as she watched Scott's deterioration fueled her anger. She was so dependent on him that were he to collapse, she would have nothing to shore up her own life. Yet nothing about their living, or their discussion of it, was ever framed helpfully. They reacted to each other out of little but impatient dislike.[265]

---

[263] Ibid., p. 651.

[264] Ibid., p. 657.

[265] A relationship based on heavy drinking might also have come into play. According to William Wasserstrom, their drinking glued the two into the will "to achieve mutuality

Socially, their former friends avoided them;[266] Hemingway, now married to Pauline Pfeiffer, pretended to be out of town much of the time. Even the Murphys wanted little to do with Zelda and Scott. Within the expatriate crowd, the Fizgeralds were still in demand, and they went on parties (often with younger Americans) and were seen where Americans gathered. When the Fitzgeralds finally met James and Nora Joyce, who led comparatively secluded lives, Scott effusively praised Joyce's writing and then turned to equally effusive praise for Nora's beauty.[267] In a repetition of the roles he and Zelda had played in the Isadora Duncan episode several years before, Scott darted through an open window to the stone balcony outside, jumped up on the 18-inch-wide parapet and threatened to fling himself to the cobbled thoroughfare below unless Nora declared that she loved him too. She hurriedly complied and later remarked—to produce a smile from her husband—"Ah, he's a good lad. I think I'll do a bunk with him some day."[268]

Partly because of this collective cold shoulder from old friends, Scott and Zelda went occasionally to Natalie Barney's salon, and mixed with her crowd of lesbians and gays. Given

---

of ruin in marriage." Wasserstrom notes that after the Jozan and Moran affairs, they did not divorce; instead, Zelda became Scott's "invalid [so he could make] ... a fetish of their love'" (William Wassertrom, Ironies of Progress (1984), pp. 174, 178).

[266] LeVot, Fitzgerald, pp. 229-30; Milford, p. 148; see Fitzgerald, summer 1930 letter in DS, DZ, p. 64.

[267] LeVot, Fitzgerald, p. 233; most accounts of the' Fitzgeralds' meeting the Joyces have Scott praising Joyce's writing, rather than his wife's appearance; SSEG, p. 252.

[268] Quoted in Fool, p. 53, front Herbert Gorman's memoir, "Glimpses of F. Scott Fitzgerald," PUL.

Scott's normal homophobia,[269] his attendance at Barney's was strange, and it led to other complications during their next year in France. J. Gerald Kennedy sees this five-month period in Paris as crucial to the Fitzgeralds' relationship:

Scott's work on the new novel sputtered, and "desolate" side trips to the battlefields at Verdun and Rheims did not relieve a domestic discontent rooted in his drinking, Zelda's compulsive dancing, and mutual suspicions of homosexuality.[270]

---

[269] LeVot, Fitzgerald, pp. 235-6; SSEG, p. 275.

[270] J. Gerald Kennedy, Imagining Paris (1993), p. 194.

SEVEN - Zelda as Artist: Dancer and Writer

If it had not been for the fact that Scott complained so constantly[271] about Zelda's dancing—her lessons, their cost, and her practicing—the two years of her study of ballet in both Philadelphia and Paris would not have assumed such importance. She had, after all, been ill with colitis, ovarian pain, and appendicitis symptoms for nearly two years before that, but Scott's impatience with her ailments had kept them out of his conversations. The visibility that his anger gave her dancing meant that all their friends also wrote about it, nearly always unfavorably. Unpredictably, the existence of Zelda's new pastime seemed to make Scott—poor and now usually drunken Scott—the object of people's sympathy.

Inscribed and reinscribed in conventional social roles, the Fitzgeralds (Scott as breadwinning husband and Zelda as supportive wife) had never been so unconventional as they

---

[271] See, for example, John Dos Passes (The Best Times (1968), p.22-1) and Gerald Murphy in Introduction to Letters from the Lost Generation, ed. Linda Patterson Miller (1991), pp. 8-9.

had liked to imagine. Zelda's role as wife had included being Scottie's mother, being the person who ran the household, and being the beautiful woman known as "Mrs. Scott Fitzgerald." Once she had stopped being only a wifely appendage, however, she became an object of criticism. Their friends seemed to unite in a chorus of "How dare Zelda become a dancer? How dare she become anything other than a wife?" More to the point, perhaps, "How dare she leave miserable Scott alone in his cups, foundering deeper and deeper into his obvious illness?"

Scott came out of this evaluation of social roles much better than Zelda did. Although he had made so little progress on his novel during the past three years that he seldom mentioned it, he was still credible in his professional role. Everyone in Paris, on the Riviera, and in New York knew he drank so much he could barely work, but somehow, fiction by "F. Scott Fitzgerald" kept appearing. More noticeably in the late 1920s, some of the fiction and essays were attributed to "F. Scott and Zelda Fitzgerald." It is well known that some of the works that were entirely Zelda's were published as being entirely the work of Scott.[272] With no record except Scott's fragmentary *Ledger* listing, it might well be that the writing partnership between Zelda and Scott had begun earlier than people thought.

The later readers of Scott's *Ledger*, like his biographers, might question that record's authenticity. In his effort to maintain control of his professional position, Scott's treatment of Zelda as an apprentice writer might have served as a cover. His notations

---

[272] See W R. Anderson, "Rivalry and Partnership: The Short Fiction of Zelda Sayre Fitzgerald," Fitzgerald/Hemingway Annual, 1977, pp. 19-42; Matthew J. Bruccoli, "Zelda Fitzgerald's Lost Stories," Fitzgerald/Hemingway Annual, 1979, pp. 123-26; SSEG, pp. 258-60.

in the *Ledger*, then, like his comments in letters to Harold Ober,[273] might be less than trustworthy.

In September of 1928, just before Scott turned thirty-two, the three Fitzgeralds once more sailed for the States. This time their entourage included Scottie's French governess, Mademoiselle, who was no favorite of Zelda's, and the objectionable Phillippe, a French boxer and cab driver who had become Scott's drinking partner. In Delaware, he would act as the family chauffeur. Glamorous in their Paris wardrobes, Scott and Zelda smiled their way through New York en route to the cavernous darkness of Ellerslie. Once back in Wilmington, Zelda resumed her ballet study with Catherine Littlefield; Scott sulked. But he filled his days with his own "training" boxing exercises and matches with Phillippe, and nights on the town with him as well.

While they were at Ellerslie this time, Zelda got back in touch with Sara Haardt, her Montgomery friend who had become a professional writer and had interviewed Zelda in 1927 for a profile (in her series of profiles of famous men's wives). Partly through Sara's efforts, Zelda had already written for *College Humor*, a better magazine than its name suggests. Now, working through both Sara and Harold Ober, and prompted by an increasingly nervous Scott who still worried about finances, Ober arranged a deal. Zelda and Scott would write a series of short stories for *College Humor*, all about different kinds of American girls. In Zelda's mind was the plan that she would eventually do a book that collected these pieces and others. She knew there was no reason she could not be a published writer.

While Zelda didn't like having to write to contract, or sharing

---

[273] See Milford, pp. 149-50.

her by-line with Scott, she had time on the train to and from Philadelphia to think about the stories. She also had agreed with an earlier suggestion of Scott's, that she earn some money to help cover her dancing expenses. So soon after they arrived back at Ellerslie and were settled, Zelda wrote "The Original Follies Girl" and "Southern Girl." Both appeared in the July 1929 issue of *College Humor*, published as if written by F. Scott and Zelda Fitzgerald.

The two are the same quasi-autobiographical account. Although Zelda was never a "Follies girl," she did burst on the New York media scene with a kind of explosive energy: "She [Gay] went to all the parties recorded in the Sunday supplement, and the press photographs of her were so startling that the mysterious notoriety about her was almost turned into vulgarity." Even though "She wasn't at all the tabloid sort of person," she attracted people—among them, "very distinguished" men—and she was able to live.[274] As Zelda charted the life of the divorced former dancer, she created the tone of the Fitzgeralds' existence. Gay, too, was given to a peripatetic life of changing addresses in a mad search for stability—and in this piece, Gay finds that tranquility. The real loneliness of Gay's life, however, was the loss of her childhood, her comfortable Southern surroundings, the narrative that opens and weaves its way through Zelda's other story, "Southern Girl."

"The Original Follies Girl" does not return to the South. Instead Gay goes to Biarritz and then comes back to New York beautifully pale and eminently stylish:

---

[274] Zelda Fitzgerald, "The Original Follies Girl," CW, p. 294.

Gay liked style, flittering, feminine style, better than anything she knew, and she never even once suspected that she had it because she dealt so completely in fundamentals—how many children you'd had or how many millions you'd made, how many roles you'd acted or the number of lions you'd tamed.[275]

Aging, forgotten by the right people, Gay died in childbirth (she "had wanted the baby"[276]) which was reported in the international press as "pneumonia." The irony of this story is that, despite Gay's being a media darling, her story was never told correctly. No one ever got it right.

Zelda's descriptions of the Jeffersonville/Montgomery setting for "Southern Girl" convey years of her memories and her love.

Wistaria [sic] *meets over the warm asphalt in summer, and the young people swim in the lukewarm creeks ... Nothing seems ever to happen in Jeffersonville; the days pass, lazily gossiping in the warm sun.*[277]

The touch of synesthesia here, and the lushness of paragraph after paragraph of just-right detail—"The roots of big water elms cracked the blocks, and we children skating home from school fell over the crevices"; "half past six on an early summer night, with the flicker and splutter of the corner streetlights going on"; "a floating stillness so complete that you could hear the grinding wheels of a trolley car climbing a hill six blocks away"[278]—show the reader why its author tried to return home to Alabama as often as she could. Reminiscent of Zelda's evocative

---

[275] Ibid., p. 296.

[276] Ibid., p. 297.

[277] Zelda Fitzgerald, "Southern Girl," CW, p. 299.

[278] Ibid., p. 300.

prose about Park Avenue, the descriptive sections of "Southern Girl" are some of her most effective work.

The "girl" of the title has some elements of Zelda but more of her friend Eleanor Browder and of other of the Montgomery girls she had grown up with. The narrative creates Harriet's romance with her Northern boyfriend, described in polarities reminiscent of Scott's early story "The Ice Palace." Ending her romance with Dan, Harriet returns to her hometown:

Five more summers and winters steamed off the slow river and passed like a gentle mist over the salvia beds and Cherokee hedges and ribbon grass of the town, and now the children she had drawn paper dolls for crowded the country club dances.[279]

Harriet, apparently happily, lived her life for her mother and for the sake of completing what she saw as her charge, "hoeing a hard row, sticking by the hopeless patchwork of the various responsibilities that were hers instead of trying to turn them into one bigger unit of a job."[280] Even though Harriet eventually finds another man to love, the courage Zelda ascribes to her stems from that central image of her facing the "hopeless patchwork" and sticking by it. In this apologia for her own years as a woman married, unable to return as often as she wanted to Montgomery, Zelda defines the way she sees her own fragmented (or patchworked) life.

There is a third story written as if part of this group. "The Girl With Talent" places the lucky actress, now a star—who was described early in her career as a woman who could not "do anything. She doesn't know how to sing or dance, and

---

[279] Ibid., p. 306.

[280] Ibid., p. 301.

she's built like a beef-eating beer bottle"[281]—into the enviable situation Zelda catches in these sentences:

Two soft blue ballet skirts formed amorphous clouds against the door and a light swung in a cage, like a golden bird, above a long mirror framed with cards and papers. Among them I saw a poem written on the back of an old program, a lacy Victorian valentine, two long telegrams for austerity, a few calling cards, a beautiful picture of a baby playing in long curly grass, and by its side a newspaper picture of a handsome young husband, rich and famous enough to have claimed a good quarter of the front page.

All these things were hers.[282]

But as Zelda's plotline makes clear, Lou the actress was prone to throw away whatever she had on one romantic whim or another. She lost the handsome husband and her carrot-soup-eating child when she disappeared for five days with a thrilling dark European, who

sat down next to Lou so softly that I had a momentary illusion that he had come down on wires from heaven. He spoke low to her, bending himself almost to his knees with each word as if forcing the words out like notes from an accordion.[283]

Years later, when she had remade her career and recovered from the scandal of her divorce, Lou once more threw it away, this time escaping her life "with a tall blond Englishman."[284]

The point of Zelda's story about talent is that, despite her romantic life, Lou always returned to her love of the dance.

---

[281] Zelda Fitzgerald, "The Girl With Talent," CW, pp. 317-18.

[282] Ibid., p. 318.

[283] Ibid., p. 323.

[284] Ibid., p. 325.

As she promised herself, "I am going to work so hard that my spirit will he completely broken, and I am going to be a very fine dancer."[285] Another effective moment in the story is the description of Lou's reverie:

She moved about under the light with preoccupied exaltation, twirling and finding it pleasant; twirling again, then heating swiftly on the floor like a hammer tapping the turns into place ... her outstretched arms seemed to be resting on something soft and supporting, so clearly did you sense their weight and their pulling on the shoulder sockets.

"I like to dance," she seemed to say. "There's nothing so much fun as this is."[286]

But the story, despite its focus on the dance, stays a romantic fantasy, and is less successful—perhaps because this was one of the stories that Scott wrote to Harold Ober about, that it was "about Mary Hay," and that it drew on material he had planned to use. As he argued with his agent about whose name would appear as author, and what price Ober should ask for which of the pieces (saying that the better ones—even though Zelda had written all of them—should receive the highest payment, and be credited to himself), he made clear the territoriality that was to surface once Zelda had written her novel, a book he found objectionable chiefly because it used up "his" material.

Zelda's fourth story, "The Girl the Prince Liked," appeared in *College Humor* in February 1930. Fitzgerald noted that it was based on the experiences of Josephine Ordway, packed with detail from their months in St. Paul. Writing about cold

---

[285] Ibid.

[286] Ibid., pp. 321-2.

weather gave Zelda the chance to describe her protagonist Helene with her "gray fur coat trailing behind her like a Greek toga, everything gray but her black suede slippers and herself. She was rose-gold."[287]

Less autobiographical than Zelda's other three stories, this one includes a description that echoes Sara Murphy's commentary about Zelda's social manner. In the fiction,

That was one of the ways she [Helene] *established social dominance over people: she would sit and watch until she frightened them, and then suddenly be friendly and free and just as charming as she had been formidable.*[288]

Another is a comment that applied to the way Zelda defined her social role: "[she] never tried much to be a good hostess; she was content always to be the perfect guest and liked saving her energies for being attractive."[289] Still another description is of Helene's memories of her popular adolescent years:

She had around her, too, lots of young boys still in college—very attractive, straight young athletes, mostly ... In summer she kissed them—on flag walks beside freshwater lakes; in the webbed moonlight spun into fragile patterns by pine needles, beside a cool wide river ...[290]

For all its resonance as descriptive fiction, "The Girl the Prince Liked" stayed too close to some external plot. Once Helene falls in love with a British prince, and begins the life of international jet-setter, her adventures have only a slight, and nostalgic, interest. She ends the story as an aging woman,

---

[287] Zelda Fitzgerald, "The Girl the Prince Liked," CW, p. 311.

[288] Ibid, p. 310.

[289] Ibid.

[290] Ibid., p. 311.

finding in the bracelet the prince had given her the memories that were both the warp, and the woof, of her existence.

Silence

For all the normalcy that no doubt marked the Fitzgeralds' lives once they were back in Wilmington, there is only a sporadic written record. Scott commented in his *Ledger* that they were back again "in [a] blaze of work and liquor." Heavily underlined, the single word Ominous stood on its own line, with the annotation below, "No Real Progress in any way and wrecked myself with dozens of people."[291] Scott's clarity about his misbehavior in France provides some insight into the reason he and Zelda could appear to be getting along. He was trying to be reasonable. He walked to the neighbors' and spoke with them; he did his banking; he tried to write.

The many tasks of keeping Ellerslie going fell, often, to him, particularly when Zelda took the train to Philadelphia for her dance lesson and was gone most of the day. Separation was a good way of avoiding their lengthy battles; another was Zelda's dedication to both her practicing and her writing. Rather than partying by creating their own weekends and inviting New York friends, Scott and Zelda saw John Biggs and his wife on occasion, and went to parties when they were invited. But they avoided their former extravagances, at least most of the time.

Their lease on Ellerslie would expire in early spring. Despite the fact that they were comfortable living there, and that the furniture and drapes and art that Zelda had purchased or made specifically for this house would be lost, Scott wanted to cut

---

[291] Scott Fitzgerald, F. Scott Fitzgerald's Ledger, quoted in SSEG, p. 282.

himself loose from the heavy expense of monthly payments. He was too worried about money, and particularly about his growing indebtedness to Scribner's, to take on any more financial responsibility. As he carped about whether or not *College Humor* should pay $250 or $500 for one of Zelda's stories, the distance between the Scott Fitzgerald who commanded $3500 for one story and this somewhat neurotic man who was willing to haggle over his wife's payment seemed irreconcilable.

Within his writerly world, Scott relied heavily on his editor, Max Perkins, and his agent, Harold Ober; he increasingly relied on his former Princeton roommate, the lawyer John Biggs, whose own novels had recently been published. That it was Biggs who received the painful phone calls from Scott—usually when he and Phillippe had been arrested or were otherwise in trouble at 3 a.m.—showed the way Scott tended to become permanently dependent.[292] Patient as the Biggses had been with both the Fitzgeralds, even John grew tired of Scott's emergencies. What was becoming increasingly clear as well was that Fitzgerald had no new friends on whom he could rely. His fame and brilliance—like his handsome appearance and his charm—were fast becoming memories.

The little that Zelda wrote about this winter in the States was cryptic, mired in a silence she did not break even in her novel. Part of her resentment was Scott's avoiding her sexually; part was his bringing Phillippe into their household and then allowing him to be "insubordinate and disrespectful"[293] to her. So she avoided everything she could about Ellerslie: "I began

---

[292] Seymour Toll, A Judge Uncommon (1993), p. 93.

[293] Zelda, letter from September (?) 1930, DS, DZ, p. 70.

158

to work harder at dancing—I thought of nothing else but that. You were far away by then and I was alone."[294]

When they let the lease expire without renewing it and sold their possessions for what they would bring, the Fitzgeralds and Phillippe took a boat for Genoa. They spent some time in Nice. Zelda's address book includes names and addresses of ballet teachers there[295]—Mme. Ourousoff at 16 avenue Shakespeare, Nevelskaya at the Hotel Polonia, Carpova at 7 his Avenue des Orangers; perhaps she was thinking of resuming her study in Nice. Scott's tendency to move almost on a whim had prepared her for any change in plans.

But they returned to Paris, and Zelda immediately resumed lessons with Egorova—in group class in the morning with a private lesson during the afternoon. She was polishing the *College Humor* stories, and she felt as if she had more money to spend than she had the year before so she brought Egorova flowers almost every day. There were some nights when she made the effort to go out with Scott, rather than listen to him complain. They started evenings at the Dingo, where Zelda had long been a favorite of Jopia Wilson's (her husband Lew owned the bar).[296] Scott and she sometimes saw people from Sylvia Beach's bookshop, Shakespeare & Company,[297]

[294] Ibid.

[295] PUL.

[296] Morrill Cody, The Women of Montparnesse (1984), p. 177.

[297] As Zelda remembered, "Sylvia Beach invited us to dinner and the talk was all of the people who had discovered Joyce; we called on friends in better hotels ... Esther [Murphy] at the Port-Royal who took us to see Romaine Brooks' studio" ("Slim\ 14',11. and Mrs. F. to Number CW, pp. 42.6-40; see Shari Benstock, Women of the Left Bank (1986), p. 88ff.

which had become so central to American expatriates that even Tallulah Bankhead[298] had asked Sylvia to publish her autobiography (following in the success of Joyce's *Ulysses*). They sometimes ran into Tallulah or other Hollywood friends like Lillian Gish and Jim Tully, or Dos Passos and his bride Katy, because people often passed through Paris.

Scott developed a friendship with young Canadian writer Morley Callaghan[299] and read him part of Hemingway's new novel, *A Farewell to Arms*, which he had in typescript. When Callaghan was reserved about its merits, Scott was unhappy. Callaghan, for his part, remembered Zelda's interfering in the conversations, demanding that he listen to her opinions and that he recognize her writing ability as well as Scott's. Because Callaghan had never read anything she had written, he was perplexed at what seemed to him to be Zelda's arrogance.

In these instances, as at other times—often with the Hemingways or, later in the summer, with Gerald and Sara Murphy, Scott took charge of Zelda's monopolizing conversations by telling her that she was tired and putting her in a cab to go home. He explained that she had ballet lessons early in the morning and that she needed rest. While the Zelda of old would never have allowed Scott to dismiss her so summarily, in the spring of 1929, Zelda (according to Callaghan's memoir) "agreed meekly … And suddenly she had said good night like a small girl and was whisked away from us—and Scott dismissed the scene almost brusquely."[300]

---

[298] Cody, *Women of Montparnesse*, p. 25.

[299] SSEG, p. 283; Milford, p. 148.

[300] Quoted in Milford, p. 149.

Robert McAlmon was another who observed the new patterns in the Fitzgeralds' lives. Married to Bryher, companion of H.D., McAlmon had published most of the American expatriates at his press—Gertrude Stein, Ezra Pound, Hemingway, H.D., William Carlos Williams, along with Ford Madox Ford and Joseph Conrad. (He had not needed to publish Scott, because he was such a successful commercial property.) McAlmon was very much a part of the expatriate scene. Discretely homosexual, he knew that Scott disliked him, but assumed it was because there had been one night when Zelda "had cast a lustful eye on him"[301]—and everyone knew that a jealous Fitzgerald was a crazy one. McAlmon also mistrusted anyone who drank as much as Scott did.

Somewhat perversely, McAlmon decided that what was going on between Hemingway and Scott had to be homoerotic, so he began telling people—including Max Perkins—that. As Gore Vidal was to write years later,

Then as now American men were hysterical on the subject of homosexuality ... McAlmon was not particularly open about his sex life but everyone knew, and he was treated with some disdain by Hemingway and Fitzgerald, two sissies in terror of being thought fairies. Whether they were or not is immaterial; many people thought they were (and perhaps they did, too) ... McAlmon did and, in his cups, he felt it his duty to reveal Ernest and Scott.[302]

Years earlier, Scott had, according to his own correspondence, saved McAlmon from a beating when they were involved in what Scott described as "some wild parties in London with a

---

[301] McAlmon, letter of June 11, 1953, quoted in Sanford J. Smoller, Adrift Among Geniuses (1975), p. 21.

[302] Gore Vidal, Foreword to McAlmon's Miss Knight and Others (1992), p. x.

certain Marchioness of Milford Haven whom we first met with Tallulah Bankhead."[303] But he was angry that McAlmon, instead of showing gratitude, was talking and writing to people about what he thought existed between Ernest and Scott.

At dinner at the Hemingways', Scott brought up the topic and Pauline scolded both men for allowing someone like McAlmon (whom she called "swine") to get under their skins; Hemingway agreed that McAlmon "was too pitiful to be beaten up."[304] The fact, however, that Paris was talking about their supposed homosexual relationship disturbed both men.

Zelda, too, was much disturbed by the possibility of same-sex attractions.[305] When she and Scott went to Natalie Barney's salon; when she chose not to go to Gertrude Stein's rather than be partitioned off "with the wives" in conversation with Alice Toklas rather than with Stein; when she and Scott went drinking with Dolly Wilde, whose heavy makeup made even cafe society seem decadent; and most of all when she realized that the only person in her life—besides Scottie—that she cared about was Egorova, Zelda was bewildered to the point of anxiety. Rumors of lesbian love affairs between the ballet students upset her; the women dancers to whom she had previously turned for help now frightened her. Zelda didn't understand what a same-sex attraction meant, and when she tried to talk with Scott about it (falling back on their intimacy in conversation, which had always been important to their relationship), he did not take her queries seriously. In her later recollection of this Paris spring,

---

[303] Scott Fitzgerald, quoted in Smoller, Adrift Among Geniuses, p. 155.

[304] Ibid., and p. 225.

[305] Zelda Fitzgerald, DS, DZ, pp. 70-1.

We came back to rue Palantine and you, in a drunken stupor told me a lot of things that I only half understood: but I understood the dinner we had at Ernest's. Only I didn't understand that it mattered. You left me more and more alone, and though you complained that it was the apartment or the servants or me, you know the real reason you couldn't work was because you were always out half the night and you were sick and you drank constantly.[306]

In the late 1920s, after the many years of drinking and frolicking and angering their friends, it was sometimes whispered that Scott and Zelda had taken on some practices of the demimonde. There is not much proof, beyond vague rumors and perhaps the Fitzgeralds' association with Dolly Wilde, the niece of Oscar Wilde who often dressed in his clothes. The fragments of memory that place Dolly—her— "'kohl-rimmed eyes' and 'total lack of discretion'"[307]—in the company of Scott and Zelda regularly are as scant as Fitzgerald's episodes in the draft of *Tender Is the Night*, where he describes the "tall rich American girl," Vivian Tauhe, a Dolly-like character. It is Scott as author who describes coming upon "Wanda [Brested] limp and drunk in Miss Taube's arms,"[308] an episode which he later deleted from the text. Earlier in the draft, Wanda Brested seems to be a

[306] Ibid.

[307] Benstock, Women of the Left Bank. Pp. 103. 180, 307; Joan Sclienkar, Truly Wilde (2000), p. 117.

[308] Schenkar, Truly Wilde, p. 118; see J. Gerald Kennedy, Imagining Paris (1993), p. 259 on the manuscript version of Fitzgerald's Tender Is the Night, and Matthew J. Bruccoli, The Composition of Tender Is the Night, vol. 2 (1963), p. 164; also Scott Donaldson, "A Short History of Tender Is the Night," Writing the American Classics (1990), pp. 177-208.

desirable heterosexual woman, but she becomes increasingly associated with the lesbian coterie.

Years later, when Zelda tried to reconstruct the last years of the 1920s, she dated Scott's sexual withdrawal from her to 1 926.[309] Given that their relationship had been grounded in sex, at least in part, his shutting her out infuriated—and frustrated—her. The jealousy Scott had professed throughout their relationship seemed to have been a facade, because if he were not able to have sex with her, if she sickened him to the extent that he pretended, then why would he be jealous of her finding satisfaction with someone else? Robert McAlmon, who had also grown up in the Minnesota Twin Cities and had known of Scott for much of his life, said that he always thought Fitzgerald "'was play-acting madder or crazier than he actually was'"[310]—he saw Scott as a performer in whatever role he took on.

In one of her fragments of a meditative essay, Zelda questioned the role of sex: "To consider: whether the sexual impulse is first activated, or whether the sexual impulse follows the emotional impetus."[311] In another unpublished essay, Zelda tried to explain why she saw her dancing and her strenuous practicing as evidence of her love for Scott—her focus on the body being unusual for the 1920s. She wrote:

To an artist, a dancer, an acrobat, a fencer or anybody communicating directly physiologically ... the first insight into the

---

[309] Zelda's letter, September (?), 1930, DS,DZ, pp. 70-1 and see p. 72, "I didn't have you to love.".

[310] McAlmon quoted in Smoller, Adrift Among Geniuses, p. 156.

[311] Zelda Fitzgerald, "A Tragic Happiness/ sketch of a temperament," essays, PUL; see DS,DZ, p. 72: "sex and sentiment have little to do with each other ...".

eloquence of ones [sic] *physical endowment is embarrassing. It's a hard thing to stand before a mirror and practice love in terms of abaresque* [sic].[312]

And in a third, she repeated the phrase describing her character's consciousness, "Haunted, uncatalogued purpose …"[313]

When Scott later wrote his description of the five years of their lives starting with February 1927 and continuing, he wrote about what he called Zelda's "utterly uncharacteristic tendencies toward lesbianism, usually with liquor." He added that she "Projects it upon husband and friends."[314] What may be most significant about this emphasis on sexuality in Zelda's incipient breakdown was the amount of space he gave it.

1 ½ years a. Feb 1927 to Aug 1928 (gestation). From the Hollywood affair [his liaison with Lois Moran]*, after which there is one side of her* [Zelda] *which her husband can never reach—a sort of brooding, a vast doubt. Husband for the most part behaving badly. (First faint hint of lesbianism-dancing teacher).*

1 ½ years b. Aug 1928 to Feb 1930 (growing obsessions). Increasing conjugal difficulties and estrangement. Increasingly in herself. Increasing ambition. World revolves around DANCING. Utterly uncharacteristic Boundless energy.[315]

Balancing on one side of Scott's scale of harsh judgment was Zelda's purported lesbianism—based on her friendship with Dolly Wilde? On his or someone else's glimpse of one kiss?—and on the other side of his scale, Zelda's "increasing ambition."

---

[312] Zelda Fitzgerald, "This Time ofnYear," essays, PUL.

[313] Zelda, essays, PUL.

[314] Fitzgerald, letter to Dr. Mildred Squires, April 4,1932, PUL.

[315] Ibid., PUL.

As his wife of nine years tried to find a way to balance her life, her art, and her broken health, Fitzgerald's summary judgment made her dilemma—and the dilemma of their marriage—seem much simpler than either was.

EIGHT - The Crack-Up, 1930

The Fitzgeralds' restless need to be on the Riviera when their friends were there, starting in the early summer of 1929, meant that Zelda's lessons with Egorova lasted only a few months. Egorova was complimentary—she knew that Zelda was making progress, particularly with her continued study in Philadelphia; she knew that in strengthening her body and her muscles, she was drawing closer to being able to use the talents she had been given. By this stage of her study, Zelda could continue to exercise and practice on her own—though not for long periods of time. She would try to take lessons in Nice.

During the summer of 1929, Scott, Zelda, and Scottie, with a nanny in tow, stayed at the Villa Fleur des Bois in Cannes. Less enthusiastic than usual about swimming and diving, Zelda was withdrawn, focusing largely on her progress in the dance. She also wrote two other stories for *College Humor*, including one ("A Millionaire's Girl") that Scott thought was so successful that he had Harold Ober withdraw it and sell it to the *Saturday Evening Post*—for Scott's usual fee of $4000. (The *Post* would pay that sum if Scott's name alone were on the story, so Scott agreed to publish it as his own; it appeared in the May 7, 1930, issue.)

"A Millionaire's Girl" involved "the Fitzgerald's roadhouse,"[316] in that the beautiful young couple—Caroline, the child married at sixteen and now divorced, and her wealthy lover Barry—visited there, so that the married Fitzgerald couple, or one of them, was the ostensible narrator. It was at the Fitzgeralds' that Barry proposed to Caroline; it was later at Ciro's that the engagement was ended, publicly, so that it could not be repaired.

Much about the golden young couple resembled Scott and Zelda: "They looked fine together; they were both dusted with soft golden brown like bees' wings, and they were tall, and the color under their skins was apricot …" Caroline suggested Zelda in her adolescence, with "her slim, perfect body" and "that lovely bacchanalian face … There was a sense of adventure in the way her high heels sat so precisely in the center of the backs of her long silk legs." Caroline resembled Zelda even in temperament: "She was ambitious, she was extravagant, and she was just about the prettiest thing you ever saw."[317]

She was also poor, so Barry's rich parents bought her off with a check and a car. When Barry angrily broke their engagement and went precipitously abroad, Caroline went to Los Angeles and won a part in a film, a part that grew to star proportions. The night of the opening, however, she attempted suicide—her ploy brought Barry back, and they were soon married. The gamble of her life, to do whatever it took to marry the man she had chosen, seemingly paid off. Zelda, however, added an admonitory last paragraph:

[316] Zelda Fitzgerald, "A Millionaire's Girl," CW, p. 329.

317 Ibid., p. 328.

She married him, of course, and since she left the films on that occasion, they have both had much to reproach each other for. That was three years ago, and so far they have kept their quarrels out of the divorce courts, but I somehow think you can't go on forever protecting quarrels, and that romances born in violence and suspicion will end themselves on the same note ...[318]

At the time Zelda wrote this story, her marriage had become little but one long quarrel, marked with probable violence and definite suspicion. In retrospect, were she thinking back to the three-year mark in their own marriage, Scottie had been born and they were just finishing their desolate months in Minnesota. *The Beautiful and Damned* had been published, with its prescient descriptions of the destruction of the young lovers. And they were heading into the Great Neck years, when quarrels, drinking, and possible infidelities became the pattern. Had the Fitzgerald marriage ended at that point, much of the 1920s—and much of both of their lives—might have been salvaged.

Zelda's second story of this group, which appeared in *College Humor* in January 1 1931, repeated the theme of the woman protagonist who is poor. In "Poor Working Girl," Eloise Everett Elkins was "carefully protected but unprovided for."[319] She had a "lyric taste in dress" but little else except "a real talent for the ukulele."[320] So when she took a job as companion to a child, thinking she would save enough money to go to New York and try for the stage, it was an adventurous beginning to her mature life. Before this time, Eloise had always slept at home; before this, she

[318] Ibid., p. 336.

[319] Zelda Fitzgerald, "Poor Working Girl," CW, p. 337.

[320] Ibid., p. 337.

had been half engaged for four years now to numerous editions of the same young man. He always had a secondhand car, a fur coat, that irregular cast of features known as an open countenance, and a gold football on his watch chain.[321]

Fired from her nanny job, instead of moving to New York, Eloise sank back into her earlier life, which to some may have looked like apathy. In Zelda's words,

she found herself at home again. She couldn't decide whether or not she was as wonderful as she thought she was, and New York seemed awfully far from the yellow frame house full of the sweetness of big Sunday meals and the noise of the cleaning in the mornings and black shadows from an open fire.[322]

Less stark in some respects than "A Millionaire's Girl," in which Caroline is not valued for herself but rather for the appearance of a self, "Poor Working Girl" dispenses with a contrived happy ending and allows Eloise to rest in obvious comfort within her familiar culture. Zelda's ending apologia for this story speaks of her protagonist's having come from "worn-out stock" since she "couldn't really imagine achieving anything."[323] The negation of that close, however, does little to spoil the tenor of Eloise's safe return home.

Even as Zelda was gaining satisfaction from the creation of her American women characters—in these six stories that were now complete—she was following a risky route psychologically. Through the varied profiles of her protagonists, Zelda was plumbing her own adolescence and womanhood. None

---

[321] Ibid., p. 339.

[322] Ibid., p. 341.

[323] Ibid., p. 342.

of the stories was "about" Zelda Sayre, yet each included elements that were germane to Zelda's life story. As Marilyn Yalom notes,

the path away from madness, like the path into it, has a specifically female lane ... the role of language as the essential medium through which the wounded narrator conveys the story of her life and gives it meaning.[324]

There is little question that Zelda was recognizing that she was, in many respects, a wounded narrator, so the act of her voicing her story lost some of its power. It certainly made her angrier than usual that "A Millionaire's Girl" was attributed entirely to the husband who had not written it, but who had moved Zelda into such a corner psychologically that she could barely write it herself. Even if contemporary psychology insists that "Words offer the possibility of reconstituting the world, of gaining mastery over one's phobias, of re-defining oneself,"[325] the process of writing does not always result in a fulfillment of that possibility.

The therapeutic role of words was to come later for Zelda. Once she had written her own story, in the novel *Save Me the Waltz* and probably in the seven or eight short stories she wrote at about the same time (stories now lost, except for their summaries in her agent's file[326]), she might have had some chance at reclaiming her story. The irony of the Scott-Zelda relationship from the start, however, was that Scott regularly usurped

[324] Marilyn Yalom, Maternity, Mortality, and the Literature of Madness (1985), p. 111.

[325] Ibid., p. 103.

[326] See Matthew J. Bruccoli, "Zelda Fitzgerald's Lost Stories," Fitzgerald/Hemingway Annual, 1979, pp. 123-6.

Zelda's story.[327] The narrative that was legitimately hers, in that she had lived it and in most cases enjoyed and cherished it, had been published in Scott's hundred short stories, and in his first three novels—even, though less obviously, in *The Great Gatsby*. For Zelda to write her story, then to recharacterize it and retell it, forced her into the position of borrowing what appeared to be her husband's story. Because of her marriage, and her relinquishing her story to Scott, she was bereft of the story she knew best, that of Zelda Sayre.

Zelda had lost not only her story; she had lost any power she might once have had in the relationship. She doggedly practiced her dance, an art her husband could not share in, and she still occasionally challenged Scott to diving contests (once Archie MacLeish had given up the competition because of an injured back, the sight of the Fitzgeralds at Eden Roc took on a more sinister tone[328]). She performed in ballet productions in Nice and Cannes, and tried to continue a social life with the Murphys and with Scott, but she found little satisfaction in anything. Gerald Murphy recalled her outright fear at a movie that included a slow-moving octopus, when she threw her body across his and screamed, "What is it? What is it?"[329]

---

[327] Clearer in hindsight, this process has been labeled injurious by all of Zelda's biographers, and others. As Elizabeth Hardwick wrote, "Zelda's greatest gift to Fitzgerald as a writer was her own startling and reckless personality and his almost paralyzing love of it" (Elizabeth Hardwick, Seduction and Betrayal (1974), p. 96). More explicitly, Carolyn Heilbrun refers to what she calls Fitzgerald's "assumption that he had a right to the life of his wife, Zelda, as an artistic property. She went mad, confined to what Mark Schorer has called her ultimate anonymity - to be storyless ... [Fitzgerald] had usurped her narrative" (Carolyn Heilbrun, Writing a Woman's Life (1988), p. 12).

[328] See Scott Donaldson, Archibald MacLeish (1992), p. 152.

[329] Quoted in Kendall Taylor, Sometimes Madness Is Wisdom (2001), p. 216.

Other people remembered her harassing Scott as he drove the narrow mountain roads, often asking him to light her cigarette at just the wrong time, harassment that culminated at the end of their stay on the Riviera when she grabbed the steering wheel and tried to force their car off the road—and over a cliff.[330]

Still, upon their return to Paris in September of 1929, no one told Zelda to see a doctor, no one told her to get help. People complained about her, her intent stares and inappropriate laughter. Scott cried to Hemingway about how difficult life was, but said nothing about Zelda; part of his letter read:

I stay alone working or trying to work or brooding or reading detective stories—and realizing that anyone in my state of mind, who has in addition never been able to hold his tongue, is pretty poor company. But when drunk I make them all pay and pay and pay.[331]

In contrast to Scott's worry about his continuing inability to write, Zelda's recollection of the summer is much more painful.

We went to Cannes. I kept up my lessons and we quarrelled. You wouldn't let me fire the nurse that both Scottie and I hated. You disgraced yourself at the Barry's [sic] party, on the yacht at Monte Carlo, at the casino with Gerald and Dotty. Many nights you didn't come home. You came into my room once the whole summer, but I didn't care because I went to the beach in the morning, I had my lesson in the afternoon and I walked at night. I was nervous and half-sick but I didn't know what was the matter. I only knew that I had difficulty standing lots of people, like the party at Wm J.

[330] This is one of the series of events that blur together; either there were many such driving episodes or one story bred other stories. See for example, Amanda Vaill, Everybody Was So Young (1998), p. 147; Milford, p. 111.

[331] Fitzgerald to Ernest Hemingway, September 9, 1929, quoted in SSEG, p. 281.

Locke's and that I wanted to get back to Paris. We had lunch at the Murphy's [sic] *and Gerald said to me very pointedly several times that Nemchinova* [one of Zelda's idols, a star of the Russian ballet who had danced the role of Aurora with Egorova in 1921] *was at Antibes. Still I didn't understand.*[332]

Zelda went on with her lessons. She did not seem to realize that Monte Carlo had become the home of a great many dancers and choreographers who had previously been with Diaghileff; that ballet had moved out of Paris. Rather, she was ecstatic to be back in Paris working with Madame.

Then in late September, Zelda received the letter that would have opened the door of professional dance. Dated September 23, 1929, Madame Sedova's letter invited Zelda to come to Naples and dance a solo in Ada, to be a part of the San Carlo Opera Ballet Company there. Given that Sedova had been a ranking Russian ballerina, a classmate of Egorova's, and was still a dancer of great distinction, her invitation was legitimate—it was a compliment to Zelda's ability.

One of the most critical gaps in the Fitzgeralds' story occurs here.[333] Even though Sedova's letter is preserved in the Fitzgerald papers at Princeton, there is no comment about whether or not Zelda answered it. There is no comment anywhere about Scott's reaction to the invitation, even in his *Ledger*, and neither is there any explanation for Zelda's staying in Paris and continuing her lessons as if she were content to be a student. In psychoanalytic terms, Zelda was comfortable with her somewhat childlike

---

[332] Zelda Fitzgerald, September (?) 1930, DS, DZ, p. 71.

[333] Letter to Zelda from Mme. Julie Sedova, September 23,1929, PUL; see Milford, pp. 156-7; SSEG, p. 228; S, p. 37.

role: she knew how to study and practice but she had no idea how to be a ballerina.

In Elizabeth Waites' assessment,

[Zelda] *declined the opportunity for reasons never clear. Given subsequent developments, both her refusal of the Naples offer and the psychotic break that followed seem to have been related to her inability to separate from Scott, no matter how chaotic their lives became.*[334]

The fruition of her lifelong dependence, first on her parents and then on Scott as replacement for at least the Judge, Zelda's fearful state of mind was a call for any help that would allow her to mature, to see the power of her own gifts, rather than be content with the same old struggles in the same old place—and that always a dependent place. Not unlike Eloise in her last-written story, Zelda "couldn't really imagine achieving anything."[335] But she had.

Zelda did not fail at becoming a ballerina. She failed at becoming an adult.

Africa, Paris, and Switzerland

The blurring of events from the winter of 1929 and 1930 to some extent mirrored those from 1927, 1928, and earlier 1929. Raucous parties, wild dinners (this time, with Zelda holding on to the edges of tables to keep herself from getting up and leaving), long nights of drinking, drinking, drinking—Paris seemed little different; Scott seemed little different. Now five years past the publication of *The Great Gatsby*, Fitzgerald was at his lowest ebb as a functioning writer. He decided he suffered

---

[334] Elizabeth A. Waites, "The Princess in the Tower," Journal of the American Psychoanalytic Association, 34 (1986), p. 657.

[335] Zelda Fitzgerald, "Poor Working Girl," CW, p. 342.

from tuberculosis, a self-diagnosis that for a time brought him some pity. At thirty-four, Scott may have subconsciously decided that the way out of his writing dilemma was death. Although he had tried to drink himself into illness, a tactic which continued, he was not tubercular—and so in late winter he decided that he and Zelda needed to find respite in yet another change of scene.

This time they traveled to North Africa, and there are a few photos of them riding on camels, Zelda's face unremittingly dour.[336] As she remembered that winter, living as she was in a body exhausted from dancing and anxiety, fifteen pounds under even her usual slim state:

We came back to Paris. You were miserable about your lung, and because you had wasted the summer, but you didn't stop drinking. I worked all the time and I became dependent on Egorowa. I couldn't walk in the street unless I had been to my lesson. I couldn't manage the apartment because I couldn't speak to the servants. I couldn't go into stores to buy clothes and my emotions became blindly involved. In February, when I was so sick with bronchitis that I had ventouses every day and fever for two weeks, I had to work because I couldn't exist in the world without it, and still I didn't understand what I was doing. I didn't even know what I wanted. Then we went to Africa and when we came back I began to realize because I could feel what was happening in others. You did not want me. Twice you left my bed saying "I can't. Don't you understand"—I didn't …[337]

Scott's analysis of the month of the African trip and the one following, which he wrote for her psychiatrist, was focused on what he called Zelda's "eccentric behavior." He described her

---

[336] SSEG, p. 288; Milford, p. 157.

[337] Zelda Fitzgerald, September (?) 1930, DS, DZ, pp. 71-2.

Definite, though intermittent irrationalities without liquor ... sleeps all day Sunday ... Writing "to pay dancing bills." Lesbianism idealized, not practiced, save for one drunken, kissing episode.[338]

Distraught as she was, it is possible in this early spring that Zelda wrote what may be one of her best, most controlled stories. Like her other six stories about women, Zelda's "Miss Ella" (published December 1931 in *Scribner's Magazine* under Zelda's name alone) told the tragic story of a Southern woman who broke an engagement because she had found another man whom she truly loved. Rather than wed Mr. Hendrix because that marriage was proper, Ella was to marry Andy Bronson, an exciting lover.

The story's opening foreshadows the abrupt ending:

Bitter things dried behind the eyes of Miss Ella like garlic on a string before an open fire. The acrid fumes of sweet memories had gradually reddened their rims until at times they shone like the used places in copper saucepans.[339]

Relinquishing the life of anything other than an "old maid," Miss Ella and her aunt, "Aunt Ella," led their traditional suitable existences together—despite the difference in their ages. The reason the lovely younger Ella was caught in the vise of Southern custom had occurred on her wedding day, just hours before the ceremony. As Zelda envisioned that day,

The southern spring passed, the violets and the yellow-white pear trees and the jonquils and cape jasmine gave up their tenderness to the deep green lullaby of early May. Ella and Andy

---

[338] Fitzgerald to Dr. Mildred Squires, April 4,1932, PUL.

[339] Zelda Fitzgerald, "Miss Ella," CW, p. 343.

were being married that afternoon in her long living room framed by the velvet portieres and Empire mirrors encasing the aroma of lives long past ... The bride cake nested on southern smilax in the dining room and decanters of port studded the long sideboard mirrors with garnets. Between the parlor and the dining room calla lilies and baby's-breath climbed about a white tulle trellis and came to a flowery end on either side of the improvised altar.[340]

Outside this island of conventional happiness, however, the dismissed suitor, the conventional Mr. Hendrix, had just shot himself in the mouth at the doorway to Ella's childhood play-house, within careful sight of her bedroom window.

In its dramatic conclusion, Zelda's seventh story about women of the modern age brings the kaleidoscope of varieties of women's life choices, their visions of romance and career, their independent decisions and their occasional successes, to a dark close. The death of Mr. Hendrix becomes a kind of mandala for the tortured Zelda, who used that resonating word "bitter" again as she wrote to Scott, "so I went on and on—dancing alone, and, no matter what happens, I still know in my heart that it is a Godless, dirty game; that love is bitter and all there is ..."[341]

Subject to nightmares, sometimes incoherent, abrupt about everything except her dance lessons and practice, Zelda was still a part of the Paris social life—though she did not participate with relish. Cheered by the fact that Charles and Xandra Kalman were to be with them in Paris, Zelda had put off her afternoon ballet lesson so she could attend the luncheon for them. But she

---

[340] Ibid., p. 348.

[341] Zelda, September (?) 1930, DS, DZ, p. 73.

grew terribly nervous about being late, so Charles offered to go with her to get a cab, and take her to the studio. (Clearly, for the Kalmans—who had known Zelda years earlier—her state of mind was anything but normal.) In the taxi, Zelda changed into her practice clothes and then, at an intersection, opened the door, left the cab, and ran down the street. Kalman returned to lunch and told Scott that Zelda needed care, that he had to see to her immediately. After months and even years of her aberrant behavior, and her own pleadings for his attention, Scott finally was moved to take action. When he wrote to Perkins about Zelda's breakdown, however, his letter emphasized what an inconvenience it had been to his writing schedule: "Zelda got a sort of nervous breakdown from overwork and consequently I haven't done a line of work or written a letter for twenty-one days."[342]

On April 23, 1930, Zelda agreed to enter Malmaison, a hospital on the outskirts of Paris. The records of her breathless, disordered statements at that time show the intense pressure she felt to earn money, to make a success of both her writing and her dancing—and, by implication, of her life. "It's dreadful, it's horrible, what's to become of me, I must work and I won't be able to, I should die, but I must work. I'll never be cured."[343] Classic anxiety symptoms, the relentless need to control her uncontrollable life, led to the usual sedation and the beginning of rudimentary therapy. She was urged to eat good food; she was not allowed to drink. By May 2, however, against Professor Claude's advice, Zelda checked herself out of the hospital, worried once more about the parties they had planned for the wedding of Ludlow Fowler's younger

---

[342] Fitzgerald to Perkins, Life, p. 181.

[343] Zelda's statements, quoted in SSEG, p. 289.

brother, Powell. Returning to their household, with Scott and his friends in the midst of hectic drinking, Zelda tried to resume lessons, despite Egorova's worried responses. She tried to lead what had become her customary life, but the breakdown symptoms continued. She quit the study of ballet. Then she resumed it. She had hallucinations, she was hysterical, she threatened suicide. Scott finally realized he could not leave her alone.

According to Donaldson, some of Scott's inattention to Zelda once they had returned from North Africa may have resulted from his friendship with Emily Vanderbilt.[344] Divorced from William Vanderbilt and now married to theatrical producer Sigourney Thayer, from whom she was separated, the former Emily Davies was in her own right one of New York's "400." Fitzgerald saw her as a valuable conquest, and evidently made little secret of his affection for her. At least, Zelda wrote to him within the month from Valmont that she herself was "much stronger mentally and physically and sensitively than Emily."[345] But Scott had said Emily was "too big a Poisson" for Zelda. In her letter, Zelda challenged his preference, asking

Why? She [Emily] *couldn't dance a Brahm's waltz or write a story—she can only gossip and ride in the Bois and have pretty hair curling up instead of thinking—Please explain—I want to be well and not bothered with poissons big or little and free to sit in the sun and choose the things I like about people.*

That Scott had been involved in what might have been another

---

[344] See Fool, pp. 56-7; Taylor, Sometimes Madness, p. 221, complicates the friend-ships by stating that Emily Vanderbilt, like Dolly Wilde, was bisexual, and that both Emily and Dolly were friends of Zelda's.

[345] Zelda's fall, 1930, letter to Scott, quoted in Fool, p. 57; see also DS, DZ, p. 94.

liaison no doubt contributed to Zelda's inability to feel secure with either their Paris friends, or with her husband.

Throughout Zelda's illness, it seemed to be difficult for Scott to allow her that illness. He wanted to manage both the illnesses and the descriptions of them. It was as if he could not allow Zelda to have anything—even sickness—that did not in some way belong primarily to him. Believing she had only to make up her mind to be well, he might have never found help for her. But with friends, Fitzgerald convinced her that she should go to Switzerland, where prestigious clinics such as Valmont were located. He was able to get her into that institution, which, though it was not a psychiatric hospital, at least offered suitable interim care.

After Zelda's admission to Valmont, Dr. H. A. Trutman and his staff called Dr. Oscar Forel for a consultation. Forel was the son of Auguste Forel, Professor of Psychiatry at University of Zurich, who was an international authority on alcoholism; his son Oscar was one of the best-trained psychiatrists in Europe and had a year earlier opened his clinic at Prangins, near Geneva. Forel agreed to accept Zelda at Prangins. The lengthy report of the Valmont physician, who recommended that Zelda be moved, emphasized that she was still frantic about the time she was losing from her active life, and that while he saw "no signs of mental illness," he did see problems in "the relationship between the patient and her husband," problems he thought were long-standing—and probably the motivation for Zelda's taking up dance in the first place. The report continued, "The husband's visits often were the occasion of violent arguments, provoked especially by the husband's attempts to reason with the patient."[346] Beyond reasoning with Zelda, Scott seemed intent on dissuading her from mentioning his possible homosexuality—a theme he was worried might be bandied about.

Luckily for Scott, Zelda's brother-in-law Newman Smith was in Europe. Although the Valmont team had thought she was willing to enter Les Rives de Prangins, when the time came, she resisted. With Smith, Scott was able to convince her that she needed the kind of attention Forel and his staff could provide.

On June 5, 1930, Zelda entered Prangins. Forel diagnosed her as schizophrenic, with "the homosexuality un symptom de la maladie."[347] It was a relatively common diagnosis for American women during this Freudian time, particularly since Paul Eugen Bleuler's 1911 book on schizophrenia had become the standard work. (Bleuler coined the term in 1908, and as Professor of Psychiatry at University of Zurich, was available to consult about Zelda at Prangins—for his customary fee of $500.) Sometimes called dementia praecox, schizophrenia was differentiated from depression or manic depression; Bleuler believed that even while schizophrenics retained their intelligence, their thoughts were disorganized. He wrote that the disease was "characterized by delusions, hallucinations, and disordered thought."[348] In his estimation, perhaps 25 percent of schizoid patients could recover.

The diagnosis came quickly, however. The usual procedure, according to the *American Psychiatric Association's Diagnostic*

---

[346] Quoted in Milford, p. 159.

[347] See Andre LeVot, F. Scott Fitzgerald (1983), pp. 195-6; SSEG, p. 291; Milford, p. 161; report dated November 22,1930, PUL.

[348] Bleuler quoted in Edward Shorter, A History of Psychiatry (1997), p. 109.

and Statistical Manual of Mental Disorders, is to observe the patient for at least six months. The primary characteristics will be "disorganized speech, grossly disorganized behavior" and "delusions or prominent hallucinations."[349] There is no mention of some of Zelda's symptoms, and whether or not she had these particular symptoms when she arrived at Prangins is unclear.

When Fitzgerald described Zelda's early months at Prangins (though he was not allowed to see her for the first months of her stay), he wrote about her incoherent letters, her "madness, wild homosexuality, toward nurses, etc., suicide threats, attempts at escape, delusions, writing and painting furiously, even tries dancing again." In a narrative about the weeks just before her going to Switzerland, he added to this summary that he had noticed her "nervous picking at fingers," and mentioned that although she was "always quiet [she] becomes abnormally so with sudden outbreaks of despair" and what he called "a violent timidity." Her "horror of people day by day [was] accentuated— [and she] honestly wants to die." He added that the "condition [was] unparalleled in husband's [his] experience for its intensity and in the way the hysteria breaks out without warning."[350]

Considering that the staff at Valmont had thought there was no mental disease, for Zelda to he quickly and confidently diagnosed with such a serious disorder might have been reason for a second, or third, opinion—or for an opinion from someone other than the Zurich group of Freudians. Historians note that there were many more diagnoses of schizophrenia with American

---

[349] See American Psychiatric Association, Diagnostic & Statistical Manual of Mental Disorders, 1st (1952) and 4th edition (1994), and Text Revision (2000), p. 273 of latter.

[350] Fitzgerald to Dr. Mildred Squires, April 4, 1932, PUL.

patients than with others. According to the view of Harry Stack Sullivan, one of the United States' leaders in treatment who practiced at Sheppard and Enoch Pratt Hospital, schizophrenia might well he prompted by "an unsuccessful reaction to anxiety." Sullivan was known for the hours of sympathetic care he gave his patients. Unlike his European counterparts, he never used electroconvulsive or insulin shock, believing it better "to leave schizoid patients untreated in the hope that these 'extraordinarily gifted and, therefore, socially significant people' could recover spontaneously."[351]

As a further indication that Zelda may have been misdiagnosed, after early treatment at Prangins, her behavior grew worse and she was soon placed in the part of the estate reserved for the sickest patients. She had tried to escape from her nurse outside the hospital grounds, behavior which damned her to confinement. Once a painful eczema began in later June, after Scottie had visited her, Zelda was in great discomfort for several months, so one must wonder where the terrible skin disorder originated, and perhaps question what treatment was being prescribed for her condition.[352] Common therapies for schizophrenia then were varied. Among them were opium and laxative cures and the use of such sedatives as chloral, bromine, Veronal and Luminal (phenobarbital). A popular therapy was the malaria cure, which

---

[351] Harry Stack Sullivan, summarized in Shorter, A History of Psychiatry, p. 176; see also Bliss Forbush, The Sheppard & Enoch Pratt Hospital, 1853-1970. A History (1971), pp. 106-7.

[352] Because of the frequent skin eruptions that accompanied Zelda's illness, modern-day physicians suggest she might have suffered, undetected, from some form of lupus, a multisymptom illness often triggered by anxiety or exhaustion.

created a fever that might lead the patient to clarity. And there was always the possibility that coma or shock treatment would be effective, though it was not specific to schizophrenia.[353] Whatever the etiology for Zelda's eczema, which at one point covered her from head to foot, nothing healed it. As she wrote to her sister Rosalind, the skin ailment "never was the sort that Cuticura soap would help. The Brussels fire brigade might have skirted the edges—". Zelda's pain was so great that she could not concentrate, and she said that "the whole vicinity of my room is covered with grease and bandages and powder and antiseptic."[354] Forel noted that he finally was able to cure the ailment through hypnosis, but a mild version of it recurred frequently—often when Scott was either present or expected to arrive.

It is to Scott's credit that he moved to Lausanne that summer; he wanted to be on call should Zelda or her doctors need him. He left Scottie in Paris with her nanny to continue school; he planned to return for a few days each month. But his behavior during the autumn that Zelda was in Prangins was otherwise not commendable. Drinking as heavily as he had in Paris, Scott began a public affair with Bijou O'Connor, an American heiress who was the daughter of English diplomat Sir Francis Elliott.[355] A month after they met, both moved into Hotel de la Paix, where Bijou remembered watching Scott write and drink gin by the bottle.

Zelda wrote with grim humor to Rosalind, "So little happens between four walls or so much—that it's hard to write a letter:

---

[353] See Shorter, History of Psychiatry, pp. 194-221.

[354] Zelda Fitzgerald to Rosalind, n.d., PUL.

[355] See Fool, pp. 57-8 and LeVot, Fitzgerald, pp. 205-6.

nothing, or a book."[356] She wrote cheerfully to Scottie in Paris, talking about the scenery and the woods (now "a flaming red and lots of the big trees are yellow in the autumn sunshine") but mostly about Scottie:

I care dreadfully at your not being here with me. The times you spent with me in the summer were the happiest of the year. It would give me so much pleasure to see you paddling in the shallow waters of the lake.[357]

She wrote with restraint about her condition, telling Scottie that she was impatient: "It got to be the limit being sick for so long and you may easily imagine how delighted I am to be better." She was, however, bored, and admitted,

Time goes on here some way. I don't know how it passes. I spent the summer walking in the woods and now that winter is nearly here there seems to be little left to do. I hope I will have more time to write you dear. It gives me great happiness to learn that you are getting along so well in school and amusing yourself so royally all the time.[358]

In a letter later in the fall, Zelda thought ahead to Christmas and asked Scottie what she could get for her—and also asked her daughter to send her "something from one of the branches [of their tree] to make you seem nearer, darling, so that I can think of you as being in the same country." She wrote with great feeling, "It seems ages and ages and ages that I haven't seen you and I want dreadfully to be with you once again and share your pleasures for the holidays."[359]

[356] Zelda to Rosalind, PUL.

[357] Zelda to Scottie, PUL.

[358] Zelda to Scottie, PUL.

[359] Ibid.

What letters remain from the Zelda-Scott correspondence are less pleasant. Zelda is angry that she is at Prangins; she knows, too, that Forel thinks Scott should be in treatment for his alcoholism, and she occasionally asks about his drinking (she says she is doing so at her doctor's request). Whenever she does, Scott replies with his characteristic defensiveness. He says it is not Zelda's role to pry into his life; he thinks his drinking is of no relevance to her illness. When he wrote a description of their lives for Dr. Forel, he blamed his own drinking on Zelda's appetite for wine with lunch, saying he had always before drunk only coffee during the day. His real point, however, is "which of two people is worth preserving."[360] He implies that his life should not be sacrificed to save Zelda's and her mania for dance. Should he give up all liquor and wine for her health? No, that he will not do. But Scott presents his dilemma in a bluster:

To stop drinking entirely for six months and see what happens, even to continue the experiment thereafter if successful—only a pig would refuse to do that. Give up strong drink permanently I will. Bind myself to forswear wine forever I cannot ... I cannot consider one pint of wine at the days end as anything but one of the rights of man.[361]

He claims in passing, and perhaps without irony, "What I gave up for Zelda was women and it wasn't easy in the position my success gave me."

Zelda defends herself and her behavior by pointing out that the world of dance was cool and beautiful, whereas

---

[360] Fitzgerald to Forel, Life, p. 197.

[361] Ibid.

at home there was incessant babbling ... and you either drinking or complaining because you had been. You blamed me when the servants were bad, and expected me to instill into them a proper respect for a man that they saw morning after morning asleep in his clothes, who very often came home in the early morning, who could not sit, even, at the table.[362]

More often, she begs him to let her leave the hospital, to return to some normal life where she could be herself again. Sadly, she writes,

Please help me. Every day more of me dies with this bitter and incessant beating I'm taking. You can choose the conditions of our life and anything you want if I don't have to stay here miserable and sick ... Please Please let me out now—Dear, you used to love me and I swear to you that this is no use.[363]

Alternately, she tells him they should get a divorce, since they will never recover their happiness, and she can no longer put up with his foibles.

During the autumn, Scott was allowed to visit Zelda every few weeks. Once her eczema had subsided, she began to improve—or so his letters to friends suggested. He wrote optimistically to Max Perkins that she was on the mend;[364] in August he had written John Peale Bishop that Zelda had had a nervous breakdown "last winter and since has had to be confined."[365] Bishop continued in a letter to Allen Tate, "Scott has been in Switzerland with Zelda ... He lies so I

---

[362] Zelda to Fitzgerald, DS, DZ, p. 86; see also DS, DZ, pp. 80-8,89-93,97-100.

[363] Zelda to Fitzgerald, DS, DZ, p. 90.

[364] Fitzgerald to Perkins in Milford, p. 170.

[365] Fitzgerald to John Peale Bishop in Milford.

could only make out that her state is serious, or at least has been. But how near actual insanity she has been or is I've no idea."[366] In December 1930, Tate asked Bishop if the Fitzgeralds were in town and went on to say that "Caroline [Gordon, his wife the novelist] liked Zelda extremely (not unreservedly, perhaps) and is sure she was a victim to Scott's delusions of grandeur in a silk hat."[367] Bishop replied on December 23, 1930:

Scott may be at Caux when we are there. He's been at Lausanne since early summer ... Zelda is still under treatment at Glion ... It's hard to make out exactly how near she's been to insanity, but I gather near enough to make her cure a long and uncertain one. Scott is probably enough to drive her or any woman crazy, but I don't really blame him, unless sexually.[368]

Autumn was filled with more recriminating letters—Scott to Zelda, Zelda to Scott—each pained, each looking for a release from guilt. Their occasional meetings were unsuccessful because they were made to bear too heavy a weight. Andre LeVot recounts one of Scott's visits to Prangins when he brought Bijou O'Connor to see Zelda, an event that was hardly calculated to improve Zelda's state of mind.[369]

Bijou left Switzerland in November.[370] Although Dr. Bleuler, at the time of his being consulted, had thought Zelda was trying

---

[366] John Peale Bishop to Allen Tate, August 9, 1930 (John Peale Bishop, The Republic of Letters in America (1981), p. 15).

[367] Allen Tate to Bishop, December 12, 1930, in ibid., p. 16.

[368] Bishop to Allen Tate, December 23, 1930, in ibid., p. 17.

[369] LeVot, Fitzgerald, p. 206.

[370] Ibid., pp. 255-6; see Fool, p. 58.

to re-enter the world too quickly, she was allowed to leave Prangins for Christmas. Unfortunately, the stress of seeing both Scott and Scottie disturbed her and she broke tree ornaments and behaved in upsetting ways, so she returned to the hospital and Scott took his daughter skiing in Gstaad. There he met another single parent, Margaret Egloff, who had taken her two children on a ski trip en route to Zurich to study with Carl Jung. Scott saw in Margaret both a kind woman and a means of learning about psychiatry—whether he wanted that information for his novel or to help with Zelda's care. According to Donaldson,

there were frequent meetings during the next six months when they spent long hours talking about literature and psychology and she came to know him "very intimately." The two of them also took trips together to the Italian lakes and to France, where they startled the John Peale Bishops by showing up on their doorstep as traveling companions. Then they went their separate ways, Margaret to remarry.[371]

Scott's life had, by that time, changed more than he admitted: in late January of 1931 his father died suddenly and Scott returned to the States for his funeral.[372] Zelda's concern for his sadness in the time they spent together before he left Switzerland cheered him, and he felt as if some part of her still cared about him. In the States he contacted friends, reporting sadly on Zelda's condition and his father's death. Dos Passos, for example, wrote to Edmund Wilson that when he saw Scott in New York,

He was in damn good shape in spite of a miserable winter, worrying about Zelda etc. He seemed to have the situation pretty

---

[371] Of Margaret Egloff, Fool, pp. 58-9.

[372] LeVot, Fitzgerald, p. 257.

well in hand—he says its actual schizophrenia—this ballet stuff was part of it and persecution ideas about people ... the question is how far she'll come back.[373]

According to Carl Jung, the death of his father may have enabled Fitzgerald to find ways to respond to Zelda's need with more maturity than he had previously shown. In Jung's *Modern Man in Search of a Soul*, he commented that, especially for a son, the death of the father "has the effect of an overhurried—an almost catastrophic ripening."[374] Perhaps such understanding led Scott to make a trip to Montgomery before he returned,[375] so that he could convey to Zelda's parents the details of both diagnosis and treatment. Inadvertently, Minnie may have sabotaged Zelda's care when she had written to Valmont that there was no mental instability in the Sayre family.[376] There was—both the Judge and their oldest child, Marjorie, had had nervous spells if not actual breakdowns, and Minnie's mother and sister had both died of suicides. Zelda had told Scott that Minnie had recently written her that she knew what the trouble was, so her mother's reticence manifested itself only officially.

That Zelda was not enthusiastic about Dr. Forel's decisions while she was a patient at Prangins becomes clear from her November 1930 letter to him. After pointing out that much of her discomfort and sadness had come from Scott's behavior, what she calls the fact that "my husband has found so agreeable

---

[373] John Dos Passos to Edmund Wilson, February 23,1931 (John Dos Passos, The Fourteenth Chronicle (1973), p. 398).

[374] Carl Jung, Modern Man in Search of a Soul (1933), p. 121.

[375] LeVot, Fitzgerald, pp. 209-10.

[376] Minnie Sayre, Milford, p. 164.

as to neglect shamefully his wife during the last four years," she closed her letter with this plea: "I am neither young enough nor credulous enough to think that you can manufacture out of nothing something to replace the song I had."[377]

[377] Zelda to Forel, November 1930, PUL.

NINE - On the Way to Being Cured

In the Zelda Fitzgerald papers at Princeton, an undated sheet of her writing illustrated her dogged need to be working. Whether she conceived this plan during her stay at Prangins or at some later time of her troubled life, she is intent on living each twenty-four hour period to the full:

6 hours study

6 hours work

6 hours play

6 hours sleep

Under "work," Zelda lists "1 hour dance technique, 1 hour dance, 2 hour design stage costume, 2 hour music composition." Under "play," "1 requisite sport 5 hours week (swimming, tennis, skating)" and under "study," "Architecture, Chemistry, Medicine, Literary composition."[378]

Her prolegomenon parallels the Diaghileff model[379] for

---

[378] Zelda Fitzgerald, essays, PUL.

[379] Serge Lifar, A History of the Russian Ballet (1954) describes the fusion of costume, music, scene, word, and the dance (pp. 241-60).

all-inclusive ballet (the combination of stage design, costume and effects, music, and dance), and suggests that Zelda might well have still been envisioning a career in dance. But more importantly, the sheet shows the anxiety that hounded her: she could leave no hour unspent, she needed to be able to say she had used her time fruitfully, she had to be working, no matter what the work consisted of. Part of her intense dislike for hospitalization was its interruption of her own significant plans.

Had Carl Jung been called in as a consultant in Zelda's case, which he might have been instead of Bleuler, her prognosis—as well as her diagnosis—might have differed. Jung insisted that the conscious and the unconscious were two halves of a healthy whole, and that therapy that attended to dreams and to prompts from the unconscious was particularly useful. As he wrote in his 1933 *Modern Man in Search of a Soul,* "The dream gives a true picture of the subjective state, while the conscious mind denies that this state exists, or recognizes it only grudgingly."[380] Damage is done to a person's mind when the unconscious is limited, restricted, by the conscious. Jung called for an "assimilation ... a mutual interpenetration of conscious and unconscious contents, and not—as is too commonly thought—a one-sided valuation";[381] in this he differed from Freud, who thought the unconscious needed to be controlled.

When Zelda found her interim salvation in dance, for herself, Jung might have analyzed that choice as her attempt to make her psyche balance, "a self-regulating system that maintains

---

[380] Carl Jung, Modern Man in Search of a Soul (1933), p. 5.

[381] Ibid., p. 18.

itself in equilibrium as the body does."[382] Any good therapy, according to Jung, existed to allow the patient "individuation ... the bringing into reality of the whole human being."[383] He often suggested creative acting out for his patients, because he had great respect for art. In his discussions of the artist, he acknowledged that "Art is a kind of innate drive that seizes a human being and makes him an instrument."[384] Complex as the drive to create art is, Jung contended that "Every creative person is a duality or a synthesis of contradictory aptitudes."[385]

Had Zelda's talent in ballet been nurtured rather than ridiculed, if her interests in writing and painting had been supported at Prangins, the outcome of her fifteen months there might have been more stable. Instead, Forel had agreed with Scott from the start of her institutionalization that she had to give up the ballet, that it was her deep commitment to dance that had led to her breakdown.[386] In fact, the two men planned together to get an assessment from Egorova that would discourage Zelda. Forel asked Fitzgerald to tell the beloved ballet teacher that it was in Zelda's best interests that Egorova be negative about her abilities. When Scott wrote to her, however, he could not bring himself to make that suggestion. So what he received from Egorova was a letter that was much more positive than

---

[382] Ibid., p. 20.

[383] Ibid., p. 31.

[384] Ibid., p. 195.

[385] Ibid., p. 194.

[386] As Phyllis Chesler noted years ago, part of Zelda's dilemma was that her husband was supported by all her doctors and therapists, so it was as if Scott Fitzgerald was her only caretaker (Phyllis Chesler, Women and Madness (1972), p. 13).

he and Forel had expected:[387] she said that while Zelda would never be "a dancer of the first rank" like Nemtchinova, she could dance with success important roles, for instance in the Ballet Massine in New York.[388]

Even as Forel and Scott delivered what they tried to color as negative news to Zelda, she understood how complimentary Egorova's letter really was. Her period of treatment, then, became a kind of mourning for the skill she had frantically developed—a skill now lost.

Regardless of how she saw her life without dance, regardless of her frustration under the care at Prangins, in January of 1931, Zelda began to improve.[389] With Scott mourning his father in the States, free from her assumption of the roles of wife, mother, good patient, Zelda took up skiing. Going to the slopes with others from Prangins, or alone, she found the sport exhilarating. She also went into Geneva, sometimes with others and sometimes alone. Although her eczema had appeared at the time of Scott's January visit, as he was leaving to return to the States, that was one of its last recurrences. Steadily, and somewhat remarkably, she was gaining ground: she even requested that Gerald Murphy visit her in the spring.

Meanwhile, in America, Scott was repeating Zelda's diagnosis to friends and family. Schizophrenia for Zelda became a kind of panacea for him: the advantages to him of her diagnosis were clear. Even while Scott saw himself as tragic and

---

[387] Mme. Egorova to Fitzgerald, quoted in SSEG, p. 302; see Life, pp. 185-6 for Fitzerald's letter of request to her.

[388] Ibid.

[389] SSEG, pp. 309-10; Milford, pp. 186-7.

loyal—he had not, after all, abandoned her, even with that dread diagnosis—he could also assume a different identity. In many ways, Zelda's illness erased much of the Fitzgeralds' past history, and legitimated at least some of Scott's objectionable behavior. In response to her diagnosis, people began recalling "crazy Zelda" stories.[390] That she might have been responding to Scott's craziness (as in his adoration of Isadora Duncan) was overlooked; all the "mad" behavior got moved into her column. Zelda's diagnosis also excused Scott's affairs, because while she was ill, he had no sex partner.

Relieved in some ways about his responsibilities to his wife, financial demands being less difficult than emotional ones, Scott made few changes in his lifestyle. It is revealing that no matter what happened to Zelda after 1930—no matter which institution she was living in, or what the circumstances of her life became—Scott continued to spend money living suitably, whether in Switzerland or in the States. Had Zelda not broken down, Scott's life by the early 1930s would have been different: he had already lost many friends, he had spent several nights in jail for drunkenness, he was making little progress on the novel which he had begun in 1925. Even he might have seen

---

[390] Nearly all the memoirists of the 1920s have, consciously or unconsciously, villified

Zelda; for example, see William Wiser, The Great Good Place (1991), where all the Fitzgeralds' car-related episodes, many of them dangerous, are based on Zelda's whims (pp. 246-7). An exception is Morrill Cody, who makes the point that even after her institutionalization, Zelda was far from "crazy" and that he found much merit in her novel, Save Me the Waltz - though he notes that the David character, supposedly based on Scott, was hardly anything like the mean Fitzgerald (Morrill Cody, Women of Montparnasse (1984), pp. 62-3)

the need to change his life. Then suddenly, he was safe. Zelda's crack-up gave him both alibi and cover.

Less directly, Zelda's absence freed Scott—not only from his guilt as she nagged him about his drinking or his failure to write; but also about his relationships with other women.[391] More importantly, it put Scottie's life and education into his hands.[392] Viewing their daughter as "his" simplified his decision-making, just as the fact of his needing to borrow money from Scribner's and from Ober, for Scottie's expenses, was seldom questioned.

Like Zelda, Scott had also feared growing old. Zelda's illness took attention away from his having entered his mid-thirties. "Illness"—no matter whose—was more appealing than "aging."

Healing in Montgomery

Once Scott returned from his trip to the States, he saw Zelda more frequently. She was often amenable to having sex with him, although about one visit he wrote to Dr. Forel, "After lunch she returned to the affectionate tender mood, utterly normal, so that with pressure I could have manoeuvred her into intercourse but the eczema was almost visibly increasing so I left early."[393] Scott's language implied a sexual contest, and as his frequent letters to Forel and the staff indicated, he did see Zelda's recovery as a challenge: he wanted to be in charge of her progress. Soon Zelda was able to go to Lausanne or Geneva

---

[391] On board ship, en route to the States for his father's funeral, for example, Scott became involved with Bert Barr, who called herself a card shark (Andre LeVot, F. Scott Fitzgerald (1983), p. 208 and Fool, p. 140).

[392] See S, pp. 45-7.

[393] Fitzgerald to Forel, quoted in LeVot, Fitzgerald, p. 201.

for an outing or for lunch with him; in July, she was allowed to go with Scott and Scottie to Annecy for fishing, swimming and tennis. In the perfect weather, she and Scott danced; and she wrote later, "It was like the good gone times when we still believed in summer hotels and the philosophies of popular songs."[394] A few weeks after that, the three Fitzgeralds visited Gerald and Sara Murphy, who with their children had taken a large house in the Austrian Tyrol.[395] Again, apparently—though there were rumors—Zelda caused no trouble. Encouraged, she and Scott talked about returning to the States, this time to live in Montgomery—a location that might keep them from resuming their foolhardy lifestyle.

On September 15, 1931, Zelda was released from Prangins with the annotation that her diagnosis had been intensified by her unreasonable ambitions, and her basic feeling of inferiority "(primarily toward her husband)."[396] So long as conflicts with Scott were avoided, her prognosis was good. The trip home on the *Aquitania* was uneventful, as were their few days in New York. Their return to Montgomery was busy, with the rental of the large frame house at 819 Felder Avenue and the hiring of an African American couple to run it, satisfying Zelda's need

---

[394] Zelda to Fitzgerald, PUL.

[395] Honoraria Murphy Donnelly, Sara and Gerald (1982), p. 150, remembers that Zelda "looked pale and drawn - so different from her tanned prettiness of the days at Antibes" [an appearance Honoraria had recalled on p. 148 as "a strikingly beautiful woman - blonde and soft and tanned by the sun. She usually dressed in pink and wore a peony in her hair or pinned to her dress"]. Contrary to the reports that claimed that the visit to the Murphys went well, however, Honoraria writes that Scott and Zelda "left abruptly one morning," leaving Scottie and her nurse with the Murphys; the rumor was that Zelda had threatened to kill herself (ibid., p. 149).

[396] SSEG, p. 313.

to make a good home for Scott and Scottie. They bought a second-hand Stutz, a white Persian cat, and a bloodhound. Her father remained ill, so she visited him and her mother frequently in the Pleasant Street house where she had grown up, and she grew to realize that the Judge would not recover. Minnie, who had already been caring for him for most of the year, was not able to help Zelda much. As might have been expected in the polite society of Montgomery, Zelda's breakdown was not discussed—indeed, it may not have been known.

What would have been obvious to Zelda's old friends and acquaintances was the fact that she had aged noticeably. Partly because of the skin damage from the intense eczema and partly because of the terrors of her treatment during the past year and a half or two years, Zelda no longer exuded that golden radiance which people remembered. She played tennis and golf, and invited people for football games and parties (in moderation) but she was quiet, reserved, and careful about her speech and her responses.

Scott's *Ledger* for the fall of 1931 in Montgomery recorded "life dull."[397] He was pleased, then, when an invitation came that he return to Hollywood to write a screenplay for Irving Thalberg. Not only did they need the money, but Scott needed a reprieve from his months of caring for Zelda and Scottie. In October he traveled to California to fulfill the eight-week contract; he would be back in Montgomery for Christmas.

Meanwhile, in his absence, Zelda wrote. The eight stories that she completed and sent to Ober have been lost, though

---

[397] Ledger, quoted in Milford, p. 193.

synopses of them remain in the agent's files.[398] They are clearly test pieces for many of the themes she is to explore in her novel *Save Me the Waltz*. Most are stories of modern-day marriage, in which the women characters are hungry for genuine caring, tired of being treated like a man's possessions. A few focus on the lives of unusually self-directed women: in "One And, Two And," the constantly-practicing ballerina loses her beau to her beautiful younger sister. (About this story Ober notes that it "Gives the feeling of the ballet—hard practice, etc."[399]) In "Duck Supper," two Southern women who had been girlhood friends compare their married lives and envy each other: "secretly each wants what the other has."[400]

Several of the stories are somewhat experimental. Two are focused on place—"Gods and Little Fishes" on the Riviera, "Getting Away From It All" on the Mid-west—but Zelda changes the predictable plotlines to capitalize on the unexpected. Ober sent the Riviera piece to *New Yorker*, but it was declined; he didn't try to market the Midwest tale. About the Riviera story, Ober's assistant noted that she "didn't understand it."[401] Neither did he try to market what he called a "sketch" about an actor who hires a double to lead his life (even to marrying a wealthy woman) while he escapes for Europe. "The Story Thus

---

[398] In M. Bruccoli, "Zelda Fitzgerald's Lost Stories," Fitzgerald/Hemingway Annual, 1979, pp. 123-6. According to W. R. Anderson ("Rivalry and Partnership," Fitzgerald/Hemingway Annual, 1977, pp. 19-42), there were at least three other lost stories - "A Workman," "The Drouth and the Flood," and "The House" - which Zelda wrote at Prangins and Scott himself tried to market.

[399] Bruccoli, "Zelda Fitzgerald's Lost Stories," p. 125.

[400] Ibid., p. 124.

[401] Ibid., p. 125.

Far" is still, in the agent's opinion, "cleverly written."[402] Another quasi-experimental narrative is "All About the Downs Case," or "Crime Passional." Perhaps drawing from the Fitzgeralds' life, but also—according to Ober's notes—from the Nixon-Nordlinger case, Zelda writes the story of the wife who falls in love with a musician, only to have her rich husband see her kiss the lover. Spiriting her off to Europe, the husband doesn't let her speak to anyone, and in a sense imprisons her in her life. Finally, to free herself, she shoots him.

This story, like several of the others, Ober tries to sell to *College Humor*, *Harper's Bazaar*, and *Delineator*. He also tries, with a few pieces, *Ladies' Home Journal*, *McCall's*, *Pictorial Review*, *Vanity Fair*, and *Saturday Evening Post*. The Southern story "Cotton Belt" he offers to *American Mercury* and *Scribner's*. Confident in the quality of Zelda's work (his synopses often begin with "Very well written"), Ober keeps marketing her fiction. About one, "Sweet Chariot," he notes: "Southern story. As good as Scott's earlier Southern stories ... Nice feeling."[403] Playing again with the themes of marriage, poverty and wealth, and the acquisition of cars, Zelda inflects more humor than usual in this narrative; this one he sends to *Redbook*, *Cosmopolitan*, *Scribner's*, *Delineator*, and the *Saturday Evening Post*.

Angry that her stories weren't selling, and as confident as Ober that—if magazines were buying—they would sell, Zelda began the exercise of reading one of Scott's short stories every night; she wrote him that although she was learning a great deal, she would never be able to write a story like his "Absolution,"

---

[402] Ibid.

[403] Ibid.

for instance. The only story of Zelda's from this autumn that Ober was able to place appeared in *Scribner* in August, 1932; it was "A Couple of Nuts," a story more like Scott's work than it was Zelda's. Plot-dominated, the tale of the two energetic and talented Americans was a story of Europe at its most corrupt in 1924. The heart of the fiction was the narrator's memory of how good the youngsters had been, before their lives abroad changed them. Like most of Zelda's stories—and Scott's—this one borrowed from her and Scott's lives:

In those days of going to pieces and general disintegration it was charming to see them together. Their friends were divided into two camps as to whose stamina it was that kept them going and comparatively equilibrated in that crazy world of ours ... Some people thought they weren't married, they were so young and decorative.[404]

Zelda also began writing her first novel and, although she said little about it to Scott, she had completed more than a third of the book before he returned in December. *Save Me the Waltz* was Zelda's bildungsroman. It was effectively, even beautifully, written; and if the lost stories were as polished as the novel, then their loss was substantial.

The novel begins in Montgomery and traces the lives of the Beggs' family: Millie, as mother, being its heart, and Austin, the judge, being the disciplinarian. Alabama, as the baby of the family, observes the romances of her older sisters and eventually has unruly adventures of her own. Much of this early section charts Alabama's wildly popular years as a belle, particularly after America enters World War I and she is courted by men

---

[404] Zelda Fitzgerald, "A Couple of Nuts," CW, p. 354.

from the military camp nearby. She describes the natty officers:

Men who were better dressed in their uniforms than ever before in their lives ... men who smelled of Fitch's hair tonic from the camp barber and men from Princeton and Yale who smelled of Russian Leather and seemed very used to being alive.[405]

Once Alabama becomes involved with David Knight, an officer who will become a fairly successful painter, she recounts their courtship, including a seminal scene in which he carved their names in the doorpost of the country club:

"David," the legend read, "David, David, Knight, Knight, Knight, and Miss Alabama Nobody."

"Egotist," she protested ... . She was a little angry about the names. David had told her about how famous he was going to be many times before.[406]

The courtship continues. Eventually they marry in New York and begin their lives among the artists and the chic in the cosmopolitan city. There is a great amount of conversation—glib, fashionable, almost surreal. (Perhaps the weakest part of the novel is its recreation of these years of the wisecrack; it foreshadows much of the dialogue in Zelda's later play, *Scandalabra*.) Their child is born and the three of them travel first-class to Europe; on board ship there is more of the oblique, fragmented conversation.

Life in Europe settles down to a focus on David's painting. In the words of his own mocking review, "we have never known in our times the touch of so strong and sure a genius as we have before us in the last canvases of one David Knight!" Petulantly

---

[405] Zelda Fitzgerald, SMTW, CW, p. 37.

[406] Ibid., p. 39.

Alabama asks, "But you're not going to work all the time, are you?" When he replies, "I hope so," she can only comfort herself with the maxim, "It's a man's world."[407]

Too energetic to sit and wait for David's company ("David worked on his frescoes; Alabama was much alone"[408]), Alabama met and grew to love "the Lieutenant Jacques Chevre-Feuille of the French Aviation." After David warned her that she had "gone Southern again,"[409] David confronts Jacques—he wants a fight. Alabama, much to her own surprise, supports David in the conflict and soon Jacques leaves for Indo-China. She shreds the letter and the photograph he leaves for her, meditating, "You took what you wanted from life, if you could get it, and you did without the rest."[410] A later line of her musing reads, "Summer and love and beauty are much the same in Cannes or Connecticut."[411]

The novel shifts to Paris in 1927; David and his art are much the rage. He has done stage settings for the Ballet Russe; he has done paintings that were hung for the Salon des Independants: "The frescoes were finished: this was a new, more personal, David on exhibit. You heard his name in bank lobbies and in the Ritz Bar."[412] References to the Knights' "open" marriage, to David's flirtations, to the society friends they party with culminate in the scene of the typical party which "poured out into the Paris

---

[407] Ibid., p. 78.

[408] Ibid., pp. 78-9.

[409] Ibid., p. 83.

[410] Ibid., p. 94.

[411] Ibid., p. 95.

[412] Ibid.

night like dice shaken from a cylinder."[413] In the throes of yet another liaison, "David opened and closed his personality over Miss Gibbs [the young actress he is pursuing] like the tentacles of a carnivorous maritime plant."[414]

Searching for a life of her own, Alabama found the ballet La Chatte, and with it, people who would introduce her to the great ballerina with whom she wanted to study. The next third of the book traces the difficult life of the ballerina in training, although at first Alabama's work in dance improves her relationship with David:

David was glad of her absorption at the studio. It made them less inclined to use up their leisure on parties ... David could work more freely when she was occupied and making fewer demands on his time.[415]

In the dialogue of the dancers in Madame's studio, in the dialogue of the frantic Americans and Europeans partying, and in the dialogue between Alabama and David, Zelda catches the atmosphere of the 1920s. The hysteria is there in the references to the avant-garde dancers, composers, painters and the bravado of people making their way into society even if their talent is limited. For Alabama, life comes to a stop—except for her dancing. As Zelda wrote,

Alabama's work grew more and more difficult. In the mazes of the masterful fouette her legs felt like dangling hams; in the swift elevantion of the entrechat cinq she thought her breasts hung like old English dugs. It did not show in the mirror. She was nothing

---

[413] Ibid., pp. 101-2.

[414] Ibid., p. 105.

[415] Ibid., p. 117.

but sinew. To succeed had become an obsession. She worked till she felt like a gored horse in the bullring, dragging its entrails.[416]

As a result of her time-consuming passion, her household "fell into a mass of dissatisfaction."[417] An angry David told Alabama she would never succeed. Alabama, however, refused to consider failure: "when she thought of giving up her work, she grew sick and middle-aged."[418] She continued to study, to practice. Months later, all but separated from David, she received a letter of invitation from Madame Sirgeva, to dance in Naples. At first she refuses, but at the last moment she goes. An important change from the largely autobiographical scaffolding which Zelda was using, in which Zelda did not take the offer, Alabama's trip to Naples—alone—brings her success: she has a good career in the ballet. But when her daughter Bonnie comes to visit, the child's presence breaks her heart—Alabama misses her child; she resents the fact that Bonnie and David are living happily in Switzerland, without her.

The ballet season continues. Then David gets word of her father's illness, but when he tries to reach Alabama, he finds that she has been hospitalized with an infection from a serious foot injury. The injury ends her dancing career. When David comes to Naples to care for her, they are reunited. In the process of surviving the blood poisoning, Zelda writes about the incredible pain of her injury. In this section she may be re-creating her own terrorizing discomfort of those fifteen months in Prangins, when there was no name for the malady that had so confounded her.

---

[416] Ibid., p. 144.

[417] Ibid.

[418] Ibid., p. 151.

Sometimes her foot hurt her so terribly that she closed her eyes and floated off on the waves of the afternoon. Invariably she went to the same delirious place. There was a lake there so clear that she could not tell the bottom from the top; a pointed island lay heavy on the waters like an abandoned thunderbolt ... Crows cawed from one deep mist to another. The word "sick" effaced itself against the poisonous air and littered lamely about between the tips of the island and halted on the white road that ran straight through the middle. "Sick" turned and twisted about the narrow ribbon of the highway like a roasting pig on a spit, and woke Alabama gouging at her eyeballs with the prongs of its letters ...[419]

The Death of Judge Sayre

Zelda occupied her time in Montgomery by visiting her parents, seeing friends, writing Scott more than thirty long letters,[420] and working on her stories and novel. She was incredibly productive. As her letters to Scott insisted, she was fine; she missed him but she loved living with Scottie and the pets, and being Minnie's daughter once more. She wrote often about the surprise she was working on—a play she had written—that would be his "welcome home" event for Christmas.

Zelda's letters were as much fiction as *Save Me the Waltz*. In them she re-created their early love, effusively, tenderly. In her novel, she created that same romance, as well as her ardor for the dance, her horror at her illness, and her knowledge that these experiences had become the center of her adult life.

---

[419] Ibid., p. 180.

[420] See DS, DZ, pp. 80ff. and unpublished, PUL.

In the midst of the joyous letters during October and November, Zelda wrote Scott one that was bluntly honest. She described the "homely lyric" of watching Scottie dress by her bedroom fire—"her long sweet delicate body and the cool of her pale hair"[421]—but then wrote him that she herself was "bad and asthmatic": "I am going to dig myself a bear-pit and sit inside thumbing my nose at the people who bring me carrots and then I will be perfectly happy." She admitted that there are nice bears, fairytale bears, "But I will be a very dirty bear with burrs in my coat and my nice silky hair all matted with mud and I will growl and move my head about disconsolately."[422] Discouraged that Ober cannot sell her stories, she is amazed at the way Minnie and the Judge continue to be noble and "civilized." She, however, is unhappy.

Then, as everyone had expected, Anthony Sayre died. Although Zelda sent Scott a wire, she told him not to travel back for the funeral. Later, she explained that she had ordered a "blanket" of flowers to cover the Judge's casket, since no one else in her family could have afforded to do so—because, she added, she knew how Scott had always felt about him.[423] Rewriting fact, Zelda here recreated Scott Fitzgerald, the loving son-in-law, a man who had never existed.

She endured the mourning and the service; she invited her family for a luncheon on Minnie's birthday, but she felt more and more alone. Zelda was also angry, though she did not admit

---

[421] Zelda to Fitzgerald, DS, DZ, p. 134.

[422] Ibid.

[423] See DS, DZ, p. 12.

to that emotion. The father she had longed to be near was now dead, without the recognition or the reconciliation she had hoped for. The husband who was to be her father's replacement in Zelda's life was not even with her for the ordeal—a man no stronger or smarter, as it turned out, than the young Zelda herself had been. With her father's death, the realization came to her that she had no more choices: now if she left Scott, she could not go home again to the father who had been so important in her life, even if she had denied that importance. Her father was dead.

Other anxieties occurred after Anthony's burial. Zelda feared losing her timorous and saddened mother—would the mother who had been there to care for her return to her former vigorous self? What would Minnie's move away from 6 Pleasant Street mean for her life, and her health? Zelda feared losing Scott, having interpreted his rare letters from Hollywood—like his failure to return for Anthony's funeral—to mean that he was once more involved with the glamorous people of the film world.

Zelda also feared losing herself, both into madness and, more simply, through the relentless process of aging and ill health. It could be that Zelda had developed a kind of "death anxiety" which added its shadow to the other darknesses she was trying to repress. According to such existential philosophers as Rollo May and Ernest Becker, "the fear of one's own death is a primal source of anxiety." The experience of losing a parent "may set in motion a lifelong inability to deal with one's own mortality except in neurotic or psychotic terms." Certain other life passages, "such as the choice of a career or the experience of childbirth, may have the paradoxical effect of reactivating and intensifying the fear of death, 'freezing' that person in psychotic time."[424]

To Florida

During the next year, when Zelda finished *Save Me the Waltz*,
she chose to bring its scenes of loss—of both career and parent—
into juxtaposition. The fantasy that David Knight did come
for Alabama when she was dying in the hospital created one
ending for the narrative, and Zelda followed that section of
the novel with the scene of the death of Alabama's father. In
the book, David and Alabama hurried back to Montgomery
to see the Judge on his death bed: what occurred there was as
disappointing as what had no doubt occurred in Zelda's own
last visits to her father—either he did not know her, or he did
not realize that any reconciliation was necessary. At his death,
then, within his possessions, there was nothing personal except
three nickels, said to be the first money he had earned. "'He
must have forgot,' Alabama said, 'to leave a message.'"[425] She
felt only more bereft.

One of the closing scenes of the novel also captures the
diminishment of her mother, as she appears to be on the same
level as her adolescent granddaughter; and then the voices of
society break into Alabama's reverie, prattling nonsense about
David's accomplishments as a painter of ballerinas:

"Nobody has ever handled the ballet with any vitality since—"
"I thought," said David, "that rhythm, being a purely physical
exercise of the eyeball, that the waltz picture would actually give
you, by leading the eye in pictorial choreography, the same sensation

---

[424] Marilyn Yalom, Maternity, Mortality and the Literature of Madness (1985), pp. 8-9.

[425] Zelda Fitzgerald, SMTW, CW, p. 188.

as following the measure with your feet."

"Oh, Mr. Knight," said the women, "what a wonderful idea!"[426]

Juxtaposing such nonsense, Zelda allowed the novel to dwindle into a modernistic melange, none of it "a wonderful idea," none of it even sensible, none of it marking a path to lead a life along. The last scene of the book is Alabama's trying to clean the house after the party, and finally, sitting in "the pleasant gloom of late afternoon" with David, the two of them "staring at each other through the remains of the party" as they prepare to travel again, leaving behind them yet another "calm living room."[427]

Like T. S. Eliot's "fragments I have shored against my ruin" at the end of *The Waste Land*, Zelda here at the end of *Save Me the Waltz* created a similarly bleak representation of the life of the artists of the impossible, people who mistakenly believed they would find "balance" in Europe and "logic" wherever they traveled, people who believed they could save themselves—far from friends and family. Instead, they found nothing.

In December of 1931 Zelda was no longer looking for the big answers, though she was desperately looking for balance. As she wrote apologetically to Scott, she felt worse, she was asthmatic, she was going to Florida for a long weekend: "I am nervous and too introspective and stale."[428] There had been too many people about, she told him, perhaps as a reminder that he had not been there during her father's funeral and its aftermath; therefore, she and the nurse were driving down Sunday for the

---

[426] Ibid., p. 194.

[427] Ibid., p. 196.

[428] Zelda to Fitzgerald, DS, DZ, p. 136.

warmth of Florida, and returning Wednesday.

In the midst of Zelda's exaggerated protestations of her love for Scott, and her missing him, throughout these more than thirty autumn letters, one paragraph of succinct and seemingly genuine emotion resonates:

I miss my Daddy horribly. I am losing my identity here without men. I would not live two weeks again where there are none, since the first thing that goes is concision, and they give you something to butt your vitality against so it isn't littered over the air like spray[s] of dynamite.[429]

In reverting to the small child's name, "my Daddy," Zelda placed herself in that dangerous role of being the daughter, the unloved daughter, she who traded father for husband—and ended up disappointed in both. In the absence of any confirming and strengthening love, rather than expressing anger, she found her own emotional bereavement and loss a sign of women's inferiority (Zelda always made herself guilty; she had never learned to be angry). The last sentence then became a metaphor about the quality of Zelda's mind, which she saw as being inferior to the mind of whatever man she lived with. While that statement is a sad reflection of gender roles in the States in the 1930s, it was personally accurate: Zelda was "losing [her] identity," for whatever reasons.

When Scott returned to Montgomery on December 20, the flurry of the holidays swamped them both: the tree, Scottie's presents for the first Christmas since she had learned there was no Santa Claus, the arrival of Scott's mother, the cooking and entertaining (since Minnie had no reason to maintain her role

---

[429] Zelda to Fitzgerald, DS, DZ, p. 142.

as family center). Without any written record of Scott's return, one can only surmise that Zelda's anticipation led sooner or later to disappointment. Of course they smoked; of course Scott drank; of course their guests did both. The atmosphere was much less healthy than it had been during the eight weeks of Scott's absence.

Scottie recalled the amazing theatricality of Zelda's decorating the tree. As she wrote,

The sunporch of our big old house was sealed off for the entire month of December and opened on Christmas Eve to reveal the history of mankind. The tree stood in the center of the room and around it circled a train which began in Egypt and stopped at Greece, Rome, the Crusades, the War of the Roses, and so forth. My mother had made tunnels through the Alps out of papier mache ... I was the envy of all my friends.[430]

As with the paper dolls Zelda designed for Scottie, this creation too showed that she did not spare herself in entertaining those she loved.

She was, however, tired.[431] Zelda had a cold. She had eyestrain; she had recurrent bouts of asthma. She also knew from experience that being so out of sorts would keep her from writing effectively. But she now had as well to run continual interference for Scott—keeping Scottie from bothering him, keeping her family from dropping in at inconvenient times, keeping her own spirits up as she saw that more and more of her life was going to maintain his schedule. At base was her realization that—no matter what she accomplished—it was

---

[430] S, p. 54.

[431] See her December, 1931, letters to Fitzgerald in DS, DZ.

Scott's writing that mattered.

In February, Scott and Zelda were driven to St. Petersburg, Florida, by their chauffeur. Although hesitant to ask Scott for help with either the stories or her novel, Zelda accepted his suggestion that the trip and the stay in a good hotel would enable them both to write. Deep sea fishing was less successful than their customary swimming and tanning, but both stayed healthy for a week. Then a spot of eczema appeared on Zelda's neck. It disappeared, but two days later another spot was visible. The fact that their having sex might prompt the skin disorder seemed never to have occurred to anyone; both Scott and Zelda saw the eczema as an indication that she was once again unstable.[432]

They were both terrified. Zelda said immediately that she wanted to return to a clinic. Absurd as her reaction was, there is no record that Scott demurred: he had been through the vicissitudes of her breakdown two years earlier; he did not want to be responsible again.

They started back to Montgomery that day. Stopping overnight, Zelda—upset and sleepless—found a flask of liquor in Scott's suitcase. She drank it. When she woke him at 5 a.m., she told him that terrible things were being done to her; he was even more alarmed at her hysteria. As they continued the drive, he telegraphed Dr. Forel in Switzerland. Forel concurred that if Zelda wanted to be hospitalized, then she should be. At Ford's suggestion, Scott consulted with Dr. Adolf Meyer at the Phipps Clinic in Baltimore; he replied that he would accept Zelda as a patient.

---

[432] Allergic reactions, like the symptoms of lupus, may well have caused the eruptions.

Soon after they arrived in Montgomery, Scott and Zelda took the train east. On February 12, 1932, she was admitted to the Johns Hopkins facility. On February 13, Scott left her to make his return trip to Montgomery.

TEN - The Phipps Clinic and Baltimore

Adolf Meyer was a follower of Bleuler, Forel, and the Freudian arm of psychoanalysis; he accepted Forel's diagnosis of Zelda without question, and began treatment accordingly. But there were other, more junior doctors at Phipps—particularly Mildred Taylor Squires, who had trained at the University of Pennsylvania Medical School, and Thomas Rennie from the Harvard Medical School—and it was their care that moderated the regime and gave Zelda more creative freedom than she remembered having had at Prangins. According to Zelda's letters to Scott, who was trying unsuccessfully to write in Montgomery so that Scottie could finish her school year before they moved to Baltimore, she was allowed to write for two hours each day.

Remarkably, in these institutional surroundings, Zelda accomplished a great deal of work on *Save Me the Waltz*. Whereas the recurrence of her illness should have made her anxious, perhaps that anxiety was erased by the fact that she felt cared for in a truly supportive way. Her bond with Dr. Squires, who had read the chapters of the novel she had brought along, was important; eventually she would dedicate *Save Me the Waltz* to her.

Gender considerations were significant: Zelda had never before been under the care of a woman doctor. She had disliked the famous Eugen Bleuler, and she referred to Dr. Meyer as an "imbecile";[433] she thought many male doctors suffered from the same pomposity as the male artists and writers she had known. But it was also likely that Zelda, by requesting institutionalization—by allowing herself to be put into the hands of the establishment, even if it meant wearing the label of "ill" was muting her tendency to speak out about the absurdities of life. The mature Zelda Sayre Fitzgerald was seldom afraid to speak her mind. What she presented in the ending section of *Save Me the Waltz*—the mockery of cocktail party conversation, and the artist David's replies which were as stupid as the questions asked of him—summarized caustically the social and personal narratives she had been trying, unsuccessfully, to live within.

That Dr. Meyer would have been somewhat amenable to letting Zelda be creative was suggested in his preface to Marion King's memoir, *A Patient's Experience in a Hospital for Mental Illness*, published in 1931 by Yale University Press. There Meyer, her doctor, noted "a salutary movement aiming to relieve the mentally afflicted of hardships inherent in the conditions of a tradition-ridden civilization."[434] For women, those traditions that spanned nearly all levels of society were housekeeping and childcare. Many practicing psychiatrists saw a correlation between female patients with mental problems and women who were married, mothers, and housewives. In her life back

---

[433] Edward Shorter, in A History of Psychiatry (1997), calls him a "second-rate thinker" p. 111.

[434] Adolf Meyer, Preface to Marion King, The Recovery of Myself (1931), p. vii.

in an institution, Zelda was free from what the months in Montgomery had showed her all too clearly was "women's work"—caring for others. She wrote to Scott from Phipps about her guilt for having her breakdown and leaving Montgomery just when Minnie was trying to move: "I ran when Mamma needed me to help her."[435] Several decades before the "antipsychiatry movement" of R. D. Laing, Thomas Szasz, and Michel Foucault, it could be that Meyer and his colleagues were becoming aware of the shortcomings of traditional Freudian psychology and were conscious too of how families of the mentally ill relied on the policing function of institutional care.

In Fitzgerald's frequent letters not only to these doctors but also to others who had cared for his wife, Zelda's care took on monumental proportions. He claimed that he had been unable to write for four years, because of worrying about and caring for Zelda, and earning money from short stories (rather than writing his novel) to keep her under doctors' care. Officious in his correspondence, Scott avoided topics that he wanted to remain unknown (like his heavy drinking).[436] He gave Dr. Meyer directions, asked for specific schedules for his wife's days, and resumed the kind of involvement that he had maintained in Switzerland.

---

[435] Zelda to Fitzgerald, PUL; in DS, DZ, p. 50, she thanks him for helping Minnie move.

[436] Fitzgerald to all Zelda's doctors, PUL. In a psychiatric commentary on Dick Diver, Fitzgerald's analyst protagonist in Tender Is the Night, Dr. David Gottlieb comments on his view of the character: Diver "wants to entertain, but he also wants to upset his wife by using the party as a vehicle. He is toying with people in a seductive and sadistic way by using his charm, his party giving ... He wants control and power over others, but cannot exert such power or control over himself." (pp. 362 and 370 of Charles R. Metzger's F. Scott Fitzgerald's Psychiatric Novel, 1989).

Writing *Save Me the Waltz*

Zelda worked every morning on her writing. In early March, Dr. Squires wrote Scott that Zelda had made remarkable progress, and that she had just finished an entire section. Freed from both the arguments with Scott and the responsibilities of life at 819 Felder Avenue, Zelda could apparently let her unconscious tell the story it had been longing to express: the narrative unfolded easily, and as she typed page after page, she was excited by her accomplishment. Then on March 9, less than a month after her admission, Zelda not only finished *Save Me the Waltz* but mailed a copy of it to Max Perkins. She wrote Scott that she had sent Perkins the book because she did not want to bother her husband, or to interrupt his work. She noted that Scribner's would not take the novel anyway. Then she promised to send him the manuscript the following Monday.

Scott wrote to Dr. Squires on March 14.[437] He had the manuscript and he was enraged. Paying for the care for his mentally ill wife, he felt as if he had been duped not only by Zelda but also by the clinic: how dare they collude in allowing her to send a novel (much of which, he said, was stolen from his current book) to his publisher without his, Scott's, permission? As if this was one of a sequence of events, he said he could no longer live with what he called such an "atmosphere of suspicion." Surprised at Fitzgerald's vehement reaction, the clinic called him with apologies.

Angry as Scott was with Zelda, he did not get in touch with her. He did not phone or telegraph, as he customarily would

---

[437] Life, pp. 209-10.

have. He did not write to her; he wrote instead to Dr. Squires, and let her convey his anger to Zelda. So the first letter between Scott and Zelda originated with his wife, and she made apologies.[438] She was deferential. She asked for his forgiveness. She repeated that she loved him "more than anything on earth" and said that "if you were offended I am miserable." She insisted that part of her sending the manuscript to Perkins was self-protective: "I did not want a scathing criticism such as you have mercilessly—if for my own good given my last stories, poor things. I have had enough discouragement."

Fitzgerald angrily edited Zelda's letter of apology, or so the copy now in the Princeton archive suggests.[439] His comments within the lines and along the margins answer Zelda in a hostile discourse: Fitzgerald is writing to himself. He does not believe a word she writes about the evolution of her manuscript, or the reasons she sent it first to Perkins. He has underlined her comment that "I was also afraid we might have touched the same material," a sentence which is, for her, just one of a complex of reasons but, for him, seems to be the primary explanation—as he put it again and again, Zelda was stealing his material. Strangely, in the midst of all Scott's anger, there is no acknowledgment in his comments that Zelda is presently in a mental hospital. His attacks would be severe even if the recipient were healthy and whole. In line with what Zelda had called his "scathing" criticism, which he evidently applied to her work "mercilessly," Fitzgerald, the angry husband, was both using his superior reputation as author and assuming that he had the right to be severe—that is, derogatory, mean,

---

[438] Zelda to Fitzgerald, DS, DZ, p. 163.

[439] PUL.

inhuman—even with his unstable wife, a woman who had never pretended to be an accomplished or a successful fiction writer.

Evidently, after Scott had wired Perkins that the novel was not to be published—but that if Scribner's was interested, the book would be rewritten and he would help with that process—Scott wrote to Zelda. He laid out the changes that had to be made, from structural ones—too many drinking and drunk scenes—to more cosmetic ones (her male character's name was Armory Blaine, the protagonist from Scott's *This Side of Paradise*; in her renaming him "David Knight," perhaps she was remembering the New York lawyer, Richard Knight, whose fairly recent admiration for her was gratifying).

Zelda's letter to Scott in reply was less apologetic; she signed it "with deepest love, I am your irritated Zelda."[440] She spoke in this letter as a writer with some authority; she would make some of the changes he wanted, she would work toward a good product, but she could not accept his revisions wholesale. *Save Me the Waltz* is her book. In fact, it is Alabama Beggs' book. In her earlier letter to Scott, Zelda had explained that she sent the book to Perkins because she could not at the time accept what she knew would he Scott's "scathing" criticism: true to her expectations, in this letter he had delivered that kind of judgment. She also explained that if her recent stories had sold, she would not have undertaken the novel. (Burned into her memory was the fact that one of her last stories, "A Millionaire's Girl," was published as being Scott's work, and that Scott had been paid $4000 for it.) The other recurring point of contention was Scott's claim that Zelda was using up his material. She

[440] DS, DZ, p. 167.

believed, in contrast, that the story of Alabama Beggs was her material. That she was making too big a draw on his store of fictional information was at the heart of his anger and of his often ingenious, and somewhat ingenuous, complaints.

This contretemps over the novel is further indication of the actual role Scott was willing to play in Zelda's writing success. He frequently professed his readiness to "help" her, and perhaps at the start of her trying to write for publication he did. But as W. R. Anderson in his thorough study of Zelda's short fiction concluded, while Scott may have nominally continued to aid her, by the time she had written most of the *College Humor* stories, his involvement was "increasingly sparing and wary." More important, as Anderson stated after studying the typescripts for these stories, Zelda "was becoming increasingly self sufficient, playing a more important part in the revisions of her work."[441]

For Mildred Squires, observing this unexpected vehemence from Fitzgerald about his wife's novel—and charged with keeping Zelda on her treatment schedule—she decided that the Fitzgeralds might be better off separated. Previously hidden issues of power and control had come to light, and Squires saw the current situation as part of what was evidently a harsh and long-standing enmity. She suggested to Scott that he should consider separating from Zelda. When he quickly replied, he said there were no problems. He placed his concern for his wife at the heart of his reasoning, saying that a separation would be "throwing her [Zelda] broken upon a world which she despises."[442]

---

[441] W. R. Anderson, "Rivalry and Partnership," Fitzgerald/Hemingway Annual, 1977, pp. 19-42; here, pp. 25-7.

[442] Fitzgerald to Dr. Squires, Life, p. 211.

One of the most consistent themes in the saga of Zelda's institutionalization and Scott's recriminations about not only her illness but also her dancing, her writing, and her spending his money is what he sees as their great, and enduring, love. Even though Zelda had said matter-of-factly in an early interview at Phipps that she and Scott "have both been absorbed in our love for each other and our hatred for each other," she would echo Scott's belief that their love was phenomenal, unlike the emotion that existed in any of their friends' marriages. Bewildered by such a fantasy—held by both patient and spouse—the physicians and psychiatrists who treated Zelda, and would have liked to treat Scott, were unclear as to the etiology of her breakdown, and unsure about possible effective treatments.

Scott Fitzgerald as Analyst

The lengthy information Scott sent to Mildred Squires dated April 4, 1932, was no doubt prompted by her suggestion that he and Zelda separate. In his double narrative of the five years before Zelda's breakdown—one part written as a year-by-year chronology, the other arranged thematically—he depicted Zelda as both jealous and competitive, but in either case always thoroughly dependent on him. In his description of their 1931 autumn in Montgomery, for example, he noted that those months for Zelda were a period "of work, strain, asthma. Intense jealousy of husband, uncaused… Jealousy concealed … nothing psychotic."[443] What is most troubling from a diagnostic standpoint is Scott's failure to equate her "intense"—and "concealed"—"jealousy" of him with "psychotic" behavior.

---

[443] Fitzgerald to Dr. Squires, PUL.

Given that he had relocated to Alabama to help her recuperate, and then had quickly left for Hollywood, there would seem to be few reasons for what he called Zelda's jealousy. What did Fitzgerald think "psychotic" meant? Did he make no connection at all between the analysis from Prangins (that Zelda felt inferior to Scott, that the hinge of her mental balance might rest in some way on a competition between the two of them) with the symptoms he included here? His letter to Squires repeats an attitude that had surfaced previously: that Zelda needed to be "rebuilt." In his judgment, nothing about her present psychological health was connected with him.

What is also at issue in this description is what Scott omits. One point is his absence from Montgomery. Another, even more significant for Zelda's state of mind, is the fact that her father died on November 17. If Fitzgerald had thought the loss of her father unimportant, he might at least have considered how much his own father's death the year before had affected him. Even if he couldn't understand Zelda's complicated relationship with the Judge, he might have seen through her complacency; after all, she had written to him candidly about the fact that she missed her "Daddy."

At the very least he might have realized how much energy it took for Zelda to help her mother and sisters with the Judge's illness and then with the funeral and its aftermath, with clearing out Minnie's Pleasant Street house and preparing for her move, and with the double weight of attending to Christmas and welcoming home not only her husband but also his mother. Zelda, a woman fragile from fifteen months' confinement in a mental hospital, was being asked to shoulder herculean labors.

Another exculpatory theme that recurs in Scott's letter to

Dr. Squires is the tenuous health of the Sayre family. His first item under the thematic narrative is "Two sisters have nervous breakdowns, a third suffers from a nervous affliction of the neck. But the patient is apparently the best balanced in the family."[444]

Much of what follows in this section is Zelda's medical history which seems, often, exaggerated. About her drinking, for example, Scott writes that she has been a

heavy but intermittent drinker and inclined to hysteria when drunk. Violent hysteria occasionally even suicidal, occured [sic] *perhaps four to seven times a year when she could only be calmed by minimum dose of morphine. No other morphine in any form ever taken (save for two weeks during peritonitis attack at age 24).*[445]

Scott's concern here seems to be that the rare use of morphine—in this description, however, much more frequent than in his other accounts—not be construed as some kind of drug addiction. He does mention that she did not drink much during the years of her ballet study, but he does not point out that for the past several years she has not been allowed to drink at all—during her stays at Valmont and Prangins, as well as in Montgomery.

He notes in this section that while Zelda had at times been a heavy smoker, she has tried to reduce the number of cigarettes she smokes. She still drinks four or five cups of coffee every day.

The Princeton archive has no response from Dr. Squires to Fitzgerald.

Later in April, Scott and Scottie moved to Baltimore, renting a house near the Turnbull family in Towson, a house ironically

[444] Fitzgerald to Dr. Squires, PUL.

[445] Ibid.

named La Paix. It was another estate-like place that was too big for their family, and certainly too big for Zelda to have to worry about. Scott visited her regularly at Phipps. Most visits ended in arguments, most of the hard feelings prompted by Zelda's work on *Save Me the Waltz*—the fact that the book existed as well as the fact that Scott was making her change it. Because the original manuscript has been lost, there is no way of telling how many changes she made.[446] A considerable amount of work was done on the galley proofs, too; those changes appear to be along the lines Scott had initially suggested.

Zelda also was writing new essays and stories, and Scott insisted on seeing those as well. She resisted. She had learned from his explosion about her novel that he was hardly an impartial editor. She held her own during the arguments, but then wept at night. She was being tormented by their arguments into the same kind of sleeplessness that had destroyed her equanimity, and her health, in Paris.

She would have been less cordial to Scott had she known that when Perkins sent her the contract for *Save Me the Waltz* in early June, it included the provision that 50 percent of the book's royalties—up to the amount of £5000—would be used to pay off some of Scott's indebtedness to Scribner's. She signed the contract on June 14, 1932. Because the book made very little money, the provision was never activated.

Two weeks later, on June 26, Zelda was discharged from Phipps Clinic.

Practiced at being tranquil in the face of upsetting

---

[446] What happened to the manuscript is another of the perplexing gaps in the Fitzgeralds' story. See SSEG, pp. 320-4; Milford, pp. 216-17, 219-26, 253-4.

circumstances, Zelda assumed the facade of a successful author—signing a contract with Scribner's was clearly a mark of her distinction. The fact that her family now lived nearby at La Paix also made continuing therapy practical, without her having to board at the clinic. Her life at home was to be as orderly as possible, under Scott's control (as agreed to by Dr. Meyer, at Scott's urging, as a condition for her release). She devoted most of July to working on the proofs of the book and improving her tennis game. She met with a therapist at the clinic once a week. She was writing a comic play; and thinking of beginning a new novel which dealt with mental breakdown.

In August, however, her mood worsened. She did not like the schedule of her life, and she particularly did not like Scott's control of everything she did. Upset with either her husband or her daughter, Zelda would go to her room—sometimes for twenty-four hours at a time. Part of her energy while she was separating herself from her family went into writing letters to Dr. Rennie,[447] and many of those were accompanied by sketches. Clearly, Rennie had become another outlet for the grief Zelda could not always diminish through her writing.

During this summer, Scott was hospitalized for nearly two weeks for what a doctor thought was typhoid fever. He was run-down, and his drinking had never been curtailed, as had Zelda's.

The Fitzgeralds' summer lasted scarcely two months. On August 29, 1932, just months after Phipps had released her, Zelda demanded to be institutionalized again.[448] A dishevelled, drunken Scott appeared with her at Phipps, where Dr. Rennie

---

[447] Zelda Fitzgerald to Rennie, PUL.

[448] Milford, pp. 260-1.

tried to calm her. She was adamant: if she could not go back to Phipps, Zelda wanted to go to Sheppard Pratt. In any case, she wanted to leave Scott, Scottie, and La Paix.

Scandalabra and Romance as Comedy

Rennie, the young Scots doctor that Zelda felt comfortable with, set up a rigid schedule for the next weeks; she promised to abide by it.[449] Somehow, the Fitzgerald household existed through the autumn and then in October *Save Me the Waltz* appeared. There was little media attention, though Zelda was interviewed. The book sold something over 1300 copies (and made $120 in royalties); reviews were mixed. Disheartened by its reception, Zelda sent Ober and Perkins her play, once again recalling Scott's wild hopes for *The Vegetable*. But Broadway was as broke as the publishing houses, and no one optioned Zelda's *Scandalabra*.[450]

The play was an effective parody of both *Scandals* and of Scott's *The Beautiful and Damned*, as well as the formality of wealthy households, in which the two rich but dissatisfied couples lived. Zelda was a good satirist. She had an ear for the wisecracking youth that comprised the wealthy echelon of New York and Paris; she had long been an astute commentator on social behavior. What she didn't have in the writing of *Scandalabra* was a sense of how long each scene or act should be.

The reasonably funny text works through outright satire of

---

[449] See the Zelda Fitzgerald-Dr. Rennie correspondence, PUL.

[450] Zelda Fitzgerald, text printed in CW, pp. 197-267. Not inferior to Fitzgerald's play The Vegetable, Zelda's play nude use of the 1920s repartee which John Dos Passos described in The Best Times (1968, p. 157), "Conversation in the early twenties had to be one wisecrack after another ... continually like the birds in badminton."

the aims, and foibles, of the rich—heavily laced with innuendo and sex. One of the two couples is devotedly happy, but needs to appear to be spendthrift and lascivious to meet the terms of an uncle's will. That couple plots to be able to stay home before the fire rather than carousing through the night spots of the city, out on separate immoral adventures. The other couple finds less satisfaction with each other, until the husband capitalizes on an accidental media situation to make his wife believe he has become a man about town. When the two couples meet on a beach outing, barely recognizing each other, the dialogue becomes even more comic. In this short scene, the stable couple, Andrew and Flower, picnic with their butler Baffles:

Andrew *Let's not spread the cloth, Flower. It's so like a winding sheet.*

Baffles *Maybe Mr. Andrew likes a little sand in his sandwiches, Miss Flower.*

Andrew *Gives 'em body.*

Flower *I should think you wouldn't be so grouchy, Andrew, now that everything's just as you suspected all along.*

She polishes his back with a vindictive gouge

Andrew *(As they begin picnic) You know, Flower, these revelations don't seem to have changed you much.*

Baffles *(Hastily) Won't you try one of these, sir? I made them myself out of papier-mache.*[451]

Across a stretch of the beach, the second couple arrives and in the misalliance between their dialogue occurs some of the play's best lines: from Andrew, "You don't know how awful it is to feel jealous—You know how you feel when you've just got

---

[451] Zelda Fitzgerald, Scandulabru in CW, p. 244

off a merry-go-round?" and Flower replies, "Oh, I think jealousy sometimes keeps a marriage from going bad," augmented by Baffles' "Acts as a sort of spiritual cellophane." In another passage, Andrew chastises Flower by saying, "you'd like us to *believe* what looks so like lies," only to have Baffles remind him, "Whether you believe it or not, Mr. Andrew, makes the only difference between fiction and reality."[452]

Scandalabra, like all good social comedies, was written to poke fun at the fabric of social convention among the moneyed classes. Had Zelda written it even five years sooner, so that Ober could have found a home for it in 1927 rather than trying unsuccessfully to do so in 1932, she might have become a playwright. As it was, Zelda could find no success.

During some of her darkest hours, she considered that Scott's interference with her dancing career had foreshadowed the years to come. Scott had written to Dr. Squires that Zelda had turned down what he described as two offers to dance professionally, one in Naples and one in Paris, because of what he called "Exterior Circumstances."[453] He explained no further. Not only was his information wrong about the sources and the number of the offers, but Scott may also have been continuing his tendency to fictionalize the events of their lives together. Now Zelda saw that since she had written and published a novel, Scott was surly and vindictive about her writing—and inhospitable to further efforts. His conscientiousness in listing the amounts

---

[452] Ibid., p. 249.

[453] One offer, according to Fitzgerald, was to debut at La Scala in Naples; "the other in Paris, premiere danseuse at Folios Begere [sic]. Exterior circumstances made her refuse both" (April 4,1932, PUL).

of money Zelda made in his *Ledger* may have been more of a goad to her sense of her promise than it was an accounting effort: setting her earnings against his, Zelda could hardly be cheered by the results of the writing she had spent much of a decade accomplishing.

Yet she still wrote. In one handwritten essay, untitled, she thought about the empowerment of playing tennis.

One has the sense of a net stretched across ultimate horizons … Tennis courts find their way to the tops of places. The air hangs high and white hot over the arena incubating latent capacities.[454]

This long essay describes the personal achievement of the player who improves, and it connects the popularity of the game with the Russian ballet. As she describes:

It hasn't been very long since tennis made its appearance in the arts. The Russian Ballet introduced the world of amateurs to the aesthetic possibilities and the spiritual gratifications inherent in a perfectly coordinated debut twelve years ago in a ballet named "The Train Bleu." People at Deauville played tennis in terms of pas-de-basque and pirouette and offered more suggestions as to the aesthetic context of the game.[455]

Without Scott's support of her writing, however, Zelda seemed to have lost the keen interest that had helped her endure the previous four or five years. What remained as evidence of her multiple talents, still sheltered within the benevolence of her husband's approval, was her painting. From her first lessons in Capri, supplemented with life drawing classes in Sarasota, Florida, Zelda's paintings appeared to have Scott's

---

[454] Zelda Fitzgerald, untitled essay, PUL, p. 1.

[455] Ibid., p. 3.

approval[456]—perhaps strangely so, because what Zelda painted was as iconoclastic and as unusual as anything exhibited in Paris during the 1920s. Scott seemed, however, pleased when she spent her afternoons painting in the garden: his image of his beautiful Southern wife may have been enhanced by her serious demeanor with her canvases and paints. At any rate, painting and drawing appeared to be what Zelda, the woman of many talents, had left.

Dr. Meyer as Analyst

In December of 1932, Adolf Meyer wrote to Dr. Forel about Zelda Fitzgerald's progress.[457] While Meyer was generally optimistic about her health, he told Forel that Scott was declining. His drinking had never diminished, even during his summer illness, and now he was taking Luminol along with his alcohol. He was under the care of another of Phipps' doctors. His moods remained unpredictable. And he had confided to Meyer that he controlled his wife's mental health absolutely. Fitzgerald had said he needed only fifteen minutes to reduce Zelda to hysteria through a "well-planned conversation" in which he would suggest that he was interested in some other woman; such a comment would "bring on her insanity again."[458] That Scott would express such a demonic idea to his wife's psychiatrist seemed to be beyond reasonable behavior, and might have fallen into the category of a challenge to the august Dr. Meyer.

In April of 1933, Dr. Meyer wrote to Fitzgerald, telling him

---

[456] See Jane S. Livingston, "On the Art of Zelda Fitzgerald," Zelda, pp. 77-85.

[457] Milford, p. 268.

[458] Fool, p. 72.

that he must either stop his drinking or forfeit any right to control Zelda's treatment. Meyer reminded Scott, "You also figure as a potential but unwilling patient" and he ascribed the poor state of Fitzgerald's mental health to "the main fact, the urge for stimulants ... alcohol."[459] Meyer wondered why Scott didn't limit his drinking and try to exercise, perhaps going riding with Zelda. But his real warning, and his evident purpose in writing, was to show Scott that his much vaunted control of Zelda's treatment was coming to an end, "The question of authority is simple. We have decided to relieve you of having to be the boss in any detailed way." Meyer pointed out that he and Scott could not reach what he called a man-to-man agreement "without a conjoint surrender of the alcohol." In response to one of Scott's suggestions, possibly that he himself take over Zelda's treatment, Meyer said his idea was "strange." He thought Zelda was satisfied with the Phipps' program.

Both the Fitzgeralds had been seeing therapists at the Phipps Clinic for nearly six months. Whether or not these joint sessions took the place of individual weekly meetings is unclear. Given that Zelda was the official patient and Scott the bill-paying spouse, their use of the clinic's facilities was surprisingly similar, as was Meyer's commenting to Dr. Forel as much about Scott as he did about Zelda. Clearly, Dr. Meyer, at least, saw Scott as a second patient.

For Zelda to have maintained her balance in the face of living at La Paix, trying to accommodate herself to the schedules of both Scott and Scottie, trying to write and paint, and staying out of the range of Scott's anger was a testimony to her having

---

[459] Adolf Meyer to Fitzgerald, April 18, 1933, PUL.

learned some effective strategies. Living at La Paix as a family, however, could not have been happy.

The Narration of Scott's and Zelda's Anger

On the afternoon of May 28, 1933, at La Paix, with Dr. Rennie and a stenographer in attendance, the Fitzgeralds tried to talk out some of their problems. The 114-page record[460] of this unusual consultation remains a tapestry of fantasy and fact, a double-sided coin of acrimony and anger that left the staff at Phipps even more bewildered about the health—or the sickness—of the relationship between Zelda and Scott.

One of the recurring topics was the issue of whose material their lives were, and Scott's charges that Zelda was usurping his fiction whenever she took characters and episodes that he had listed in his notebook—whether or not she knew what was in his notebook. The anger that *Save Me the Waltz* had provoked still seethed, and because their disagreement ran so deep—with Zelda unable to accept that the autobiographical record of her life was Scott's material—there was no conclusion. It seemed futile to try to bridge this ever-widening chasm. In Scott's words,

It is a perfectly lonely struggle that I am making against other writers who are finely gifted and talented. You [to Zelda] *are a third rate writer and a third rate ballet dancer.*

Her quiet response was, "You have told me that before."

In Fitzgerald's thinking, because he was "a professional writer, with a huge following. I am the highest paid short story writer in the world … one in ten million," he had the right

---

[460] PUL in total; pages of typescript not given. Subsequent quotations are from this source.

to everything they had done, thought, investigated, and lived through together: "Everything we have done is my ... I am the professional novelist, and I am supporting you. That is all my material. None of it is your material." That Zelda retorted calmly, saying that he was making "a rather violent attack on a third rate talent," only infuriated him.

The page-by-page transcription of the interchange reads as if most arguments have no ending point. Whether or not Dr. Rennie saw his role as convener or moderator is unknown; what directions he had from Dr. Meyer are unclear. Perhaps his job was only to supervise and allow the lacunae of dead-end argument to be recorded. For in almost every case, as the voices of Scott and Zelda grow more and more tense, no one intercedes and the dialogue dwindles into insult.

Zelda: "*I remember the night you broke my nose and you had to get a doctor out there.*"

Scott: "*A nosebleed.*" *(He explained that he was putting her to bed.)*

Zelda: "*You said I said your father was an Irish policeman, a thing I never said, and I have never understood it ... and you came in and threw a lot of things into the fireplace, and hit my face, and completely alienated my sister from you ... You came home from Princeton so drunk, on a weeping jag ... Scott threw a blue vase into the fireplace ... My sister* [Rosalind] *left the house in the middle of the night.*"

Scott: "*You don't accept any responsibility ... and that is why you have got a nurse at $50 a week.*"

Then, backtracking, Scott apologized and said he did not mean to start a quarrel, to which Zelda replied "it has been a quarrel for the last ten years."

Later, again in discussion about whose talents are professional,

Scott said he has been a professional writer since he was ten, and that when he was only seventeen, he was writing Triangle Club shows at Princeton. He taunted Zelda with the insult that when she was seventeen [which she was when they met] "she was just boy-crazy. She read the Rubiat of Omar Khayyam." In his frustration, Scott frequently interjected snide comments as a personal attack, as if he were trying to shake Zelda's composure. In one of those interchanges, her retort to his question "What does being a writer mean?" was "If it means drinking yourself to death and being crazy all the time, I don't want it."

Scott frequently turned to the statement that when he was writing *The Great Gatsby*, "doing the best work of [his] my life," Zelda had tried to destroy him. He implies that she fell in love with Jozan as an intentional ploy to hurt his writing. Zelda then told him seriously that "As far as destroying you is concerned I have considered you first in everything I have tried to do in my life."

Her criticism of Scott focused on his drinking; he defended his behavior as

what was characteristic of the day. I would go out once a week, and I would maybe drink too much, and sometimes would stay out all night. Zelda, during that time, had almost a hundred doctors, I figure, who gave her bromides, morphine—

She quickly replied that Scott's statement was "not true," and he changed the figure to "fifty," but added that all of them gave her "morphine injections." In another interchange about drinking, he moved even more quickly to insult her: "I never drank until I was sixteen years old. The first time I met her I saw she was a drunkard." He also added that Zelda, at least mentally, was a prostitute.

One of Scott's areas of attack was what he called Zelda's foolish ambition to be a ballet dancer, for which he paid $300 a month to Egorova. He claimed that the payment was her reason for encouraging Zelda in her lessons. Recounting Egorova's letter, he said flatly, "You could not dance." Zelda's retort was

That is not so. She said I could dance a leading role in the Mazarine Ballet ... What she said was that I started too late to be a star. You know what being a star in the Russian Ballet means. There are about six of them.

Scott frequently moved to the defense that because Zelda was having sex with him, all her complaints were unfounded. As he had in his letters to her various doctors, he charted their happiness and unhappiness in terms of when and how often they had what he called "sexual relations."

Zelda: "You have mistreated me continuously. There has not been one day since I have been in this house [La Paix] *that you have not done something unpleasant to me ... Since Alabama?"*

Scott: "I have supported you."

Zelda: "Yes, you supported me, and you have been reproaching me for that."

Scott: "That is all very recently. I have supported you. Our sexual relations were very pleasant."

She responded noncommittally.

Scott: "When did you cease to enjoy them? Jesus, it is just like talking to a circus clown."

Zelda: "You won't allow me to sleep in bed ... I say nice things, and it is a dog and cat, terrible." She continued that she could get along without sex, but that he could not. She added that he had been drinking hard all winter.

This scene circled back to another in which Scott used their lack of intercourse to explain her morose comment that unless she was writing, she would "rather be dead."

Scott: "You would rather be dead?"

Zelda: "Why not?"

Scott: "Well, we have had no relations for more than three or four months."

She took him to task abruptly for that easy solipsism:

Zelda: "You accuse me of everything in the world, with having ruined your life, not once, but over and over again … Last fall. You sat down and cried and cried … You said I had ruined your life, and you did not love me, and you were sick of me and wished you could get away. It is impossible to live with you. I would rather be in an insane asylum, where you would like to put me."

Then, in an apparent turn to Rennie, Zelda continued, "He told Scottie when she was twelve … Your mother is crazy, and you are bad, and I wish I was dead."

Needing to retaliate after this onslaught, which he evidently could not deny, Scott attacked Zelda's illness.

Scott: "Can't you stop your 'I's'? Who are you? You are a person of six or seven different parts. Now, why don't you integrate yourself?"

Zelda: "Listen, Scott, I am so God damned sick of your abuse that honestly I don't know what I will do … .One reason I have to do things behind your back is because you are so absolutely unjust and abusive and unfair, that to go to you and ask you anything would be like pulling a thunderbolt down on my head. I would not ask you for five cents."

As she had earlier said, again apparently to Rennie, "Scott has continuously reproached me absolutely for the fact that he has to pay for [clinics] and states that I have ruined his life." She defends her own writing as a way to pay some of those expenses.

Scott interjects, "You are just a useless society woman, brought up to be that."

Zelda: "That is what you want me to be."

Scott: "No, I don't."

Zelda: "Well, what do you want me to be?"

Scott: "I want you to do what I say."

By the time of the last thirty pages of the transcription, much of the invective was repeated, but there were moments of silence when either Scott or Zelda tried to reach the other with a particularly harsh comment. At one point, for example, Scott insulted Zelda by telling her, "Your memory is like a sieve." To which she answered, "My life has been so miserable that I would rather be in an asylum. Does that mean a thing to you?" And he answered, "It does not mean a blessed thing." A few pages later, Zelda told him, "I don't want to live with you, because I want to live some place that I can be my own self."

The progression from that point on was even more disorderly. Scott defended his drinking by saying that he drank only three or four drinks a day (although if he were following his usual practice, he was not counting wine or beer). Zelda contended that she saw nothing to do but "get a divorce, because there is nothing except ill-will on your part and suspicion." It was not the first time in the interchange that she had made that suggestion; this time Scott appeared to have heard what she was saying. But when he reminded her of their good marriage, saying "We were about the most envied couple in about 1921, in America," she replied, "We were awfully good showmen."

Frustrated as he was by Zelda's increasingly direct statements, Scott tried to end the discussion by blackening her character, announcing "You were my mistress before we were married." To that Zelda only replied, "I dropped a whole lot of other people."

Whether or not he read the situation correctly, Scott felt that Dr. Rennie was giving more credence to Zelda's story than to his. He wrote Rennie warning him of Zelda's persuasive charm,[461] and she continued to write to Rennie herself. The month after the transcribed interview, Zelda tried to burn some old clothes in an unused fireplace upstairs, and started a house fire that could have done much more damage than it did. Reminiscent of her burning the clothes she had made in Hollywood, this episode was treated as an innocent mistake by everyone involved—but Scott wondered.

In early June, Zelda's play *Scandalabra* went into production by the Vagabond Junior Players of Baltimore. After its opening, which ran until 1 a.m., the cast and Scott and Zelda met each night after the production and, with Scott's help, cut—from scene one through to the end—so that after a week, the play was running in a reasonable amount of time. It could not, however, be salvaged—reviews from the start were bad, and the fantasy-farce mode was outdated in the most severe years of the Great Depression. Disappointed, Zelda felt that Scott's mandate that she not work on her psychiatric novel (so that she not use up "his" material) was keeping her from important writing. She put a lock on the door of the room in which she wrote, but she was afraid to resume the fiction.

Then in August, her mother wrote about her brother Anthony's breakdown.[462] Six years older than Zelda, Anthony

---

[461] Fitzgerald letter quoted in Milford, p. 282.

[462] Minnie Sayre to Zelda, August 9, 1933, PUL.

had become depressed after losing his job; he and his wife Edith searched for private treatment, but finally when he had not improved, Edith told Minnie. Angry that she had not known of his condition, Minnie took him to Asheville, North Carolina, to Dr. Thorington, who "did for Anthony what he would do for his own son—viz—took him to Mobile to Dr. Eugene Bondurant, a distinguished nerve specialist."

Minnie's letter continued that Anthony's tests had come back "toxic from malaria and bile." His wife Edith had gone to visit her family in Rome; she would return when Anthony was better.

A few days after Zelda received Minnie's letter, however, came the news that Anthony was dead. He had jumped from the window of his Mobile hospital room.

Now Zelda's life was complicated with fears that she and her brother shared the same set of maladies. Scott's life was complicated by the fact that the novel on which he had worked so long had been sold to *Scribner's Magazine* as a serial and, now titled *Tender Is the Night*, would begin appearing in January of 1934. He had to finish the book now; he had no choice—he had spent all the years of advances, and more.

After the fire in the upstairs fireplace, Scott used the poor condition of La Paix as reason to move. Their smaller townhouse at 1307 Park Avenue was modest. At Dr. Meyer's suggestion, Scott and Zelda took a vacation to Bermuda, but the constant rain there set Scott back with pleurisy. As if trying to balance his work with some attention to Zelda's life, Scott arranged an exhibit of her paintings at a friend's gallery in New York.[463]

---

[463] Milford, pp. 283-4.

Instead of being pleased, she was infuriated: she said her paintings were too personal to he shown.

She may have also been resentful because Scott was again directing her life—giving the art world access to her work, even if she did not want that work shown. She had also read the first, and perhaps the second, installment of her husband's novel; she had realized once more how much of her life was the substance of his fiction. In his modeling Nicole Diver's mental instability upon her own, Zelda recognized both her letters, and her symptoms.

Zelda went to bed.

On February 12, 1934, two years after her first admission to Phipps, Zelda was readmitted as a patient. Kept under a suicide watch[464] and on bed rest, sedated, ordered to gain at least fifteen pounds, Zelda Sayre Fitzgerald gave up the struggle to exist in the outside world, a world dominated, inevitably, by Scott.

---

[464] Milford, pp. 286-7; Kendall Taylor, Sometimes Madness Is Wisdom (2001), pp. 284-5.

ELEVEN - Zelda as Patient

"I left my capacity for hoping on the little roads that led to Zelda's sanitarium," Scott wrote in his *Notebooks*.[465] There is slight reason to think Fitzgerald's almost continuous references to Zelda's mental illness were entirely self-serving; he did not refer to her and her condition as a means of getting attention, nor did he use her breakdowns as a way of legitimating his heavy drinking. Despite his cruelly defensive remarks when he was made to face her, particularly in the company of her doctors or psychiatrists, Scott Fitzgerald in 1934 was forced to realize that his carefully orchestrated life as the male half of a celebrated couple had ended. His "life" as he had created it was gone. Left with the care of not only his wife but also his daughter, his mother, his professional reputation as one of the great contemporary writers, and himself, Fitzgerald at scarcely thirty-seven was bereft of confidence—both emotional and financial. He had assumed he and Zelda would be partners throughout their lives. Now he knew they would not be.

---

[465] Scott Fitzgerald, The Notebooks of F Scott Fitzgerald (1980), p. 204.

When Fitzgerald had mentioned Zelda's "sort of nervous breakdown"[466] to Max Perkins in the spring of 1930, her illness received scarcely more space than the wedding of Ludlow Fowler's brother. When Zelda signed herself out of Malmaison, Fitzgerald seemed less than alarmed. Taking her to Valmont several weeks later showed his deeper concern, but again he wrote to friends as if the situation was temporary. In the transfer of Zelda to Prangins, Fitzgerald grew more concerned; but again, he assumed she would recover. As he wrote to Dr. Forel in the summer of 1930, "due to your [Ford's] tireless intelligence and interest, there is a time in sight when Zelda and I may renew our life together on a decent basis, a thing which I desire with all my heart."[467] He wrote then to Edmund Wilson, himself recovering from a breakdown, "She is now almost 'well,' which is to say the psychosis element is gone. We must live quietly for a year now and to some extent forever."[468]

But Scott was wrong.

It was another year before Zelda was released from Prangins. His hopes escalated again: his bringing her back to the States, with Scottie, and settling them in Montgomery with the Sayres and Zelda's siblings, was another step ahead to normalcy. All would be well. Zelda was cured.

That state lasted less than six months before the frantic trip by train to Johns Hopkins, and the long saga of stormy institutionalization at the Phipps Clinic. *Save Me the Waltz* was written and published. Scott's months at La Paix wore on. Finally, however, he entered in his *Notebooks* some recognition of Zelda's state:

---

[466] Fitzgerald to Perkins, Life, p. 181.

[467] Fitzgerald to Dr. Forel, Life, p. 196.

[468] Fitzgerald to Edmund Wilson, Life, p. 199.

Her letters are tragically brilliant on all matters except those of central importance. How strange to have failed as a social creature … the insane are always mere guests on earth …[469]

As the decade of the 1930s continued, Scott came to see that Zelda's "breakdown" might become permanent, a condition that would only be intensified by medications and particularly by the intermittent electroconvulsive or other shock treatments used as a last measure. For the creative and imaginative Zelda, the loss of many of her memories—a primary result of shock treatment—was to constitute the loss of the more significant parts of her life.

Sorting through the various motivations of both Zelda and Scott Fitzgerald has prompted more than a dozen biographical studies, and many more essays. The conundrum of their "love" for each other—however that emotion was defined over the years—piques our troubled fascination even as it is admittedly complicated by both of their needs to drink heavily, as well as by Zelda's institutionalization in mental hospitals. Few of the assumed facts in the couple's history during the 1930s are stable: even when the biographer works directly from letters between them now preserved in the Princeton Fitzgerald collections, the material increasingly shows the eroding tensions their lives as a couple produced. Aggravated by their living together, their hostility is either expressed—as when Zelda wrote to Scott, "You had other things: drink and tennis, and we did not care about each other. You hated me for asking you not to drink"[470]—or denied, as in much of Scott's correspondence, particularly to his friends, or to Zelda's troublesome (for Scott) admirer Richard Knight.

---

[469] Fitzgerald, Notebooks, p. 335.

[470] Zelda Fitzgerald to Scott, DZ, DS, p. 72.

In that letter, Scott claimed, "In another year, Deus volens, she [Zelda] will be well. For the moment she must live in a state of Teutonic morality, far from the exploits of the ego on its own."[471]

Both Scott and Zelda were people proud of their intellectual capacities. Zelda, for example, soon after her institutionalization at Phipps in February or March of 1932, wrote to apologize for Scott's having to "leave" his novel again, and then wrote about her assessment of what their lives needed—tranquility:

I wish we could reach some static placidity that would run like a Gregorian chant through our lives and bolster up the services a little. I s'pose we could if we had accepted some inviolable premise of human conduct and could consider our deviations from it as such, instead of finding it necessary to change all our conceptions to fit every unexpected develloppment [sic] *of our selves. My cat thoughts have eaten so many mice that they have grown quite gray ...*[472]

Zelda's tactic was to figure it out for them; Scott's was to inundate her doctors with all the information he could recall. It is clear that both Scott and Zelda were working to get to the heart of their dilemma—regardless of whether or not they had the learning to do so. What is also clear is that neither of the Fitzgeralds had much patience.

The Place of *Tender Is the Night*

To claim that Zelda was so depressed over having read the installments of *Tender Is the Night* available to her in February

---

[471] Fitzgerald to Richard Knight, Scott Fitzgerald, The Letters of F. Scott Fitzgerald (1963), pp. 500-1; in apologizing for calling Knight a "fairy," he terms him "neurotic." See Exiles, p. 194.

[472] Zelda to Scott, unpublished and undated, PUL.

of 1934 is oversimplification. But psychological patterns are repetitious. She was familiar with such intense reactions; her analysis at both Valmont and Prangins had included the element of her feelings of inferiority toward Scott. Psychiatrists and doctors at both hospitals attributed the intensity of her need to succeed in the ballet to that motivation—her challenging herself to become a star in an art Scott could not compete in. Her almost frantic training for the ballet was the opposite condition of the avolitional state that characterized many schizophrenics.

Fitzgerald's scheduling her exhibition of paintings and drawings at Cary Ross's gallery to coincide with the serialization and publication of *Tender Is the Night* was his admission that Zelda would probably he so affected. (In fact, in a letter to her several months later, he admonishes her not to read *Tender Is the Night* again: "I feel very strongly about your re-reading it. It represents certain phases of life that are now over."[473]) Perhaps he remembered that her collapse in Florida two years earlier had followed discussions about the characters of Nicole and Dick in the novel-in-progress, the book which became *Tender Is the Night*.

Admittedly, there was traumatic fallout from Zelda's reading the novel, but it was not entirely autobiographical. Part of the real harm in Fitzgerald's creation of—and presentation of—Nicole Diver in the book was the "fact" of her having been sexually abused by her father. Thoroughly accepting as he was of Freudian psychoanalysis, Fitzgerald believed the trauma of Nicole's psychosis would need to be as dramatic as possible: father-daughter incest

---

[473] Fitzgerald to Zelda, Life, p. 257.

was the most horrific plotline he could imagine.[474]

He acknowledged to Zelda that he had made up this scenario. (Zelda's friends were irate; one wrote that Zelda was "certainly never raped by her father."[475]) As so many critics have noted, however, because Scott took phrases and ideas from Zelda's actual letters to him, readers would likely assume that all parts of the Nicole story were based on the facts of Zelda Sayre's life.

The blackening of the character of Nicole-Zelda-Sara Murphy (Sara, said by Scott to have been the model for Nicole, was always indignant about the book, despite its dedication to her and Gerald) was perhaps the less egregious insult: as a result of the plotline, the person who became the monster within the novel was Nicole's father, not the disintegrating, ineffectual Dick Diver, for whom the reader maintained some sympathy. It was the character of Judge Sayre that Fitzgerald, through his fiction, denigrated. The beloved if austere Judge, revered by everyone who knew him (as Zelda had recently witnessed at his funeral in 1930) and, in Scott's perhaps unconscious resentment, the man who was his primary rival for Zelda's heart, had been permanently defamed. This use of her father, this attack on a person so crucial to Zelda's being, was far worse than Scott's practice in *Gatsby* of naming the yacht captain Dan Cody, after one of Zelda's early suitors.

---

[474] Part of Scott's need to control stemmed from his belief that order, representative of the rational, was the highest good. He was seldom comfortable with any kind of disorder, or with behavior be found disruptive.

[475] Exiles, p. 212.

Problems of "Reading" the Fitzgerald Story

One of the dilemmas throughout Zelda's treatment had been the presumed definiteness of her diagnosis. Yet even though the Forel-Bleuler-Meyer group agreed on schizophrenia as the basic malady, Squires—and to some extent Rennie—treated Zelda more as if she needed encouragement rather than any kind of rebuilding or psychoanalysis. According to descriptions of schizophrenia in the *Diagnostic and Statistical Manual of Mental Disorders*, the 1994 edition (IV, Text Supplement 2000),[476] the condition is marked by at least a one-month period of delusions, hallucinations, and disorganized speech—which occurs within a six-month period of illness. Other germane characteristics are disorganized behavior (sometimes, forms of catatonia) and affective flattening, an emotional shutdown, along with avolitional behavior. There are, of course, a great many variants of these states, but for the mental health observers who knew anything about Zelda's history, she seemed to exhibit behaviors more characteristic of mania (perhaps a bipolar condition), or of a "substance-induced psychotic disorder"[477] (stemming from her overuse of both alcohol and nicotine: Zelda smoked throughout her breakdowns and hospitalizations), or perhaps the more physiologically based "Psychotic Disorder Due to a General Medical Condition."[478] For example, Zelda's pervasive eczema and her battery of fatigue symptoms were more easily recognized as markers

---

[476] See American Psychiatric Association, Diagnostic and Statistical Manual of Mental Disorders, 1994, IV, and Text Supplement, 2000, pp. 297-340; this, p. 312.

[477] Ibid., p. 298.

[478] Ibid.

of systemic lupus erythematosus. Of lupus patients today, it is thought that 15 percent of them have been erroneously diagnosed as schizophrenic.[479]

Taken dramatically to first Valmont and then Prangins as she was in 1930, the wife of a man reasonably famous on the international scene, Zelda fit at least some of the descriptors for schizophrenia. It seems clear, however, that early in her hospitalization she might more easily have been diagnosed as having a "schizoaffective disorder," a "schizophrenic disorder" or—if the symptoms of hallucinations or delusions were brief (or non-existent)—a "brief psychotic disorder."[480] While the prognosis of cure in classic schizophrenia is small,[481] patients can recover so thoroughly from ailments within the schizoid family that there might be no accompanying "decline in functioning,"[482] the most serious outcome of schizophrenia.

So far as hospital records indicate, any investigation of Zelda's illness as substance-induced or as related to her overall physical health—as in lupus—was not made. And the diagnosis of schizophrenia was given well before the six months period of her illness had expired.

Other traits associated with a schizoid patient—physical awkwardness, the "word salad" of disassociative speech, or a lack of interest in life[483]—do not describe Zelda Sayre Fitzgerald. While there is no way to return to 1930 and begin observation

---

[479] Ibid., p. 336.

[480] Ibid., p. 298, 309.

[481] Ibid., p. 309: "Complete remission is probably not common.".

[482] Ibid., p. 298.

[483] Ibid., pp. 300, 306.

and medication over again, the specificity of the diagnosis, and the speed with which it was given, raise questions that remain unanswered. Unfortunately, as recently as the year 2000, the American Psychiatric Association stated, "No laboratory findings have been identified that are diagnostic of schizophrenia."[484]

Another difficulty in telling the Fitzgeralds' story accurately is tracking cause-and-effect relationships in the events of their lives through their chary record-keeping. Zelda seldom dated any of her letters; neither kept a journal or diary, and even Scott's *Ledger* was to end in 1936. Combined with their frequent moves, which was their pattern long before Zelda's illness, the paucity of accurate information keeps most conclusions tentative. As Alice Hall Petry points out, biographers and critics often "do not make the expected connections between [Zelda's] declining of the job offer from Italy and the notorious steering wheel incident, or between the publication of 'A Millionaire's Girl' as the work of Scott Fitzgerald and the mental collapse of' the woman who actually wrote it."[485]

Petry scrutinizes the sequence of events to build a cause-and-effect timeline; an underlying critical problem, however, is that most observers of these events have been looking at the

---

[484] Ibid., p. 305.

[485] Alice Hall Petry, "Women's Work," Literature-Interpretation-Theory, 1989, p. 69. She builds a formidable case in the opening of the essay. "item: On 23 September 1929, ... Zelda Sayre Fitzgerald, wife of the famous young author F. Scott Fitzgerald, received a formal invitation to join the San Carlo Opera Ballet Company in Naples, Italy. As her debut with the San Carlo, she was to dance a solo role in Aida, with other solo performances as the season progressed. She turned down the offer. A few days later, while Scott was driving along the Corniche - that treacherous stretch of road that claimed the life of Grace Kelly - Zelda grabbed the steering wheel and attempted to force the car off the cliff.".

Fitzgeralds' lives from the perspective of Scott's point of view, not Zelda's.

Similarly, Shoshana Felman uses the paradigm of social value based on gender to explain why women in twentieth century culture are so quickly labeled mad. Because women are conditioned to become adults through "serving an image, authoritative and central, of man," any deviation from that role is considered "crazy."[486] But, as Zelda Fitzgerald's behavior suggests, becoming mad is neither a rebellion or a "contestation": rather,

madness is the impasse confronting those whom cultural conditioning has deprived of the very means of protest or self-affirmation ... "mental illness" is a request for help, a manifestation both of cultural impotence and of political castration. This socially defined help-needing and help-seeking behavior is itself part of female conditioning.[487]

Craig House: Coming and Going

One example of the difficulty of finding all the pieces of any one segment of the Fitzgeralds' story is Zelda's transfer to, and two months' stay in, the luxurious Craig House sanitorium in upstate NewYork. Fitzgerald had been told about Craig House before and he had written to inquire about care and cost;[488] once Zelda's behavior at Phipps during February of 1934 did not improve, he decided to move her to the more expensive facility. The cost, $175 a week, was considerably more than he paid at Phipps.

Zelda's letters from whichever institution she was staying in

---

[486] Shoshana Felman, "Women and Madness: The Critical Phallacy," *Diacritics*, 1974, p. 2.

[487] Ibid.

[488] Scott to Dr. Clarence Slocum, May 16, 1932, PUL.

were one long lament over how much her hospitalization cost. As she wrote Scott once she had arrived at Craig House,

I am miserable that this added burden should have fallen on your shoulders. All the beauty of this place must cost an awful lot of money and maybe it would be advisable to go somewhere more compatible with our present means. Please do not think that I don't appreciate the strain you are under.[489]

She asks him, however, not to stop Scottie's piano lessons. She also asks him if she is allowed to resume her writing, or would he prefer she stay with painting?

The letters from Zelda's brief stay at Craig House show that both the Fitzgeralds were behaving true to their patterns: on March 12, 1934, Scott had written to Dr. Slocum a brief history of Zelda's illnesses, including her colitis, the appendectomy nearly ten years before, and what he counted as two bouts of asthma, which he attributed to the deer hair from the trophy heads in the Montgomery rental. His primary concern in this early letter, however, was to let Slocum know he was to restrict Zelda's discretionary spending—Scott wrote that by the time he sent her $50 a month for painting supplies and a typist, "she is getting about 8/10ths of the family income."[490]

According to Dr. Slocum's reply to Scott, when he gave Zelda her husband's letter to read, she had a "slight hysterical outbreak" as a result of what she called "the receipt of your letter."[491] She was under pressure to finish a story she was writing for Scott,

---

[489] Zelda to Scott, DS, DZ, pp. 180-1.

[490] Scott to Dr. Slocum, March 12, 1934, PUL.

[491] Dr. Slocum to Fitzgerald, March 19, 1934, PUL.

for publication, and even though Slocum wanted to treat her for exhaustion, and put her on a week of bed-rest, she would not hear of that until she had her writing finished.

On March 16, Scott telegraphed Zelda: "If you can't finish article please send what you have. Love, Scott."[492] Clearly, Zelda's interpreting Scott's attitude as pressure was reasonable; clearly, Scott's calling the piece an article and Zelda's naming it a story suggests that it is one of her last-published light essays for the *New Yorker* or *Esquire*, probably "Show Mr. and Mrs. F ..." Their slight interchange shows how tense all acts of both the Fitzgeralds were.

On March 26, Dr. Slocum writes Scott that Zelda is a good patient; there have been "no episodes of any kind."[493] He orders that she have breakfast in bed, and then a massage and a half-hour rest after that. Zelda protests, however: Slocum reports that she "thinks this is not the way to make good, because she wants to be as active as possible in her work."[494]

During Zelda's first month at Craig House, on March 29, her art exhibit opened in New York. Scott asked Dr. Slocum whether a nurse might bring Zelda into New York (for the opening, for Max Perkins' lunch, and to see her friends who would come to the gallery), and then return with Zelda to Craig House that night by train.[495]

Again, there was a difference of opinion. After her return, Dr. Slocum saw a Zelda who was pleased with the exhibit and the

---

[492] Scott to Zelda, telegram, March 16, 1934, PUL.

[493] Dr. Slocum to Fitzgerald, March 26, 1934, PUL.

[494] Ibid.

[495] Scott to Dr. Slocum, March 22, 1934, PUL.

friends who came,[496] whereas Scott said Zelda seemed "sunk" the day of the exhibit.[497] Slocum disagreed. Then Scott wrote with the suggestion that Zelda be "re-educated" rather than be allowed to rest. His idea was somewhat self-serving, as his letter continued:

my great worry is that time is slipping by, life is slipping by, and we have no life ... her passionate love of life and her absolute inability to meet it, seems so tragic that sometimes it is scarcely to be endured.[498]

To this suggestion, Slocum replied that Zelda was so fatigued that she was not strong enough for intensive therapy. He wants more and more bed-rest for her. He admits to Fitzgerald, however,

I do think, however, that Mrs. Fitzgerald has a leaning toward a feeling of inferiority, which does disturb her. I think that she tries to overcome this by producing something that is worth while and in this effort she became fatigued and most of her reactions ... are distinctly fatigue symptoms.[499]

Unlike the psychiatrists at both Prangins and Phipps, Dr. Slocum of Craig House runs his own ship. Scott's suggestions fall on seemingly impenetrable ears. If Zelda here, as she was at Valmont, strikes a set of trained observers as a woman miserably fatigued (rather than schizophrenic), then years of treatment may have been in error. When the record is studied, the most damaging act of Zelda's pre-breakdown life appears to have been her passionate study of the ballet. If her study is considered "delusional" or "hallucinatory," it may seem a symptom of illness. But if Zelda's aim to succeed as a ballerina is read as

---

[496] Dr. Slocum to Fitzgerald, April 11, 1934, PUL.

[497] Scott to Dr. Slocum, April 8, 1934, PUL.

[498] Ibid.

[499] Slocum to Fitzgerald, April 11, 1934, PUL.

an unusual but possible goal, as the correspondence with both Egorova and Sedova suggests, then her continuing—like her initial—hospitalization is only tragic. How Zelda's dedication to the dance is labeled makes all the difference.

If, as is possible, Zelda was using her clear proficiency in ballet as a way to show Scott that she was a talented woman, as a means of reclaiming her own ability after the years she had devoted herself to him and his professional career, then her behavior makes a great deal of sense. Instead of being delusional, it becomes reasonable.

The third interchange with Dr. Slocum at Craig House comes with Scott's decision to move Zelda away from the luxury and competence of its care, and put her into the larger institutional hospital that abutted their lawn at La Paix. Sheppard and Enoch Pratt Hospital had a good psychiatric program, but like most city hospitals, it was overcrowded. Fitzgerald's embarrassed admission that he could no longer afford Zelda's care at Craig House came in a letter he wrote to Slocum on May 14. (Even though he and Zelda knew long before that date that she was moving out, Scott pretended that the decision had just been taken; he then excused Slocum's not knowing that Zelda was leaving by saying that he had telegraphed Slocum earlier. He probably had not.) What he explained on May 14 was that because there had been no movie rights sold for *Tender Is the Night*, he therefore needed to move Zelda to "a more modest environment."[500]

In his letter, he also asked Dr. Slocum to allow him terms for paying his wife's existing bill at Craig House. He offered to pay "$400 now, $400 next week, and the balance a week after that."

---

[500] Fitzgerald to Slocum, May 14, 1934, PUL.

At $175 a week, very little of Zelda's two-month stay had been paid for.

In his *Ledger*, however, Fitzgerald wrote the word katatonic.[501] Considering the extensive correspondence about Zelda's being moved in order to save money, Fitzgerald's seemingly explanatory *Ledger* entry might be read as misleading.

Zelda was moved to Sheppard and Enoch Pratt Hospital. That facility, while considered excellent, provided few of the luxuries Zelda had grown accustomed to having; it housed between 200 and 300 patients in its mental wards. With one of the ironies that haunted the Fitzgeralds' lives, as Zelda is taken to Sheppard and Enoch Pratt, Scott's *Tender Is the Night* appears on the *New York Times* Best Seller list.

The Years at the Sheppard and Enoch Pratt Hospital

Zelda was treated as all patients were at the Towson, Maryland, institution: an unvarying daily schedule with frequent periods of observation and inspection, meals of wholesome foods, treatment with drugs new to the American market, and the new methodology of shock treatments. From May 19, 1934, to April 7, 1936, Zelda lived in a sternly institutional setting, bothered by noises from the bare-floored corridors and the intrusion of terribly ill—and often sedated—fellow patients. Even though Zelda had earlier told Scott that she was so ill it didn't matter which hospital she was in,[502] she realized after the first body inspection—when her cigarettes, lighter, makeup, and money were taken—that

---

[501] Scott Fitzgerald, F. Scott Fitzgerald's Ledger (1972), p. 188.

[502] Zelda to Scott, May 1934, DS, DZ, p. 196.

she had spoken out of ignorance. She had never been housed in a mental hospital before.

Sheppard and Enoch Pratt had long been considered a premier hospital. Harry Stack Sullivan had done important research there on schizophrenic patients;[503] he was gone, however, and because he had been a hard man to get along with, much of his work was being ignored. He had worked with patients in a private six-bed ward; by 1934, Zelda would be one of her doctor's thirty patients. (In 1934, 369 patients were admitted to the hospital; 373 in 1935.)

Dr. William Elgin was chief of women's services—and Zelda's doctor. With her characteristic quick response to male doctors, Zelda decided she did not like either him or his authority.

She particularly did not like the hospital's practice of giving every admitted patient a thorough physical within 24 hours of his or her arrival, an examination followed within ten days by a comprehensive medical history examination. The reports from "the attending physician, the oculist, dentist, and other specialists" were all placed in the patient's file. Then

as complete a personal history of the patient as securable was taken, including his early environment, family, childhood, and adolescent days. The story of his maturity included domestic life, personal attributes, business activities; and any traumatic events experienced.[504]

It was what historian Bliss Forbush called A "searching investigation."[505]

---

[503] Bliss Forbush, The Sheppard and Enoch Pratt Hospital (1971), pp. 106-7.

[504] Ibid., p. 90.

[505] Ibid.

Only then did treatment begin. "The use of massage, hydrotherapy, light treatment, special exercises, special diet when required, and the application of electricity ... was all a part of the healing process."[506]

During the 1930s, a new part of the healing process was "the use of metrazol as a convulsive treatment, and insulin shock treatment." Reserved for the cases that were considered hopeless, metrazol shock[507] was administered only after letters were sent to the person in charge of the patient's care, asking for permission to use this treatment. Once the family consented, the patient received another thorough physical.

Unfortunately, Zelda was at Sheppard and Enoch Pratt during the years when they experimented with this shock treatment. By 1940 they had stopped its use, realizing that drug therapies "had a similar effect, and were cheaper and less dangerous."

In the Princeton collection of Zelda Fitzgerald's correspondence is a letter to Scott, dictated by Zelda to a friend at Sheppard who is writing for her. Dated February 25, 1935, the letter states that she cannot see because her eyes have "clotted up with blood." ("I hope to be all right soon. Let's hope so. The doctors are doing everything they can do but that isn't much.")[508] She finished a painting of a bunch of tulips while she still had the use of her eyes. She misses him. Zelda's winter was plagued with

506 Ibid.

507 Ibid., p. 123.

508 Zelda to Scott Fitzgerald, February 25, 1935, PUL. "Peggy," the amanuensis, added her note to Scott that Zelda is "getting along really well, when you consider what she's going through." See also Exiles, pp. 214, 275.

general disability, infected fingers, and maladies that only added to her recurring depression, and to her increasing reliance on religion and on the Bible.

In contrast, during the summer and fall before (1934) she had written Scott about playing a lot of tennis, being home-sick for him and Scottie, and taking part in "pea-shelling and singing."[509] Arriving at Sheppard, she had written wryly, "you know this is a very regimented system we live under with every hour accounted for."[510] She also noted, "I'm sad because I can't write."[511]

As with most of her institutionalizations, there were moderate periods and bad ones. For the 1934 Christmas holidays, Zelda was allowed to leave Sheppard to spend time with Scott and Scottie. Unfortunately, Christmas Eve became stressful because Scott had invited Gertrude Stein and Alice Toklas to visit them:[512] they were in Baltimore with Gertrude's maternal relatives, on their triumphal tour that followed Stein's *The Autobiography of Alice B. Toklas*. Some of Zelda's paintings were displayed, and Scott offered any of her choosing to Gertrude. The two which Stein chose—Tulips and Crossing Roses—were favorites of Zelda's too, and she replied that she had earmarked those works as gifts for her doctor. Stein chose a different painting. It is an evening famous for Scott's obsequious behavior to

---

[509] Zelda to Scott, after June 14, 1934, DS, DZ, p. 206.

[510] Ibid., p. 205.

[511] Zelda to Scott, late summer/early fall, 1934, DS, DZ, p. 209.

[512] See Fitzgerald to Stein, December 29, 1934, Scott Fitzgerald, The Letters of F. Scott Fitzgerald (1963), p. 518; Linda Wagner-Martin, "Favored Strangers": Gertrude Stein and Her Family (1995), p. 219.

Stein, and for his putting Zelda's talents on display as a kind of self-aggrandizement.

By the summer of 1935, Zelda wanted out of Sheppard and Enoch Pratt. Whatever the course of her treatment had been, it had brought her at times to speak of—and attempt—suicide: there were periods when she was under constant suicide watches.

Sometimes she saw Scottie, who could bike over from Turnbulls', their neighbors when they were still living at La Paix. She saw Scott rarely: during the summer of 1934, he had begun making North Carolina his homebase, whether Tryon, Asheville, or Hendersonville.

In the summer of 1935, Zelda was allowed to go home to Montgomery to Minnie, but not to be transferred to Highland Hospital in Asheville, North Carolina. During the spring of 1936, that move was accomplished. She was relieved to be in a less regimented care facility, and it had been her assumption that, by being located in western Carolina, she would see Scott more often. Her pique in this undated letter to him, reproduced here in its entirety, shows her disappointment—and also the fact that she has begun writing again.

Dear Scott,

Do as you like about the story: it is perhaps too light to merit the corrections of a famous author. Why don't you just tear it up?

Thanks for the flowers: they are a pretty color. When I liked anything at all I liked yellow. It's so clear.

I don't need anything at all except hope, which I

can't find by looking either backwards or forwards, so I
suppose the thing is to shut my eyes.
  Zelda
  Also, I would like very much to see you to ask you
to arrange some things that are very important, since I
will probably be here a long time. When it is conven-
ient for you, of course.[513]

Zelda Fitzgerald was enough recovered to notice that her
devoted spouse was hardly ever in attendance. She could not
help but be hurt by his absence.

---

[513] Zelda to Scott, Summer, 1936, PUL.

TWELVE - The Crack-Up, 1936

The statement is sometimes made that Zelda Fitzgerald wrote no letters during most of her time in the Sheppard and Enoch Pratt Hospital. The implication of that conjecture is that she was mired in such depression and madness that her normal patterns of reaching out to Scott, to Scottie, and to her mother had disintegrated.

One of the problems with accepting this concept—besides the obvious fact that letters from Zelda at Sheppard to Scott do exist—is that it allows the years 1934, 1935, and 1936 to disappear from the Fitzgeralds' short history. Given Scott's debacle of drinking, having affairs, worrying about his health, and lying to his publishers and friends, the relative oblivion of those years in published accounts is kind. But the months of the summer of 1934 and 1935 cannot be expunged from the record because, even if Zelda were safe within the walls of Sheppard and Enoch Pratt, Scott was not. The experiences he had during Zelda's years of hospitalization in Baltimore are what led to his writing "The Crack-Up" essays for *Esquire*; they probably also contributed to his death.

Memoirs of F. Scott Fitzgerald during these mid-1930s years are plentiful. Whether written by Laura Guthrie Hearn, Dorothy Parker, Caresse Crosby, or Tony Buttitta, they show a man so wrecked by drinking and depression that his behavior is hard to fathom. When he seeks out the young Buttitta in his basement bookshop in Asheville's George Vanderbilt Hotel, Fitzgerald is searching for a friend. For Buttitta, who had previously thought that going to Chapel Hill and drinking with a few of the students and teachers at University of North Carolina was literary mecca, his hours with Fitzgerald in the summer of 1935 were unbelievably significant. Of course he kept a journal—not only of the important author's drunken escapades, but also of his opinions about other writers, books, life in New York, and his own personal history.

It is in Buttitta's memoir that the reader finds Scott admitting the way he taunted Zelda to make something of her talents ("I can be a bastard when it comes to taunting and accusing people"[514]), and his hypothesis that Isadora Duncan's unexpected death sent Zelda back to her passion for ballet ("Isadora was an extraordinary woman. One in the limelight, one she [Zelda] would like to have been. Isadora did it on her own. It was Zelda's insane wish to do the same. Replace Isadora now that she was dead, and outshine me at the same time."[515]) It is also in this memoir that Fitzgerald recalls the horror of Zelda's long bout of eczema in Prangins.[516]

---

[514] Quoted by Tony Buttitta, The Lost Summer, A Personal Memoir ([1974] 1987), pp. 122-3.

[515] Ibid., p. 129.

[516] Ibid., p. 122.

Buttitta also tells the story of Fitzgerald's sexual relationship with a mulatto prostitute[517] from the Asheville area, and recounts that woman's assessment of whatever difficulties Scott had experienced during intercourse. But once Scott began an affair with a married woman who was staying at the Grove Park Inn, as he was, his dependence on Buttitta as a confidant lessened. It is in the journal of his interim secretary, Laura Hearn,[518] that the vivid history of his sexual impropriety is recorded. Hearn also records Fitzgerald's attempts to stop drinking by replacing his customary gin with extravagant numbers of beers—sometimes thirty—each day. The details of Fitzgerald's North Carolina life illustrate the discrete summary Scott Donaldson chooses to give in his biography:

In the decade after Zelda's breakdown in 1930 he attracted the love and admiration of many women, including members of two particular professions. "Excepting for trained nurses," as he observed in one of his last stories, "an actress is the easiest prey for an unscrupulous male." It was a generalization based on experience. As his health declined and he tried to dry out from drinking, Fitzgerald frequently required nursing—in Baltimore, in Asheville, and in Hollywood.[519]

The usual practice in writing about Scott Fitzgerald, however, is less to rehearse the experiences of a man who was for many years an alcoholic—with all the failures of morality and conscience that term implies—than to chart his life as author, even through the very years which showed him at his professional nadir.

---

[517] Ibid., pp. 113, 132, 135, 172-73.

[518] Laura Guthrie Hearn, "A Summer with F. Scott Fitzgerald," Esquire 62, 1964, p. 162.

[519] Donaldson, Fool, pp. 58-9.

Much of what Fitzgerald wrote between the publication of *Tender Is the Night* in 1934 and his death in 1940 was failed work. Many of his stories did not find publishers, even with Ober's assiduous efforts: at least some of the Count Philippe series, the Gwen stories, the Basil and Josephine stories, and the various rewrites of stories from the 1920s, or of the Fitzgeralds' lives from those years (that is, "Image in the Heart," the Zelda-Jozan story, "a chaste liaison," published in *McCalls*, 1936). Yet as Jennifer McCabe Atkinson points out, "between 1931 and 1939, he wrote and published 48 stories ... Even the slim years were not bone dry."[520]

Fitzgerald's turn to the essay was itself not unusual: he and Zelda both had been glad to supplement his income from fiction by writing nonfiction for any market available. Much of the disillusion that seemed to surprise readers by the time of "The Crack-Up" essays in 1936 had been in evidence at least a decade earlier ("Does a Moment of Revolt Come Sometime to Every Married Man" [*McCalls*, March, 1924];—"Why Blame it on the Poor Kiss if the Girl Veteran of Many Petting Parties is Prone to Affairs After Marriage?" [New York American, February 24, 1924]; "What Kind of Husbands Do Jimmies' Make?" [Baltimore American, March 30, 1924]). The fact that Scott Fitzgerald was willing to write at all for the new low-paying magazine *Esquire* showed his desperation:[521] for the standard fee of $250 an essay, he gave Arnold Gingrich prose that was, eventually, to be considered some of his best work.

---

[520] Jennifer McCabe Atkinson, "Lost and Unpublished Stories," Fitzgerald/Hemingway Annivii, 1977.

[521] Stephen W. Potts, The Price of Paradise (1993), pp. 43, 91.

Collected throughout his notebooks, too, were the kind of often anguished statements that readers claimed not to recognize when they read the essays. For instance, Fitzgerald on gender:

When I like men I want to be like them—I want to lose the outer qualities that give me my individuality and he like them. I don't want the man [sic] *I want to absorb into myself all the qualities that make him attractive and leave him out ... When I like women I want to own them, to dominate them, to have them admire me.*[522]

For the Fitzgerald in the notebooks, ownership was visceral: "The feeling that she was (his) began between his shoulders and spread over him like a coat going on."[523] Once man and woman comprise a family, however, Fitzgerald assesses:

Family quarrels are bitter things. They don't go according to any rules. They're not like aches or wounds; they're more like splits in the skin that won't heal because there's not enough material.[524]

"The Crack-Up," February, March, April, 1936

It is this sense of imagery that Fitzgerald, living in relative poverty in a Hendersonville, North Carolina, hotel, brings to his *Esquire* essays. The first of these essays creates the drama of the author's possible illness: "I had sat in the office of a great doctor and listened to a grave sentence."[525] The next paragraphs describe his search for solitude, for an acute loneliness: he wanted his time to himself. The mastery of Fitzgerald's prose comes in the two quick reversals:

---

[522] Scott Fitzgerald, The Notebooks of F Scott Fitzgerald (1980), p. 146.

[523] Ibid., p. 172.

[524] Ibid., p. 192.

[525] Scott Fitzgerald "The Crack-Up," The Crack-Up (1945), p. 71.

—And then suddenly, surprisingly, I got better.

—And cracked like an old plate as soon as I heard the news.[526]

The reader goes from sorrow to joy, and then to stunned disbelief. The strong narrative pull of this inward-turning prose takes the reader from the opening calm abstractions over an emotional precipice. Into even the most ordered life, such an explosion may come.

Fitzgerald's cracked plate became the touchstone image for his seemingly inexplicable crash—and for the two essays that followed. It was one of his gifts as writer that many readers—Gertrude Stein and Edith Wharton among them—appreciated. Rather than the self-consciously spare, terse, rhythms of a Hemingway paragraph, Fitzgerald's deft sequences of often poetic words kept the reader with him.

"That is the real end of this story," he announces, but then he writes for another three full pages. Recognition of his disaffected moods and his hopeless outlook carries the reader past any kind of literal identification into a kind of subversive empathy. When the author's energetic friend advises him to "Buck up" and stop feeling sorry for himself, we readers behave like he does: we dislike her and all her energy. We disdain to ask her for any of her vitality. We stand, with Scott Fitzgerald, holding a similar "tin cup of self-pity"—and walking "very carefully like cracked crockery."[527]

Fitzgerald opens the second essay, "Pasting It Together," which appeared in the March, 1936, *Esquire*, by listing some uses for the cracked plate, assuming it has been kept in the pantry. The

---

[526] Ibid., p. 72.

[527] Ibid., p. 74.

early turn in this piece comes as he titles the later pages, "a cracked plate's further history." It is here that he joins the plate metaphor with the subdued tones of the dark night of the soul. When it is three o'clock in the morning, even small problems loom large and, in the author's accepting words,

in a real dark night of the soul it is always three o'clock in the morning, day after day.[528]

What the numbness of this pain of understanding has brought him to is withdrawal, "a vast irresponsibility toward every obligation, a deflation of all my values."[529] In this well of both apathy and silence, the author moves on to the third essay, "Handle With Care."

According to the essay, some of his spirit was creeping back. He felt forced into a search for meaning. On a "harassed and despairing night,"[530] he traveled a thousand miles, looking for space to think about "why I had developed a sad attitude toward sadness, a melancholy attitude toward melancholy and a tragic attitude toward tragedy—why I had become identified with the objects of my horror or compassion." For him, his "self-immolation was something sodden-dark."[531] With Swiftian irony, Fitzgerald despairs of being an admirable whole man; he is content to be only a writer. Relinquishing a bevy of aims, that writer also has come to accept the premise that "the natural state of the sentient adult is a qualified unhappiness."[532]

---

[528] "Pasting It Together," The Crack-Up, p. 75.

[529] Ibid., p. 78.

[530] "Handle With Care," The Crack-Up, p. 80.

[531] Ibid., pp. 80-1.

[532] Ibid., p. 84.

Fitzgerald's cracked plate and three o'clock dark took on somber life as images of the Great Depression, where cultural promise had met with only resistance, and lives felt truncated, blocked, even while they continued.

For one of the first times in his writing career, Fitzgerald appeared to be speaking in a voice other than his own.

People read the essays. Hemingway wrote to Max Perkins about them—several times—objecting to Fitzgerald's confessional mode;[533] Dos Passos lamented his publishing the essays at all. When James Laughlin at *New Directions Press* later asked Edmund Wilson to edit a Fitzgerald commemorative, he suggested that the nucleus of the collection be the three "Crack-Up" essays. In retrospect, in 1945, Dos Passos remarked "how well those articles read that annoyed me so ... [how] reasoned and deliberate"[534] they were.

Critic Marc Dolan emphasizes in his *Modern Lives, A Cultural Re-reading of "The Lost Generation"* how central both Fitzgerald's essays and Zelda's were. One of his points is that while much of the Fitzgeralds' nonfiction was designed to increase their celebrity, "The Crack-Up" essays were unusually impersonal. (In contrast, Zelda's last two published essays—both of which appeared under Zelda and Scott's joint by-line—made the opposite move, into the very personal. "Show Mr. and Mrs. F. to Number—" appeared in *Esquire* for May-June, 1934, after Zelda finished writing it at Craig House; "Auction—Model 1934"—a literal ragbag

[533] Scott Donaldson, Hemingway vs. Fitzgerald (1999), pp. 194-200.

[534] John Dos Passos to Edmund Wilson, July 19, 1945, John Dos Passos, Fourteenth Chronicle (1973), p. 533.

of pieces of the couple's lives—was published in *Esquire* in July.) Dolan's comment about "The Crack-Up" essays is that they are strangely unpopulated. Neither the author's wife nor his child is mentioned: instead he clearly situates himself alone in the small Southern town. Yet it is at this period in Fitzgerald's history that he is realizing the great, and permanent, loss of Zelda. (As George Jean Nathan was later to write, "Zelda's illness left Scott in a state from which he never fully recovered."[535])

For Dolan, like Alfred Kazin and Robert Sklar, Fitzgerald's seemingly disclosive essays, then, can be seen as highly fictional: "battlegrounds between self-creation and self-confession."[536] For John W. Crowley, both Fitzgerald's essays and *Tender Is the Night* must be named "the locus classicus of American drunk narratives" with their plot being "a drunkard's tragic downfall."[537] In the case of the essays, Crowley contends, information is withheld; instead of a confession, the essays become apologia, and ask the reader to participate in a game of discovery.[538] For Michael Nowlin, writing more directly about the mental patient covered with eczema in *Tender Is the Night*, the information being withheld may have less to do with drinking than with the male ego's frustration with domineering, emasculating women. As he notes, "The female artist-figure signifies the consequences of refusing the

---

[535] George Jean Nathan, "Memories of Fitzgerald, Lewis and Dreiser," Esquire, October, 1958, p. 149.

[536] Marc Dolan, Modern Lives (1996), pp. 142, 146.

[537] John W. Crowley, The White Logic, Alcoholism and Gender (1994), p. 67.

[538] Ibid., p. 71.

ethos of feminization. Unlike Rosemary and Nicole, she was not 'happy to exist in a man's world.'"[539] One might return to Fitzgerald's own disclosive paragraph in his *Notebooks*:

Once when you were strong, you gave me the luxury of loving you most, of even being cruel in a small little vain or impartial way. When you were weak, you came to me, nosing into my arms like a puppy. But later it was different. You used your strong times to edge away from me—break out a new world of your own where I was excluded. Your weak times belonged to me, but you had forgotten all the words that had melted me.[540]

The fantasy that Scott was Zelda's primary caretaker, and that she was his, continued.

After "The Crack-Up"

Zelda was moved to Highland Hospital in April, 1936, but settling into Dr. Robert Carroll's routine took some time. Much of the seventy patients' days were built around physical exercise, culminating in their taking a hike of several miles up the mountain. Gorgeous as the North Carolina spring could be, learning to participate in all the physical routines of Highland was difficult. And there were experimentations with medication, and shock treatments.

Scott had had to stay in the Baltimore area to help care for his mother, who had suffered a stroke. He asked the Ohers to be Scottie's guardians so she could use their home, and their care, as an interim center for her life (she was to board at the

---

[539] Michael Nowlin, -The World's Rarest Work,- College Literature, 25 (1998), p. 72.

[540] Scott Fitzgerald, The Notebooks of F. Scott Fitzgerald (1980), pp. 318-19.

Ethel Walker School in Connecticut in the fall).[541] When he did move to Asheville in July, he broke his shoulder diving into the Grove Park Inn pool. The bad break necessitated a waist to fingertip cast, and caused him a miserable summer and fall; when his mother died in September, he was so incapacitated he could not travel to her funeral.

Part of the time at Highland, Zelda was thriving—hiking, playing tennis and hall, painting, writing, recapturing her enjoyment in the beauty of the Smoky Mountains which she had loved as a child in Saluda. As she became comfortable with this more individualized treatment plan, despite Dr. Carroll's continuation of shock therapy, her religious mania began to diminish: she turned back to her painting. During her early months of care at Highland, Zelda wrote to Scottie,

As a painter, I experiment in achieving all color values by the juxtaposition of red, blue and yellow—which are the three primaries. It's more fun to be a painter with five little pots of paint than to own a great many tubes of shades which I contend can be rendered by rhythms and placement of the primaries ...[542]

Whether or not her daughter was interested enough in art to understand how radical Zelda's approach was, in the opening of her letter is a series of visuals she evokes for Scottie:

I love Christmas. There's a cold and silver Christmas of ice and starlight and light blue and laurel that I have painted and Christmas of the Holy Lands of aureoles of dust and olive trees and the holiness of eternity and there is Christmas of our story books of bright red mittens and of holly.

---

[541] DS, DZ, pp. 219-20 (editors' notes).

[542] Zelda Fitzgerald to Scottie, undated, PUL.

It is in what might be called the eye of Zelda's painterly imagination that she seems to have become a painter who not only paints but who thinks like one who paints. At Highland, Zelda had found encouragement beneath its institutional regime, an encouragement that allowed her to find her own way of seeing, and being in, the world.

In other respects, however, moving to Highland was a disappointment. She saw her mother and her sisters, but she seldom saw Scott. Once his mother's estate was settled, he sent her some unexpected money for which she thanked him, saying she would buy a decent suit. But even with Zelda in Asheville and Scott living in a cheap hotel in Tryon, North Carolina, their paths seldom crossed. Part of the explanation was that—despite Scott's illnesses and broken shoulder—he had never stopped drinking.

Both Matthew J. Bruccoli and Scott Donaldson note Fitzgerald's desperate maneuvers to hide that fact.[543] After two bouts of delirium tremens in 1934, he had written less often to either Perkins or Ober about his health: he sometimes hired trained nurses to help him avoid alcohol. Then, in the autumn of 1936, a few months after "The Crack-Up" essays, journalist Michel Mok published a damning four-page interview with Fitzgerald in the *New York Post*: Mok had come to North Carolina around the time of Scott's fortieth birthday, and Fitzgerald—medicated and drinking—had given Mok fuel for his harsh piece, which ran under the headline "The Other Side of Paradise/ Scott Fitzgerald, 40/ Engulfed in Despair …"

---

[543] SSEG, p. 410; Donaldson, Hemingway vs. Fitzgerald, pp. 235, 237; DS, DZ, p. 235, editors' notes.

Horrified with the portrait when it appeared, Fitzgerald unsuccessfully overdosed on morphine, his suicide attempt existing only in his letters.

One of the most egregious displays of his drunkenness occurred later in 1936 at a Christmas tea dance he gave for his daughter in Baltimore: although Scott was so drunk everyone could see his condition, he insisted on dancing with Scottie's girlfriends. Then he abruptly sent everyone home, and soon checked himself into a hospital to dry out. Scottie went by train to stay with Zelda in North Carolina.[544]

Fitzgerald's writing continued to suffer. He felt great relief when friends vouched for his state of mind and health so that MGM offered him $1000 a week for a six-month contract, beginning in July of 1937. Except for vacations with Zelda and Scottie, after the summer of 1937 Fitzgerald's trips back east were rare: it was as if his existence had become something other than that of Scott Fitzgerald, husband and father. And even as Zelda continued to write letters to him saying that she missed him, both she and Scottie gradually made new lives for themselves.

The Last Scott-and-Zelda Stories

Living in Hollywood and soon involved with Sheilah Graham, a divorced London chorus girl now turned gossip columnist, Fitzgerald worked on what were considered important screenplays and good movie scripts. MGM renewed his contract in December, 1937, and raised his weekly salary to $1250.[545] He had money to repay his borrowings, although he did not succeed

---

[544] Sally Cline, Zelda Fitzgerald (2003), p. 363.

[545] Ibid., p. 456 and see p. 367.

in doing that. (Bruccoli estimates that his work in Hollywood garnered $85,000, on which he paid modest income taxes.[546] He had money for vacations with Zelda, and occasionally with both Zelda and Scottie. From Highland Hospital, Zelda traveled alone—to visit her mother in Saluda and Montgomery, to visit Rosalind in Manhattan—and with Dr. and Mrs. Carroll, once for three weeks to Sarasota, Florida, so she could take art classes. But traveling with Scott meant that she once again assumed the role of his needy, dependent wife.

Two of the Fitzgeralds' last vacations were particularly disastrous. The last family trip, in March 1938,[547] was Scott's taking Zelda and Scottie to Virginia Beach and then to visit relatives in Norfolk. Zelda and Scottie argued; Scott drank and became so abusive that Zelda reported him to the hotel manager before she returned—alone—to Asheville. (A few months later, Zelda traveled east for Scottie's graduation from the Ethel Walker School; Scott did not attend, but he funded Zelda's and her sister Rosalind's trip to Connecticut.)

The last Scott and Zelda trip was in April 1939,[548] and it was made at Zelda's suggestion—that she and Scott go to Cuba. Scott was on edge because MGM had dropped his contract after he had traveled to Dartmouth with the young writer Budd Schulberg, drunk the entire time (Schulberg's novel *The Disenchanted* is a fictionalized version of the debacle).

Back in California, worried about money and the prospect of

---

[546] SSEG, p. 450.

[547] Ibid., p. 367; DS, DZ, p. 367, editors' notes.

[548] Cline, Zelda Fitzgerald pp. 367-8; DS, DZ, p. 369, editors' notes; SSEG, pp. 446, 450-2.

having to support himself by freelancing, Scott had a terrible row with Sheilah, threatening her with a revolver. He also gave her a check for 2000, as if he were paying her off. From that scene, he flew east to meet Zelda; he arrived in North Carolina drunk. Once they were in Cuba, Scott kept drinking and eventually got into a fight. Zelda arranged their transport back to New York, where she—with the help of Clotilde and John Palmer—got him safely into a hospital. After borrowing money from friends, she returned, quietly and alone, to Asheville.

It was another Fitzgerald story buried under layers of silence.

It was also the last time she and Scott were to see each other.

THIRTEEN - Endings

F. Scott Fitzgerald, April 1939 to December 1940

With the survival instinct that had saved him at other times during the 1930s, Scott Fitzgerald realized once he returned to California that he had reached bottom. If he was ever going to write seriously again, he must act to save himself. Accordingly, he hired the young, inexperienced (and, luckily for him, talented) Frances Kroll as his secretary. By mid-summer, he was at work on the manuscript which would become *The Last Tycoon*, the story of the brilliant Irving Thalberg, Hollywood novice who had yet won through to phenomenal success on sheer talent.[549]

Kroll's unflinching memoir of the last year and a half of Fitzgerald's life shows the way the role of writer served as a catalyst for the man's increasingly fragmented personality. When Scott is writing well, dictating to Frances, pacing the room in his worn bathrobe, he can control his drinking, to some extent. After he is reconciled with Sheilah, he can assume some stability,

---

[549] SSEG, pp. 462-4; see chart SSEG, p. 474.

although much of Frances' work consists of doing errands that relate to Sheilah or to Scottie (whom he is to see only once more in his lifetime), and more rarely to Zelda. Seldom driving, inclined to feed his damaged physical system on sweets and the fudge he cooked for himself in the kitchen,[550] Scott saw his body generally give way. In Kroll's words,

Yet, Scott was a writer—always. That's all he wanted to be. His hope was to attain a measure of immortality in the literary world and that stubborn objective repeated itself throughout his lifetime.[551]

Krill also makes vivid how little Scott could actually work. His energy had been depleted in parallel with his physical deterioration and his nerves were sapped with his belief that his incipient tuberculosis had returned; therefore, he planned carefully for even a few hours of writing time during a day.

Life kept interrupting his work. In the spring of 1939, Scottie feared she had appendicitis, and from California Scott supervised the doctors' appointments and plans for a possible surgery. Zelda, along with her family, badgered Scott to allow her to be released from Highland Hospital. Finally, after months of letters—particularly between Scott and Dr. Carroll, Scott and Zelda, Scott and Minnie, and Dr. Carroll and Minnie[552]—Zelda was released to live—not independently, as she had asked,

---

[550] Robert Westbrook, Intimate Lies (1995), p. 249; Frances Kroll Ring, Against the Current (1985), p. 41.

[551] Kroll Ring, Against the Current, p. 37; this memoir became the text for the 2001 film, Last Call.

[552] As Carroll wrote to Zelda's mother, "The facts remain unchanged-that she [Zelda] has been mentally injured, that her central nervous system is peculiarly susceptible." PUL.

but with her mother in the small house on Sayre Street in Montgomery. One of the saddest letters she was to receive was Scott's directive that, upon her leaving Highland, she not come to California but rather that she go to her mother's.[553]

Admitting that their marriage now existed in name only, Scott had months before sworn his daughter to secrecy about Sheilah.[554] Despite his sometimes violent behavior to her, and his anti-Semitic insults when he called her Lily Shiel, Scott seemed to realize that her love for him was to be valued.

Scott's Encino household also included a cook and, at times, a nurse. In the year and a half that Kroll records, Scott clearly tried to bring his life under control. Parts of the Monroe Stahr novel were written; some sections were fully developed. But by May of 1940, Scott knew he could no longer live in a remote location. He moved into an upper-floor flat at 1402 North Laurel in Hollywood near Sheilah's apartment on North Hayward.[555] In November, in Schwab's drugstore, he had a frightening coronary attack and was ordered on bed-rest. To avoid the stairs at his address, he moved into Sheilah's first-floor apartment. On December 19, he wrote Zelda and sent her a small Christmas check.[556] Another attack occurred on December 20; and on December 21, 1940, Scott Fitzgerald died.

The first of his Princeton friends to publish a novel, the first to marry, the first to live entirely on the income from his

---

[553] SSEG, p. 81.

[554] See ibid., p. 488.

[555] Ibid., pp. 483-4.

[556] DS, DZ, pp. 382-3.

writing, Fitzgerald was also the first to die. He was only three months past his forty-fourth birthday.

Zelda Sayre Fitzgerald as Widow

Zelda, living in Montgomery, was notified of Scott's death in time to help John Biggs, the executor of the estate, decide on the burial location and the service. As she later wrote to Frances Kroll, who with typical efficiency and tact had taken care of everything connected with having Scott's body moved east to Bethesda, Maryland, vacating the apartment, and following the instructions which Biggs sent her, "Though I knew that he was ill, his death was a complete shock to me, and so heart-breaking that I am inadequate to his last necessity for me."[557]

As her letter made clear, Zelda was unable to attend Scott's burial in the Episcopal cemetery in Rockville; she asked Newman Smith to represent her and her family, and she sent pink gladioli. That she knew her life would be vastly different without the support, the income, or the pressures to conform to that relentless role of Mrs. Scott Fitzgerald seemed clear in her notes to the people who did carry the burden of Scott's funeral—the Ohers, the Perkinses, the Turnhulls, the Murphys, the Biggses, Ludlow Fowler, and of course Scottie.[558]

Although it took several years, Zelda eventually got a monthly check of slightly under $50 from the annuity John Biggs purchased for her from her share of Scott's estate, something a bit over $44,000.[559] She received $35 a month from

---

[557] Included in Kroll Ring, Against the Current, pp. 120-1; also PUL.

[558] Milford, p. 350; SSEG, pp. 488-9.

[559] SSEG, p. 489.

veterans benefits. Because Biggs did his work for the next decade without a fee, Zelda and Scottie were supported by the small estate as much as they possibly could have been.[560] In the words of Biggs' biographer, the Judge spent the decade "trying to be Zelda's informal guardian ... father surrogate to ... Scottie ... and literary executor."[561]

Zelda was often impatient with her small income, with her mother's fussing over her and her activities, with her inability to travel—and she was sometimes less than a model convalescing adult (and Minnie's youngest child). Zelda and Scott's daughter Scottie once told a biographer what the strain of dealing with Zelda as convalescent was like:

She would start out her old self, charming, gay and witty, but after we had gone shopping and had lunch and perhaps gone swimming in the afternoon ... she would start to slide visibly out of the exterior world into her own interior one and this was very upsetting.[562]

Minnie Sayre kept Zelda as comfortable as she could, but the small house was confining, and some days were not conducive to Zelda's working in the garden. The outdoors was Zelda's place—she prayed and read near the flowers; later, she wrote Ludlow Fowler that she kept "a cage of doves who sing and woo the elements."[563] As her mother told a friend, "Flowers were Zelda's hobby ... she worked off nervous attacks in her flower garden."[564] Aside from her life with Minnie, Zelda occasionally

---

[560] Seymour Toll, A Judge Uncommon (1993) , pp. 183-4.

[561] Ibid.

[562] S, p. 86.

[563] Zelda Fitzgerald to Ludlow Fowler, PUL.

[564] Minnie Sayre to Mrs. John R. Raimey, PUL.

went out with women she had grown up with; other of her Montgomery friends visited; Scottie (and then Scottie's husband, Jack, and then Tim, their first child) visited, as did her sisters Clotilde and Rosalind. For the most part, however, Zelda led a life so quiet that one day was indistinguishable from the next.

She sketched. She painted. Then she painted over those canvases, or sometimes donated her finished paintings to be used for their canvas—other practicing artists were instructed to paint over her work. She drew; she did watercolors. During 1942, she had several exhibitions of her work in Montgomery, one at the Museum of Fine Arts, another at the Woman's Club.[565] Of the several assessments of Zelda's art, one of the most cogent is that of art historian Jane S. Livingston, who takes all of Zelda's work seriously—paintings, gouaches, drawings, paper dolls. She sees this medium as the one in which Zelda continued to study, learn, and practice. Despite the large quantities of her work lost in fires—the 1933 fire at La Paix as well as the Highland Hospital fire in 1948, and the destruction of other paintings, perhaps by Zelda's hand or by her sister's—Livingston concludes that Zelda as graphic artist "had a kind of supernally *innate*, and fecund, giftedness."[566]

Added to Livingston's assessment must be the quality Zelda often evinced, of seeing life around her with a painterly eye. Her fiction and her essays are often suffused with concrete description, much of it spatial; and they are just as regularly heightened with details of color. From her unpublished manuscript headed "Notes for a Calendar," for example, Zelda evokes the dying autumn:

---

[565] Milford, p. 369.

[566] Jane S. Livingston, "On the Art of Zelda Fitzgerald," in *Zelda*, p. 78.

The world is bare and musical for Thanksgiving; brown leaves play quietude across a heaven strung with bare gray trees.

The world is expensive in November; there should be intricacies of chrysanthemums and the associational beauty of amber and quiet amber wines and Chinese odors symbolized in amber; amber for appraisal ...[567]

She concludes the vignette by calling this glimpse of fall "a still life."

In contrast to the gray tones of November, Zelda notes, "September's a browner month" and as she meditates about picking apples "from a rusted mountain top," she accents the scene with "purple asters" used to "deepen" the horizons.

Throughout her many notes for ballet configurations—colors coupled with stage decor—Zelda repeats this combination of shape and shading. On a sheet labeled "Design for the Ballet," she draws a silver-blue spire, its height intersecting with a line marked "white/ gratitude" and the caption "black metallic" listed below the horizontal line. The page is headed "God is the Perfect Comprehension."[568]

Zelda Fitzgerald as Writer

To Livingston's conclusion that Zelda was most talented and proficient as a graphic artist, the biographer must point to the equally impressive quantity of Zelda's writing. Whether in unpublished essays, letters, and lost stories or in the published oeuvre, Zelda's writing consistently shows her almost invincible ease with language. She wrote authoritatively to Scott about

---

[567] Zelda Fitzgerald, "Notes for a Calendar," PUL.

[568] Zelda Fitzgerald, PUL.

the artists she admired (saying of Picasso that "his work is an idea, not a painting"[569]); she wrote, from Prangins, that Scott needed to send her something to read besides Joyce ("Not in French, since I have enough difficulty with English for the moment and not Lawrence and not Virginia Woolf or anybody who writes by dipping the broken threads of their heads into the ink of literary history"[570]): Zelda was astute in her opinions and her self-assessments, and confident in her expression of them. In one unpublished essay from the Princeton archive, for example, she wrote about the way such American writers as Frank Norris, Theodore Dreiser, Sinclair Lewis, Sherwood Anderson, "and all sorts of authors in Scribners Magazine and the American Mercury" had taken as their subject "the undistinguished, the banal, the blatantly uninteresting."[571] If this approach to the realistic was new, she in contrast would create something more challenging.

In Zelda's writing of the later 1920s, her own highly descriptive stories of young America's women began to form a collective portrait of characters usually written about—even by Scott Fitzgerald—stereotypically. Scott himself recognized the value and the originality in her *College Humor* pieces, advising her shortly after her third breakdown that she should compile a collection of the stories. In his letter of June 13, 1934,[572] he suggested *Eight Women* as a possible title for the manuscript of 50,000 words; he would write an introduction for the book.

---

[569] Zelda to Scott, DS,DZ, p. 152.

[570] Zelda to Scott, DS, DZ, p. 102.

[571] Zelda Fitzgerald, untitled, PUL.

[572] Scott to Zelda, DS, DZ, pp. 203-4.

In Zelda's reply, she thought *Eight Women* "is too big a steal from Dreiser [referring to his 1919 *Twelve Men*]." Instead, she suggested *Girl Friends*. Again, Zelda knew what she liked, and could support her choices. She wrote in that same letter, making reference to the continuing Aristotelian wisdom that "all emotions and all experience were common property" but saying that, in her words, "the transposition of these into form was individual and art."[573] Zelda then broke away idiomatically, and conveyed some of her own aesthetic questions:

But, God, it's so involved by whether you aim at direct or indirect appeals and whether the emotional or the cerebral is the most compelling approach, and whether the shape of the edifice or the purpose for which it is designated is paramount ... At any rate, it seems to me the artists business is to take a willing mind and guide it to hope or despair contributing not his interpretations but a glimpse of his honestly earned scars of battle and his rewards.[574]

Then, to conclude this unusually abstract commentary, Zelda made a strangely isolated reference to *Save Me the Waltz*, her first novel which had brought such trouble to the Fitzgeralds' already troubled marriage. She wrote: "That was what I was trying to accomplish with the book I began: I wanted to say 'This is a love story—maybe not your love story—maybe not even mine, but this is what happened to one isolated person in love. *There is no judgment*'" [italics this author's].[575]

Despite the apparent strength of Zelda's aesthetic convictions, the Fitzgeralds' history shows that she did not publish

---

[573] Zelda to Scott, DS, DZ, p. 206.

[574] Ibid., p. 205.

[575] Ibid., p. 206.

Girl Friends, nor did she manage to write a second novel. On a personal level, Zelda had been terribly scarred by her husband's reaction to her writing *Save Me the Waltz*; even *Scandalabra* was a somewhat desperate risk. She had originally taken Fitzgerald at his encouraging best: he had said that he wanted her to become a successful writer. Writing *Save Me the Waltz* was her effort to find wholeness in her own persona. But that effort only angered Scott. According to psychologist Elizabeth Waites, Zelda's accomplishment in the novel was that she had written "seriously and in depth about her own life."[576] She had, in effect, claimed that life as her own, an action which threatened Fitzgerald both as writer and as man.

The Story of *Caesar's Things*

Several of the Fitzgeralds' biographers[577] have suggested that the novel Zelda wanted to work on at both Phipps Clinic and Craig House was *Caesar's Things*, the fragmentary manuscript now in the Princeton archive. Internal evidence has long proved that text to be a product of the 1940s, a book Zelda began only after Scott's death. Even though in 1934 Scott was encouraging Zelda to publish the story collection, there is no answer extant to her question to him about whether or not she was allowed to write a novel, since his *Tender Is the Night* had finally appeared. She was obviously assuming that her proposed novel about madness could no longer use up the material he had wanted to keep for his 1934 novel.

---

[576] Elizabeth A. Waites, "The Princess in the Tower: Zelda Fitzgerald's Creative Impasse," Journal of the American Psychiatric Association, 34:3, 1986, p. 658.

[577] Sally Cline, Zelda Fitzgerald (2003), p. 326; Milford, p. 261; SSEG, p. 347.

What exists of *Caesar's Things* is, however, not "about insanity." The novel Zelda wanted to write during the 1930s was probably about the great dancer, Nijinsky, and his madness. In creating this book, she would once again have been able to represent the worlds she knew so intimately—that of professional ballet, one of the clear successes of her *Save Me the Waltz*—as well as the painful existence of mental breakdown. By transferring her autobiographical experiences to a character who was male, Russian, and famous, she could draw on her own life in disguise; she could engage in a kind of artistic self protection.

Perhaps part of the difficulty Zelda had with the later manuscript she called *Caesar's Things* was trying to repress the memory of Scott's anger over her first novel. It was many months after his death before she began the novel; she could not get past the memory of his censure, his hostility, his contempt for her efforts. Even as she wrote to their friend Margaret Turnbull that she was beginning a novel, the description of it as a book about religious belief—with "the thematic intent of inducting the Biblical patterns of life into its everyday manifestations"[578]— was inaccurate. Although she spoke of her trouble organizing the work, one might assume she had written very little of it.

Once she did begin the novel, it is evident that she found herself back in the very personal territory she had explored in *Save Me the Waltz*. One might say that the story of the last seven years of Zelda's life accrues in the fragments of the book she called *Caesar's Things*, marking the division by her choice of title between the seemingly valued things of the materialistic world and the truly valuable elements of the spiritual world.

---

[578] Zelda Fitzgerald to Margaret Turnbull (1941), PUL.

The spiritual, however, is captured through the calm nostalgia of an earlier Montgomery, Alabama, a place where the fictional narrator could remember,

When I was little there … admonitory hedges fenced the personal rights of the citizenry. Cotton was sold in the public square on Saturdays and wine dispensed from cubby-holes under the rickety iron stair-ways and bunting-strung balconies of downtown stores … Debutante young men made overtures of gala traditions to a waltz-time world; existence was charming.[579]

What Zelda values most is the fact that

There was so much time in the world. Girls polished their shoes and watched their hair drying in the sun and clothed the summer afternoons in organdy … the town swam with story.

Much of the novel is disproportionately about the childhood of Janno [the Zelda character]:

We played out in the twilight under the arc-lights and the dusty moon, planning poetically and harmoniously through the mystery and reverence of the haunted moths-shattered hours after supper. We made clover chains under the sycamore in the sandy rutted alley and told the passing season on the fading of sickly-sweet summer vines.

While elements of racially mixed Montgomery are visible, there are only a few places where black life seems threatening— Janno alone by the railroad tracks, Janno alone near the hospital. When Zelda draws scenes of fear, she uses a dreamlike effect: is her recreation of possible sexual threat based on what she has learned in treatment about the importance of recalling dreams, or is she softening memories she has previously worked to repress?

---

[579] Caesar's Things (manuscript, PUL); all further references from this text; no page numbers available.

That many of the scenes which differ from the materials she used in *Save Me the Waltz*—often, scenes that make Janno vulnerable rather than aggressively in charge—are unfinished in the manuscript suggests Zelda's inability to polish them. Or perhaps the suggestion is that she cannot bear to do so.

In contrast, some of the manuscript of *Caesar's Things* is quite finished. Zelda's recollections of her adventurous sisters' lives, for example, introduce her accounts of their several romances and marriages. She sets up these sections with a summarizing section:

Janno remembered the day when her sisters made up their minds that life was indeed in a rut what with waiting around for cosmic destinies which never happened and stubbing their toes over traditions which had already been. They went to work. This was an awesome and horrifying experience to the child [Janno] producing equivalent results to waking Daddy from his mid-day nap or scaling the back fence now that she was too big a girl.

The first months at the office, her sisters went to work with veils pulled down over the face; then they decided that women should or shouldn't work and that they would live honestly, so they pulled up their veils and before the year was out they were eating their lunch in a public place downtown.

Zelda had learned a lot about gender and power since writing *Save Me the Waltz*. Her chapters about Janno's love for her husband Jacob benefit from an ironic awareness about Jacob's vulnerabilities: there is humor here which was never visible in the earlier book. Most comfortable when he is entirely dominant, Jacob here is a painter, not a writer; he has swept Janno away from Montgomery and into his own highly stratified world; their happiness as a couple depends upon his thinking she lives in awe of him:

Jacob went on doing whatever it was that Jacob did; he was always doing something with pencils or pieces of string or notebooks or things which he found in his wallet; this made him absent-minded and preoccupied ... He was more important than Janno; she always felt as if she should be helpful about his tinkerings; they were intricate enough to need an assistant.

She repeats what becomes a refrain: "She didn't really do anything but wait on his will."

He owned her; bundled her up and sat her in taxis beside him, danced her around the gilded edges of many fashionable hours, showed her off to an inclusive set of college friends and made a big success of being impersario [sic] *His friends were admiring and affectionate.*

While Janno makes the best of her circumstances, Jacob becomes restive:

Jacob had other theories of life. Jacob didn't really like the sitting around in a wet bathing suit and he hated the taste of sand. He liked expatiating about values and origins and was exhaustive in his way of making the stories of people fit into his impetuous pre-conclusions about them. He kept nagging and asking and third-degreeing his acquaintances till it all made acceptable continuity with what he thought it ought to be dramatically.

Again, Jacob's power is largely gender-based.

Jacob's policy concerning women was that they were charming unless they tried to exercise authority. Jacob literally could not stand a woman's prerogative: to him women were agents of his own grace ... He hated his sister. She was a lovely girl whom he hated—largely because he never could find out what it was about her he so heartily resented. He hated his mother because ... he blamed her for the failure of his life. He hated Janno for the same

292

reason but this did not come to light until many years later when it really had become difficult to make money ...

Caesar's Things contains a great deal of pain, perhaps more pain than anger. There is a long section, for example, on Janno's forbidden love for the French flier, and on Jacob's locking her away for much of the summer. But largely, as in her letters to friends after Scott's death in 1940, Zelda here managed to salvage their remarkable early years. For her too, in this last reprise of their lives as "the Fitzgeralds," they were the couple beloved of each other, of their friends, and of their culture. Not the starkly materialistic pair of Scott's novel *The Beautiful and Damned*, Zelda's Janno and Jacob are gently melancholic survivors, perhaps undamaged by their journeys in the euphoric wastelands of the 1920s, lovers with their abilities and their promise intact. As she notes in one passage from the novel,

None of them, in their fervor and necessity to contribute to their brilliant and embittered world, remembered the fact that what counts is not the kiss but the loyalties which are broken; the threads of fidelity which are frayed ... Spiritual responsibility often seems to be a matter alone of the courage of one's faith...

Zelda's Returns to Highland

Zelda's calm, private life with her mother in Montgomery lasted more than three years before her first return for care to the Asheville hospital. Several mentions of the year 1942 in the *Caesar's Things* manuscript mark it as a product, unfinished as it was, of that stretch of comparative health. World War II occupied much of every American's energy; in the winter of 1943, Scottie Fitzgerald married Jack Lanahan while he was back in the States

293

on leave.[580] That July, Zelda spent a week in New York with her daughter—a trip that was too filled with events and excitement to be relaxing for either of them. In August she returned to Highland Hospital, and remained there until February of 1944.

By this time in the history of psychiatry, the use of insulin and electroconvulsive shock treatment was common. The young Honoria Murphy remembers a visit from Zelda to the Murphys several years later, when Zelda admitted to Sarah that she did not remember much about the 1920s.[581] By this time, her various courses of shock treatment—which had begun during her stay at the Sheppard and Enoch Pratt Hospital in the mid-1930s—had made her impairment noticeable: loss of memory, for an artist like Zelda, was tormenting. In her art more so than in her writing, she turned often to subjects from that steadily darkening past: during the 1940s, she painted watercolors of the cities where she and Scott had lived as if she were attempting the graphic reconstruction of what memories could be captured.

Recent biographers of Zelda[582] have tried to present her life in Montgomery from 1940 on as remarkable for her productive activity. Kendall Taylor lists her participation in Red Cross work, her occasional dance lessons (and continuing practice) with Amelia Harper Rosenberg, her painting, her vigorous walking—and her constant interaction with Scottie, now a New York journalist. Perhaps these biographers protest too much: Zelda found solace in her religion and in her garden,

---

[580] See Kendall Taylor, Sometimes Madness (2001), pp. 350-1; S, p. 154; Zelda, letters to Scottie, PUL.

[581] Honoria Murphy Donnelly, Sara and Gerald (1982), p. 150.

[582] Taylor, Sometimes Madness, pp. 349-5 2; see also Cline, Zelda.

but she was never completely well—nor could her mind ever recover from the disabling shock treatment it had received.

Sara Mayfield, the Fitzgeralds' biographer who also grew up in Montgomery and had herself experienced some of the elements of Zelda Sayre's life, catches the tone accurately: "It is true that she [Zelda] lived quietly, but her years from 1941 to 1948 were neither as tormented nor as rash and improper as one would infer from the biographical and fictional accounts."[583] Mayfield reminds the reader of the dailyness of commonplace life: for both Zelda and her mother, each day was a span of time to be experienced—and, at times, endured—marked by meals, prayers, the state of both yard and house, and the chores demanded by them. Neither woman was wealthy. Their lives, in fact, were placid and home-bound partly because of their limited finances.

Letters from Zelda in Montgomery to Scottie in the East show the comparative good humor with which both mother and grandmother bore their separation from Scottie. Attentive to the young wife's interests, Zelda often wrote about house-keeping, recipes, budgets.

Your cottage sounds like enchantment … I wish that I could be there to help you and enclose a page of advice … about how to make things meet one's spiritual purpose.[584]

Despite her lead-in about spiritualism, Zelda talks in this letter about cooking,

don't exhaust yourself in remembrance of the Ritz. Simple meals are more enjoyable in simple surroundings and I would rather

---

[583] Exiles, p. 281.

[584] Zelda Fitzgerald to Scottie, undated correspondence, PUL (subsequent quotations and references from this file of letters).

have a good baked potato than almost anything. You put them in a hot oven for an hour and stick a broom straw through … Rub the salad bowl with garlic, pour equal parts of oil and vinegar over the lettuce, a little salt and a teaspoonful of mustard and weep with gastronomical delight.

She also sends recipes for baked apples, cooked prunes, grits, and "the redemption of peas," a vegetable she doesn't much care for.

In other letters to Scottie from the 1940s, Zelda divides the property from the estate, transferring to Scottie all the silver, china, linens, phonograph records, scrapbooks, and art (a Picasso etching, a Marie Laurencin reproduction, as well as family portraits). In her words, "that which you want to use is unconditionally yours." And again,

Whatever things are left of our many house-keeping enterprizes [sic], *I want you to have. Do not consider these mine; your life contributed the greatest solace and the deepest pleasure of our domestic venture …*

She advises Scottie about lamps and cushions, and offers to make drapes and curtains for her windows, as she had done at Ellerslie and other places. She reminds Scottie, too, of her personal "spiritual obligation," and the need for prayer. Zelda hopes, however, that life will use her daughter "far less inexorably than it has used me, but should it prove harder to master in later years than at present seems probable," the practice of prayer will be comforting.

When Zelda thinks of her own future, as she occasionally does in this thoughtful correspondence, her mode is reassuring. She sees herself (after Minnie's death) buying "a cottage in Carolina where land is cheap and skies are high … [and then]

wasting away under the pine trees." The site of so many of her late watercolors, the peace of Zelda's childhood summers in Saluda, North Carolina, colors her imagination.

In regard to the promise Zelda saw in living long, as her mother had done and was doing, the greatest tragedy of her life was the fire that destroyed Highland Hospital. Zelda Sayre Fitzgerald was identified as being one of the nine women who died on the upper floors from smoke inhalation; she was taken to Maryland for burial beside Scott. Ironically, she was about to leave the hospital. She had returned to Highland only twice more once in 1946, so that she was there when Scottie's first child was born (but she saw Tim, her beloved grandson, several times during 1946 and 1947) and again at the end of 1947, a stay that lasted until the March 11, 1948, fire. The insulin shock treatments which she was receiving during the winter of 1948 had improved her outlook, and she was just days from resuming her life in Montgomery, the place she still considered home.

At the time of her death, Zelda Sayre Fitzgerald was forty-eight years old. She had spent much of her thirties in sanatoriums, and had found security at Highland Hospital during some months of her last decade. Throughout these painful years, Zelda had always chosen to go into institutions; she had never been committed. She had outlived her husband by more than seven years; she had learned to know and appreciate her daughter and others of her immediate family. She had developed her artistic talents, and she had come to experience a religiosity that was crucial to her sense of herself Zelda's religious beliefs might have made others uncomfortable, but they added immensely to her own existence. As she once wrote to Scottie,

I simply must ... offer you whatever my tragic experience has

297

mercifully indicated to be the best way of life: whatever will yield the deepest spiritual reward for what you put in. It isn't just a frustrate inhibited desire to assert myself, but my deepest love that makes time want you to love God and pray.

Bibliography

Primary

Fitzgerald, F. Scott. *Flappers and Philosophers*. New York: Charles Scribner's Sons, 1920.

—*All the Sad Young Men*. New York: Charles Scribner's Sons, 1926.

—*Taps at Reveille*. New York: Charles Scribner's Sons, 1935.

—*The Crack-Up*, ed. Edmund Wilson. New York: New Directions, 1945.

—*The Beautiful and Damned*. New York: Charles Scribner's Sons, 1950.

—*The Stories of F. Scott Fitzgerald*, ed. Malcolm Cowley. New York: Charles Scribner's Sons, 1953.

—*Tender Is the Night*. New York: Charles Scribner's Sons, 1962.

—*The Letters of F. Scott Fitzgerald*, ed. Andrew Turnbull. New York: Charles Scribner's Sons, 1963.

—*Thoughtbook of Francis Scott Key Fitzgerald*. Princeton: Princeton University Library, 1965.

—*The Great Gatsby*. New York: Charles Scribner's Sons, 1969.

—*The Last Tycoon*. New York. Charlie, Scribner's Sons, 1969.

—*This Side of Paradise*. New York: Charles Scribner's Sons, 1970.

—*Dear Scott/Dear Max: The Fitzgerald-Perkins Correspondence*, ed. John Kuehl and Jackson R. Bryer. New York: Charles Scribner's Sons, 1971.

—*F Scott Fitzgerald: In His Own Time*, A Miscellany, ed. Matthew J. Bruccoli and Jackson R. Bryer. New York: Popular Library, 1971.

—*As Ever, Scott Fitz—: Letters Between F Scott Fitzgerald and His Literary Agent, Harold Ober, 1919-1940*, ed. Matthew J. Bruccoli and Jennifer M. Atkinson. Philadelphia: Lippincott, 1972.

—*F Scott Fitzgerald's Ledger: A Facsimile*. Washington, D.C.: Microcard, 1972.

—"Fitzgerald on 'The Ice Palace': A Newly Discovered Letter," *Fitzgerald/Hemingway Annual*, 4 (1972), pp. 59-60.

—*The Basil and Josephine Stories*, ed. John Kuehl and Jackson R. Bryer. New York: Charles Scribner's Sons, 1973.

—*The Cruise of the Rolling Junk*. Bloomfield Hills, MI: Bruccoli Clark, 1976.

—*The Vegetable*. New York: Charles Scribner's Sons, 1976.

—*The Price Was High, The Last Uncollected Stories of F. Scott Fitzgerald*, ed. Matthew J. Bruccoli. New York: Harcourt, Brace, Jovanovich, 1979.

—*Correspondence of F. Scott Fitzgerald*, ed. Matthew J. Bruccoli and Margaret M. Duggan. New York:

Random House, 1980.

—*The Notebooks of F. Scott Fitzgerald*, ed. Matthew J. Bruccoli. New York: Harcourt, Brace, Jovanovich, 1980.

—*Poems, 1911-1940*, ed. Matthew J. Bruccoli. Bloomfield Hills, MI: Bruccoli and Clark, 1981.

—*The Short Stories of F Scott Fitzgerald*, ed. Matthew J. Bruccoli. New York: Scribner, 1989

—*F. Scott Fitzgerald: Manuscripts*, ed. Matthew J. Bruccoli. 16 vols. New York: Garland, 1990-94.

—*F. Scott Fitzgerald: A Life in Letters*, ed. Matthew J. Bruccoli. New York: Scribners, 1994.

—*The Love of the Last Tycoon: AWestern*, ed. Matthew J. Bruccoli. Cambridge: Cambridge University Press, 1994.

—and Zelda Fitzgerald. *Bits of Paradise, 21 Uncollected Stories*, ed. Matthew J. Bruccoli and Scottie Fitzgerald Smith. New York: Charles Scribner's Sons, 1973.

and Zelda Fitzgerald. *The Romantic Egoists: A Pictorial Autobiography from the Scrapbooks and Albums of F. Scott and Zelda Fitzgerald*, eds. Matthew J. Bruccoli, Scottie Fitzgerald Smith, and Joan P Kerr. New York: Scribner's, 1974.

and Zelda Fitzgerald. *Dear Scott, Dearest Zelda: The Love Letters of F Scott and Zelda Fitzgerald*, eds. Jackson R. Bryer and Cathy W. Barks. New York: St. Martin's Press, 2002.

Fitzgerald, Zelda. *Save Me the Waltz*. London: Grey Walls Press, 1953.

—*The Collected Writings of Zelda Fitzgerald*, ed. Matthew

J. Bruccoli. New York: Charles Scribner's Sons, 1991; reissued Tuscaloosa: University of Alabama Press, 1997.

—*The Art of Zelda Fitzgerald: Alice in Wonderland and Other Fairy Tales*, ed. Heidi Kunz Bullock. Lynchburg, VA: Maier Museum of Art, Randolph-Macon Women's College, 1998.

—"Caesar's Things." Unpublished novel (Princeton University Firestone Library).

Secondary

Agnew, Ellen Schall. [Essay on Zelda Fitzgerald's art.] *The Art of Zelda Fitzgerald: Alice in Wonderland and Other Fairy Tales*. Lynchburg, VA: Maier Museum of Art, 1998, n.p.

Allen, Joan. *Candles and Carnival Lights: The Catholic Sensibility of F. Scott Fitzgerald*. New York: New York University Press, 1978.

American Psychiatric Association. *Diagnostic and Statistical Manual of Mental Disorders*, first edition. Washington, D.C.: American Psychiatric Association, 1952; fourth edition, 1994. Text Revision, 2000.

Anderson, VV. R. "Rivalry and Partnership: The Short Fiction of Zelda Sayre Fitzgerald," *Fitzgerald/Hemingway Annual* 1977, pp. 19-42.

Atkinson, Jennifer McCabe. "Lost and Unpublished Stories of F. Scott Fitzgerald," *Fitzgerald/Hemingway Annual* 1977, pp. 32-63.

Bankhead, Tallulah. *Tallulah, My Autobiography*. New York: Harper and Brothers, 1952.

Benjamin, Jessica. *The Bonds of Love: Psychoanalysis,*

Feminism, and the Problem of Domination. New York: Pantheon, 1988.

Benstock, Shari. *Women of the Left Bank, Paris, 1910-1940*. Austin: University of Texas Press, 1986.

Bishop, John Peale. *The Republic of Letters in America, The Correspondence of John Peale Bishop and Allen Tate*, ed. Thomas Daniel Young and John J. Hindle. Lexington: University Press of Kentucky, 1981.

Blackshear, Helen F. "Mamma Sayre, Scott Fitzgerald's Mother-in-Law," *Georgia Review* (Winter 1965), pp. 465-70.

Boyd, Ernest. *Portraits: Real and Imaginary*. New York: Doran, 1924.

Brodie, Janet Farrell. *Contraception and Abortion in Nineteenth-Century America*. Ithaca, New York: Cornell University Press, 1994.

Bruccoli, Matthew J. *The Composition of Tender Is the Night: A Study of the Manuscripts*. Pittsburgh: University of Pittsburgh Press, 1963.

—"Zelda Fitzgerald's Lost Stories," *Fitzgerald/Hemingway Annual* 1979, pp. 123-6.

—*Some Sort of Epic Grandeur, The Life of F. Scott Fitzgerald*. New York: Harcourt, Brace, Jovanovich, 1981; second revised edition, University of South Carolina Press, 2002.

Bryer, Jackson R., ed. *The Short Stories of F. Scott Fitzgerald: New Approaches in Criticism*. Madison: University of Wisconsin Press, 1982.

Bush, Wanda. "Zelda and Scott," *Montgomery Advertizer Journal, Sunday Magazine* (March 28, 1965), n.p.

Buttitta, Tony. *The Lost Summer, A Personal Memoir of F. Scott Fitzgerald*. New York: St. Martin's Press, 1987, reissue from 1974.

Chesler, Phyllis. *Women & Madness*. New York: Doubleday, 1972.

Clemens, Anne Valdene. "Zelda Fitzgerald: An Unromantic Vision," *Dalhousie Review* 62 (Summer 1982), pp. 196-211.

Cline, Sally. *Zelda Fitzgerald: Her Voice in Paradise*. New York: Arcade, 2003.

Cody, Morrill with Hugh Ford. *The Women of Montparnasse*. New York: Cornwall, 1984.

Comely, Nancy R. "Madwoman on the Rivieria: The Fitzgeralds, Hemingway, and the Matter of Modernism," *French Connections: Hemingway and Fitzgerald Abroad*, ed. J. Gerald Kennedy and Jackson R. Bryer. New York: St. Martins Press, 1998.

Crosby, Caresse. *The Passionate Years*. New York: Dial, 1953.

Crowley, John W. *The White Logic, Alcoholism and Gender in American Modernist Fiction*. Amherst: University of Massachusetts Press, 1994.

Dardis, Tom. *The Thirsty Muse: Alcohol and the American Writer*. New York: Ticknor and Fields, 1989

Davis, Simone Weil. *Living Up to the Ads, Gender Fictions of the 1920s*. Durham, NC: Duke University Press, 2000.

Djos, IvIatts. "Alcoholism in Ernest Hemingway's *The Sun Also Rises*: A Wine and Roses Perspective on the Lost Generation," *A Casebook on Hemingway's The*

Sun Also Rises, ed. Linda Wagner-Martin. New York: Oxford University Press, 2002, pp. 139-53.

Dolan, Marc. *Modern Lives: A Cultural Re-reading of "The Lost Generation."* West Lafayette, IN: Purdue University Press, 1996.

Donaldson, Scott. "Scott Fitzgerald's Romance with the South," *Southern Literary Journal* 5 (Spring 1973), pp. 3-17.

—*Fool for Love: F. Scott Fitzgerald.* New York: Congdon & Weed, 1983.

—"A Short History of *Tender Is the Night*," *Writing the American Classics*, ed. James Barbour and Tom Quirk. Chapel Hill: University of North Carolina Press, 1990, pp. 177-208.

—*Archibald MacLeish, An American Life.* Boston: Houghton Mifflin, 1992.

—*Hemingway vs. Fitzgerald: The Rise and Fall of a Literary Friendship.* Woodstock, New York: Overlook Press, 1999.

Donnelly, Honoria Murphy with Richard M. Billings. *Sara and Gerald: Villa America and After.* New York: New York Times Books, 1982.

Dos Passos, John. *The Best Times.* New York: Signet, 1968.

—*The Fourteenth Chronicle, Letters and Diaries of John Dos Passos*, ed. Townsend Ludington. Boston: Gambit, 1973.

Durr, Virginia Foster. *Outside the Magic Circle: The Autobiography of Virginia Foster Durr*, ed. Hollinger F. Barnard. Tuscaloosa: University of Alabama Press, 1985.

Eble, Kenneth E. "Touches of Disaster: Alcoholism and Mental Illness in Fitzgerald's Short Stories," *The Short Stories of F. Scott Fitzgerald: New Aproaches in Criticism*, ed. Jackson R. Bryer. Madison: University of Wisconsin Press, 1982, pp. 39-52.

Ellison, Emily. "The Fitzgerald Connection," *Atlanta Weekly*, 27 September 1981, pp. 8-11,44-7.

Epstein, Joseph. "F. Scott Fitzgerald's Third Act," *Commentary* 98:5 (1994), pp. 52-7.

Felman, Shoshana. "Women and Madness: The Critical Phallacy," *Diacritics* (Winter 1975), pp. 2-10.

Forbush, Bliss. *The Sheppard and Enoch Pratt Hospital, 1853-1970. A History*. Philadelphia: J. B. Lippincott, 1971.

Foucault, Michel. *Madness & Civilization*, trans. Richard Howard. New York: Vintage-Random, 1965.

Fryer, Sarah Beebe. *Fitzgerald's New Women: Harbingers of Change*. Ann Arbor, MI: UMI Research Press, 1988.

Fulkerson, Tahita N. "Ibsen in 'The Ice Palace,'" *Fitzgerald/Hemingway Annual*, II (1979), pp. 169-71.

Germain, Adrienne, King K. Holmes, Peter Piot, Judith N. Wasserheit, eds. *Reproductive Tract Infections: Global Impact & Priorities for Women's Reproductive Health*. New York: Plenum, 1992

Gilligan, Carol. *In a Different Voice*. Cambridge: Harvard University Press, 1982.

Gilman, Sander L. *Difference and Pathology: Stereotypes of Sexuality, Race, and Madness*. Ithaca, NY: Cornell University Press, 1985.

Gilmore, Thomas B. *Equivocal Spirits: Alcoholism and*

Drinking in 20th Century Literature. Chapel Hill: University of North Carolina Press, 1987.

Gish, Lillian. *The Movies, Mr Griffith, and Me*. New York: Prentice-flail, 1969.

Going, William T. "Two Alabama Writers: Zelda Sayre Fitzgerald and Sara Haardt Mencken," *Alabama Review* 23 (January 1970), pp. 3-29.

Goldhurst, William. *F Scott Fitzgerald and His Contemporaries*. New York: World, 1963.

Gordon, Mary. "Introduction" to *Zelda Fitzgerald, The Collected Writings*, ed. Matthew J. Bruccoli. New York: Charles Scribner's Sons, 1991, pp. xv—xxvii.

Gottlieb, David I. "Afterword" to Charles R. Metzger's *F Scott Fitzgerald's Psychiatric Novel*. New York: Peter Lang, 1989, pp. 359-77.

Graham, Sheilah. *College of One*. New York: Bantam, 1968.

—*The Real F Scott Fitzgerald*. New York: Grosset & Dunlap, 1976.

Hackl, Lloyd C. *F Scott Fitzgerald and St. Paul: "Still Home to Me."* Cambridge, MN: Adventure Publications, 1996.

Haardt, Sara. *The Making of a Lady*. New York: Doubleday, 1931.

—*Southern Album*, ed. H. L. Mencken. New York: Doubleday, Doran, 1936.

—*Southern Souvenirs (Selected Stories and Essays)*, ed. Ann Henley. Tuscaloosa: University of Alabama Press, 1999.

Hardwick, Elizabeth. *"Zelda," Seduction and Betrayal, Women and Literature*. New York: Random House,

1974, pp. 87-103.

Hart, Livye Ridgeway. "A Profile of Zelda," unpublished manuscript. *Sara Mayfield Collection*, University of Alabama, Tuscaloosa, Alabama (n.d.).

Hartnett, Koula Svokos. *Zelda Fitzgerald and the Failure of the American Dream for Women*. New York: Peter Lang, 1991.

Hearn, Laura Guthrie. "A Summer with F. Scott Fitzgerald," *Esquire* 62 (December 1964), pp. 160-5,232 ff.

Heilbrun, Carolyn G. *Writing a Woman's Life*. New York: Ballantine, 1988.

Hemingway, Ernest. *A Moveable Feast*. New York: Scribner's, 1964.

—Ernest Hemingway: *Selected Letters, 1917-1961*, ed. Carlos Baker. New York: Scribner's, 1981

Holman, C. Hugh. "Fitzgerald's Changes on the Southern Belle: The Tarleton Trilogy," *The Short Stories of F. Scott Fitzgerald: New Approaches in Criticism*, ed. Jackson R. Bryer. Madison: University of Wisconsin Press, 1982, pp. 53-64.

Hook, Andrew. *F. Scott Fitzgerald, A Literary Life*. Basingstoke: Palgrave Macmillan, 2002.

Hudgins, Andrew. "Zelda Sayre in Montgomery," *Southern Review* 20 (1984), pp. 882-4.

Irwin, Julie M. "F. Scott Fitzgerald's Little Drinking Problem," *American Scholar* 56 (Summer 1987), pp. 415-27.

Israel, Lee. *Miss Tallulah Bankhead*. New York: Putnam's Sons, 1972.

Johnson, Owen. *The Salamander*. New York: A. L. Burt, 1914.

Jung, Carl G. *Modern Man in Search of a Soul*. Trans. by W. S. Dell and Cary F. Baynes. London: Kegan Paul, 1933.

Kellner, Bruce. *Carl Van Vechten and the Irreverent Decades*. Norman: University of Oklahoma Press, 1968.

Kennedy, J. Gerald. *Imagining Paris: Exile, Writing, and American Identity*. New Haven: Yale University Press, 1993.

—"Fitzgerald's Expatriate Years and the European Stories," *The Cambridge Companion to F. Scott Fitzgerald*, ed. Ruth Prigozy. New York: Cambridge University Press, 2000, pp. 118-42.

—and Jackson R. Bryer. "Preface: Recovering the French Connections of Hemingway and Fitzgerald," *French Connections: Hemingway and Fitzgerald Abroad*, ed. J. Gerald Kennedy and Jackson R. Bryer. New York: St. Martin's Press, 1998, pp. vii—xv.

Kluver, Billy and Julia Martin. *Kiki's Paris, Artists and Lovers 1900-1930*. New York: Harry N. Abrams, 1989.

Kramer, Peter D. "How Crazy Was Zelda?" *New York Times Sunday Magazine* (December 1, 1996), pp. 106-9.

Kuehl, John. "Psychic Geography in 'The Ice Palace,'" The Short Stories of F. Scott Fitzgerald: New Approaches in *Criticism*, ed. Jackson R. Bryer. Madison: University of Wisconsin Press, 1982, pp. 169-79.

—*Scott Fitzgerald: A Study of the Short Fiction*. Boston: Twayne, 1991.

Lanahan, Eleanor. *Scottie: the Daughter of ... .* New York: HarperCollins, 1995.

—ed. *Zelda: An Illustrated Life. The Private World of Zelda Fitzgerald.* New York: Harry N. Abrams, 1996; includes Jane S. Livingston, "On the Art of Zelda Fitzgerald," pp. 77-85.

—"Introduction," *Dear Scott, Dearest Zelda,* eds. Jackson R. Bryer and Cathy W. Barks (New York: St. Martin's Press, 2002), pp. xxiii—xxxi.

Lehan, Richard. "F. Scott Fitzgerald and Romantic Destiny," *Twentieth Century Literature* 26 (Summer 1980), pp. 137-56.

—"The Romantic Self and the Uses of Place in the Stories of F. Scott Fitzgerald," *The Short Stories of F. Scott Fitzgerald: New Approaches in Criticism,* ed. Jackson R. Bryer. Madison: University of Wisconsin Press, 1982, pp. 3-21.

LeVot, Andre. Translated by William Byron. *F Scott Fitzgerald, A Biography.* Garden City, NY: Doubleday, 1983.

Lewis, Roger. "Ruth Sturtevant and F. Scott Fitzgerald (1916-1921)," *Fitzgerald/ Hemingway Annual,* 1979, pp. 3-26.

Lifar, Serge. Translated by Arnold Haskall. *A History of the Russian Ballet: From its Origins to the Present Day.* London: Hutchinson, 1954.

MacKie, Elizabeth Beckwith. "My Friend Scott Fitzgerald," reprinted from *Fitzgerald/ Hemingway Annual,* 1970, in *F. Scott Fitzgerald,* ed. Kenneth E. Eble. New York: McGraw-Hill, 1973, pp. 7-18.

MacLeish, Archibald. *Archibald MacLeish: Reflections*, ed. Bernard A. Drabeck and Helen E. Ellis. Amherst: University of Massachusetts Press, 1986.

Mayfield, Sara. *Exiles from Paradise, Zelda and Scott Fitzgerald*. New York: Delacorte Press, 1971

McAlmon, Robert. *Miss Knight and Others*. Albuquerque, New Mexico: University of New Mexico Press, 1992.

—and Kay Boyle. *Being Geniuses Together, 1920-1930*. London: Hogarth, 1984.

McCullers, Carson. *Illumination & Night Glare, The Unfinished Autobiography of Carson McCullers*, ed. Carlos L. Dews. Madison: University of Wisconsin Press, 1999.

McDonough, Kaye. *Zelda: Frontier Life in America, A Fantasy in Three Parts*. San Francisco: City Lights, 1978.

McDowell, Edwin. "Fitzgerald-Fuller Affair Recounted," *New York Times*, November 9, 1984, Section C, 21.

McLenciem, Winzola. "Scott and Zelda," *Ladies' Home Journal* 91 (November 1974), pp. 58, 60,62,170-1.

Mellow, James R. *Invented Lives, F Scott and Zelda Fitzgerald*. Boston: Houghton Mifflin, 1984.

Meredith, Cary. "*Save Me the Waltz* as a Novel," *Fitzgerald/Hemingway Annual*. Detroit: Gale, 1976, pp. 65-78.

Metzger, Charles R. *F Scott Fitzgerald's Psychiatric Novel*. New York: Peter Lang, 1989.

Meyer, Adolf. "Preface" to *Marian King, The Recovery of Myself: A Patient's Experience in a Hospital for Mental Illness*. New Haven: Yale University Press, 1931, pp.

vii—xi.

Meyers, Diane Tietgens. *Subjection and Subjectivity, Psychoanalytic Feminism and Moral Philosophy*. New York: Routledge, 1994.

Meyers, Jeffrey. *Scott Fitzgerald, A Biography*. New York: HarperCollins, 1994.

Milford, Nancy. *Zelda, A Biography*. New York: Harper & Row, 1970; reissue, 2001.

Miller, Alice. Translated by Ruth Ward. *The Drama of the Gifted Child (Prisoners of Childhood)*. New York: Basic, 1981.

Miller, Jean Baker. *Toward a New Psychology of Women*. Boston: Beacon, 1976.

Miller, Linda Patterson, ed. *Letters from the Lost Generation: Gerald and Sara Murphy and Friends*. New Brunswick: Rutgers University Press, 1991.

Mitchell, Ted. "The Doom of the Mountains," *Our State* (NC) (March 1999), pp. 70-3.

Mizener, Arthur. *The Far Side of Paradise: A Biography of F. Scott Fitzgerald*. Boston: Houghton Mifflin, 1951.

Moses, Edwin. "F. Scott Fitzgerald and the Quest to 'The Ice Palace,'" *CEA Critic*, 36 (January 1974), pp. 11-14.

Nanney, Lisa. "Zelda Fitzgerald's *Save Me the Waltz* as Southern Novel and Kunstlerroman," *The Female Tradition in Southern Literature*, ed. Carol S. Manning. Urbana: University of Illinois Press, 1993, pp. 220-32.

Nathan, George Jean. "Memories of Fitzgerald, Lewis and Dreiser," *Esquire*, October 1958

—"Profiles of Other Writers: F. Scott Fitzgerald (1896-1940) and Zelda Fitzgerald (1900-1947)," *A George Jean Nathan Reader*, ed. A. L. Lazarus. Rutherford, NJ: Fairleigh Dickinson University Press, 1990, pp. 156-60.

Nathan, Peter E. "Alcoholism in America: Extant, Diagnosis, Etiology, Treatment, Prevention," *States of Mind, American and Post-Soviet Perspectives on Contemporary Issues in Psychology*, ed. Diane F. Halpern and Alexander E. Voiskounsky. New York: Oxford University Press, 1997, pp. 169-97.

Nowlin, Michael. "'The World's Rarest Work': Modernism and Masculinity in Fitzgerald's *Tender Is the Night*," *College Literature* 25 (1998), pp. 58-77.

Nussbaum, Martha C. *Love's Knowledge*. New York: Oxford University Press, 1990.

Page, Dave and John Koblas. *F. Scott Fitzgerald in Minnesota: Toward the Summit*. St. Cloud, MN: North Star Press, 1996.

Pattillo, Edward. *Zelda: Zelda Sayre Fitzgerald Retrospective*. Montgomery, AL: Montgomery Museum of Fine Arts, 1974.

Petry, Alice Hall. "Women's Work: The Case of Zelda Fitzgerald," *Literature—Interpretation—Theory* (December 1989), pp. 148-59.

Piper, Henry Dan. *F. Scott Fitzgerald: A Critical Portrait*. New York: Holt, Rinehart &Winston, 1965

Polier, Rex. "Fitzgerald in Wilmington: The Great Gatshy at Bay," *Philadelphia Sunday Bulletin* (January 6, 1974), Section 4.

Potts, Stephen W, *The Price of Paradise, The Magazine Career of F Scott Fitzgerald*. San Bernadino, CA: Borgo Press, 1993.

Prigozy, Ruth. "Introduction," *The Cambridge Companion to F. Scott Fitzgerald*, ed. Prigozy. New York: Cambridge University Press, 2000, pp. 1-27.

Quick, Jonathan. *Modern Fiction and the Art of Subversion*. New York: Peter Lang, 1999.

Reagan, Leslie J. *When Abortion Was a Crime: Women, Medicine and Law in the United States, 1867-1973*. Berkeley: University of California Press, 1997.

Ring, Frances Kroll. *Against the Current: As I Remember F Scott Fitzgerald*. Berkeley, CA: Creative Arts, 1985 (basis for film, *Last Call*, 2002).

Robertson, Elizabeth. "Speaking from the Place of the Other: Identity and Narrative Form in the Life and Art of Zelda Fitzgerald," *Denver Quarterly* 19 (Summer 1984), pp. 130-9.

Rodgers, Marion Elizabeth, ed. *Mencken and Sara: A Life in Letters—The Private Correspondence of H. L. Mencken and Sara Haardt*. New York: McGraw-Hill, 1987.

Runyan, Keith. "The Fitzgeralds in Montgomery, Alabama," *The Courier-Journal and Times*. Louisville, KY, 24 March 1974, Sec. G: 1, 14.

Schenkar, Joan. *Truly Wilde*. New York: Basic, 2000.

Schiff, Jonathan. *Ashes to Ashes: Mourning and Social Difference in F. Scott Fitzgerald's Fiction*. Selinsgrove: Susquehanna University Press, 2001.

Shorter, Edward. *A History of Psychiatry, From the Era of the Asylum to the Age of Prozac*. New York: John

Wiley, 1997.

Skemer, Don C. "Loveless in Louisville: F. Scott Fitzgerald's Verses to Mildred McNally, 1918," *Princeton University Library Chronicle* 58 (1997), pp. 320-4.

Sklar, Robert. *F. Scott Fitzgerald: The Last Laocoon*. New York: Oxford University Press, 1967

Smith, Scottie Fitzgerald. "Princeton and My Father," *Princeton Alumni Weekly* 56 (March 9, 1956), pp. 8-9.

—"Introduction," *Letters to His Daughter by F. Scott Fitzgerald*, ed. Andrew Turnbull. New York: Scribner's, 1965, pp. ix—xvi.

—"Introduction" to Zelda, Zelda Sayre Fitzgerald *Retrospective*, Montgomery Museum of Fine Arts (1 9 74) .

—"Introduction," *Bits of Paradise*, ed. Matthew J. Bruccoli and Scottie Fitzgerald Smith. New York: Scribner's, 1976.

—"The Colonial Ancestors of Francis Scott Key Fitzgerald," *Maryland Historical Society Magazine* (Winter 1981), reprinted as "Afterward" in Bruccoli, *Some Sort of Epic Grandeur, the Life of F Scott Fitzgerald*. New York: St. Martin's Press, 1987, reissue from 1974, pp. 495-507.

—"The Maryland Ancestors of Zelda Sayre Fitzgerald," *Maryland Historical Society Magazine* (Fall 1983), pp. 217-28.

Smaller, Sanford J. *Adrift Among Geniuses: Robert McAlmon, Writer and Publisher of the Twenties*. University Park: Pennsylvania State University Press,

1975.

Spender, Dale. "Zelda Fitzgerald (1900-1947): A Paradigm of Plain Theft," *The Writing or the Sex? Why You Don't Have To Read Women's Writing To Know It's No Good*. New York: Perganson, 1989, pp. 175-92.

Stein, Gertrude. *The Autobiography of Alice B. Toklas*. New York: Harcourt, Brace, 1933.

Stern, Milton R. *The Golden Moment: The Novels of F. Stott Fitzgerald*. Urbana. University of Illinois Press, 1970.

Stewart, Grace. *A New Mythos, The Novel of the Artist as Heroine, 1877-1977*. Montreal: Eden Press Women's Publications, 1981.

Stovala, Thomas J. *Scott Fitzgerald: Crisis in an American Identity*. New York: Barnes & Noble, 1981

Tavernier-Courbin, Jacqueline. "Art as Woman's Response and Search: Zelda Fitzgerald's *Save Me the Waltz*," *Southern Literary Journal* 11 (Spring 1979), pp. 22-42.

—"The Influence of France on Nicole Diver's Recovery in *Tender Is the Night*," *French Connections: Hemingway and Fitzgerald Abroad*, ed. J. Gerald Kennedy and Jackson R. Bryer. New York: St. Martin's Press, 1998, pp. 215-32.

Taylor, Kendall. *Sometimes Madness Is Wisdom: Zelda and Scott Fitzgerald, A Marriage*. New York: Ballantine, 2001.

Taylor, Littleton. "A Letter from Zelda Fitzgerald," *Fitzgerald/Hemingway Annual*, 1975, pp. 3-6.

Toklas, Alice B. *What Is Remembered*. New York: Holt, Rinehart, and Winston, 1963.

Toll, Seymour I. *A Judge Uncommon: A Life of John Biggs, Jr.* Philadelphia: Legal Communications, 1993

—"Biggs and Fitzgerald: An Untold Story," *F. Scott Fitzgerald Society Newsletter* 8 (December 1998), pp. 10-15.

Tomkins, Calvin. *Living Well Is the Best Revenge.* New York: Viking, 1962.

Turnbull, Andrew. *Scott Fitzgerald.* New York: Charles Scribner's Sons, 1962.

Tytell, John. *Passionate Lives.* New York: Carol Publishing, Birch Lane Press, 1991, pp. 74-141.

Ussher, Jane M. *Women's Madness: Misogyny or Mental Illness?* Amherst: University of Massachusetts Press, 1991.

Vaill, Amanda. *Everybody Was So Young: Gerald and Sara Murphy, A Lost Generation Love Story.* Boston: Houghton Mifflin, 1998.

Valentine, Kylie. *Psychoanalysis, Psychiatry and Modernist Literature.* Basingstoke: Palgrave Macmillan, 2003.

Van Vechten, Carl. *Parties: Scenes of Contemporary New York Life.* New York: Knopf, 1930.

Vidal, Gore. "Foreword" to Robert McAlmon's *Miss Knight and Others.* Albuquerque: University of New Mexico Press, 1992, n.p.

Wagner, Linda W. "A Note on Zelda Fitzgerald's *Scandalabra*," *Notes on Contemporary Literature* 12 (May 1982), pp. 4-5.

—"*Save Me the Waltz*: An Assessment in Craft," *Journal of Narrative Technique*, 12:3 (Fall 1982), pp. 201-9.

Wagner-Martin, Linda. *"Favored Strangers": Gertrude Stein and Her Family*. New Brunswick: Rutgers University Press, 1995.

Waites, Elizabeth A. "The Princess in the Tower: Zelda Fitzgerald's Creative Impasse," *Journal of the American Psychoanalytic Association* 34:3 (1986), pp. 637-62.

Waldhorn, Arthur. "The Cartoonist, the Nurse, and the Writer: 'An Alcoholic Case,'" *New Essays on F. Scott Fitzgerald's Neglected Stories*, ed. Jackson R. Bryer. Columbia: University of Missouri Press, 1996, pp. 244-52.

Wasserstrom, William. *The Ironies of Progress: Henry Adams and the American Dream*. Carbondale: Southern Illinois University Press, 1984.

West, James L. W., III. "Did F. Scott Fitzgerald Have the Right Publisher?" *Sewanee Review* 100 (1992), pp. 644-56.

—"Prospects for the Study of F. Scott Fitzgerald," *Resources for American Literary Study* 23:2 (1997), pp. 147-58.

—"Almost a Masterpiece" (on Trimalchio), *Humanities Penn State*, 21:1 (January—February 2000), pp. 15-20.

Westbrook, Robert. *Intimate Lies: F. Scott Fitzgerald and Sheilah Graham, Her Son's Story*. New York: HarperCollins, 1995.

White, Ray Lewis. "Zelda Fitzgerald's *Save Me the Waltz*: A Collection of Reviews from 1932-33," *Fitzgerald/ Hemingway Annual*, 1979, pp. 163-8.

Wilson, Edmund. *The Shores of Light, A Literary Chronicle of the Twenties and Thirties*. New York:

Farrar, Straus and Young, 1952.

—*The Higher Jazz*, ed. Neale Reinitz. Iowa City: University of Iowa Press, 1998.

Wiser, William. *The Great Good Place: American Expatriate Women in Paris*. New York: Norton, 1991

Woolf, Virginia. *On Being Ill*. Ashfield, MA: Paris Press, 2002 (reissue from 1930).

Yalom, Marilyn. *Maternity, Mortality, and the Literature of Madness*. University Park: Pennsylvania State University Press, 1985.

Yorke, Lane. "Zelda: A Worksheet," *Paris Review* (Fall 1983), pp. 210-63.

Acknowledgments

Once again, I am deeply indebted to the Rockefeller Study and Research Center at Bellagio, Italy, where time for writing is not only available, but inviolate. I also thank the University of North Carolina-Chapel Hill, for a gift of a Kenan semester free from teaching, and the Institute of Arts and Humanities on the same campus for the good fellowship of other faculty participants during my term there.

This study of the Fitzgeralds draws from the knowledge of a number of scholars—among them, Rose Marie Burwell, Jackson Bryer, Scott Donaldson, Kirk Curnutt, and a quantity of other readers of the work of both the Fitzgeralds. At the Princeton Library, I thank Anna Lee Pauls; at Scribner's, Lydia Zelaya; at Harold Ober Associates, Craig Tenney; at the F. Scott and Zelda Fitzgerald Museum in Montgomery, Robert Delk and Wesley Newton. With special thanks to Eleanor Lanahan. For psychiatric and medical information I thank Dr. Einar Arnason, Dr. Karen E. Lasser, and Dr. Watson A. Bowes, Jr. I am also indebted to research help from Lindsey Smith and Bryan Giemza, doctoral students at the University of North Carolina-Chapel Hill.

Unpublished materials are published by permission of Harold Ober Associates Incorporated. Copyright 2004 by Eleanor

CPSIA information can be obtained
at www.ICGtesting.com
Printed in the USA
LVHW111651061122
732497LV00002B/410